# THE MIDDLE EAST
*A Social Geography*

40

# THE MIDDLE EAST
## *A SOCIAL GEOGRAPHY*

### STEPHEN H. LONGRIGG

Second Edition
with revision and incorporating new material
by James Jankowski

*Read not to contradict and confute, nor to
believe and take for granted, nor to find
talk and discourse, but to weigh and consider*
Francis Bacon (1561–1626)

ALDINE · ATHERTON
CHICAGO / NEW YORK

*First published June* 1963
*Revised edition* 1970
*Fourth Printing* 1971


© Stephen Longrigg 1963, 1970

Library of Congress Catalog Card No. 75-91722
SBN 202-10008 (Cloth)
SBN 202-10013 (Paper)


Aldine·Atherton, Inc.
529 South Wabash Avenue
Chicago, Illinois 60605

Printed in the United States of America

# CONTENTS

# LIST OF ILLUSTRATIONS

## ACKNOWLEDGMENTS

Photographs have been supplied by kind permission of the following:

| | | | |
|---|---|---|---|
| *BP* | British Petroleum Co. | *KOC* | Kuwait Oil Co. |
| *BS* | Black Star | *PE* | Persian Embassy |
| *FS* | Miss Freya Stark | *PH* | Paul Hartman, Paris |
| *IE* | Israeli Embassy | *PP* | Paul Popper |
| *IOP* | Iran Oil Participants | *SG* | Sudan Government |
| *IPC* | Iraq Petroleum Co. | | |

No. 57 is reproduced from Asad: *The Road to Mecca* by permission of The
Bodley Head Ltd.; Nos. 56 and 60–63 from Stark: *Seen in the Hadhramaut* by
permission of John Murray Ltd.; Nos. 9–18 from *Turkey in Pictures* (Duckworth).

## MAPS by R. W. FORD

# PREFACE

THE pages here following are, in my intention, far from constituting a text-book of Middle Eastern geography or society, or a political analysis of its many problems, or an orderly statistical or economic review; they are, indeed, no nearer to being a substitute for all or any of the many excellent books already published on these subjects than are the sketch-maps to taking the place of the large-scale atlas which, I hope, readers will have open at their elbows. I have felt compelled to pass over important aspects of the Middle Eastern region and its component countries, almost or entirely in silence: among such aspects being those of military resources, prominent personalities, constitutional or legal issues, budgets and balances of trade. And even on matters upon which I have tried to say something fairly specific—topography, races and languages, religions, climates, natural resources and agronomy, industry, communications—too little detailed information can be given in the compass available to satisfy a reader (perhaps, in this case, a student) desirous of a full picture of a given aspect of things in this or that territory. For most of such detail, and not less for an appreciation which may be widely different from mine, he can very easily look elsewhere: the literature of these countries, as of today, is abundant and accessible. My attempt has been to offer an objective but informed account of the different races and social forces found in Middle Eastern environments, urban and rural, in terms of the particular circumstances, problems and hopes of the dozen separate and more or less divided states of the region. It is my hope that the non-specialist reader may from all this learn something true and perhaps suggestive, while the expert may find not too much to offend him. The views expressed are those of one whose personal experience of these countries has been extensive, I hope receptive, and certainly sympathetic. In fully half of the territories covered, and particularly those of the Fertile Crescent, I have, as a long-term resident, had many friends over many years.

At the time of writing, much of the region is, as notably as any in the world, in a continuing state of visible, often revolutionary, change in almost every field—social, cultural, economic, political. Time will, henceforward, greatly modify the conditions here presented. I have intended, therefore, chiefly to emphasize those aspects which, being the least ephemeral, are likely to remain valid for some years, and, I hope, to indicate the areas in which, and the lines on which, change, on indications already visible, is most to be expected. And if in the near future country A acquires or suppresses country B, country C changes its form of government to become a republic or a dictatorship, or discovers oil, and country D becomes a satellite of the U.S.S.R., the reader will at least be informed of the conditions out of which—or because of which—such change occurred.

In the method of spelling oriental names I have, like other orientalists anxious to avoid the appearance of pedantry, tried to compromise between correct and popular spellings—with results which, as usual, will certainly fail to please everybody.

The arrangement of relevant material to the best advantage and the reader's convenience has proved a particularly puzzling problem: was it to be on a regional, or a country-by-country, or a subject-by-subject basis? And how were dullness and repetition to be best avoided? The solution adopted, one of inconsistent compromise, will not suit all tastes; but to the dissatisfied I recommend the use of the two indices provided, whereby they will find, I hope, most of what there is to find.

The kindly individuals and corporations who have made their photographs available for these pages, to an extent which the list thereof will make plain, are hereby most cordially thanked.

S. H. L.

*15th November*, 1962.

## PREFACE TO SECOND EDITION

A Second, revised and 'up-dated', Edition of this book having been demanded by its publishers, this has now been prepared and is offered to the public, seven years after original publication. In this work I have enjoyed the kind and efficient help of my friend James Jankowski, Assistant Professor of History at the University of Colorado. To him I have left, with relief and gratitude, by far the greater part of the work of incorporating herein, within sadly rigid limits of space and pagination, the main features, developments and events of the most recent years, since 1962.

S. H. L.

# CHAPTER ONE

# THE REGION

## 1. *Scale and Orientation*

IN a region of the earth where much is dubious, and little undisputed, the content of its very designation, 'Middle East', is the first controversy to be met. The term was invented, half a century ago, by an American admiral, and seemed to fill a need; it gained ground, become respectable, and was accepted, largely thanks to 1939–1945 wartime usage, in official (especially military and political) as well as popular circles. Less generally in the western hemisphere, where 'Near East' still prevails, but very widely now in the eastern, the phrase has taken its place with other convenient titles—Eastern Europe, French Africa, Soviet Bloc, South-East Asia—as meaning something conveniently thus expressed.

But what, and how to be delineated? If on lines of pure geography, one's northern boundaries must be the Caspian, Caucasus, Black Sea and Marmara: the western, the Aegean, eastern Mediterranean, Suez Canal and Red Sea; the southern must be the Arabian Sea and Gulf of Oman: the eastern, perhaps, a line across the horrific desert that covers east-central Persia across most of its narrow waist from the Caspian to the Makran coast. But the area so defined would include Russian Transcaucasia, which nobody claims today as Middle East, and would exclude Turkey-in-Europe, Egypt and the Sudan, and the eastern one-third of Persia. To correct this, therefore, one must add to geographic some cultural and political criteria, on which agreement is no matter of course. Thus guided, we shall omit Transcaucasia: bring in Cyprus, a slightly dubious recruit: enrol obviously Egypt, and less obviously the Sudan, while leaving its southern, pagan, purely African provinces largely out of account, and shut the door, with some hesitation, on Libya, whose Cyrenaican province, up to the great Sirte divide, could well pass as Middle East. All of Persia must come in. It is doubtfully logical to omit, as we do, Afghanistan, but this is more Central Asian: and it is tempting perhaps, but not quite sufficiently, to admit the Islamic, part-Arabian Somalis.

Our area then, in the end, is that of the Egyptian and Sudanese

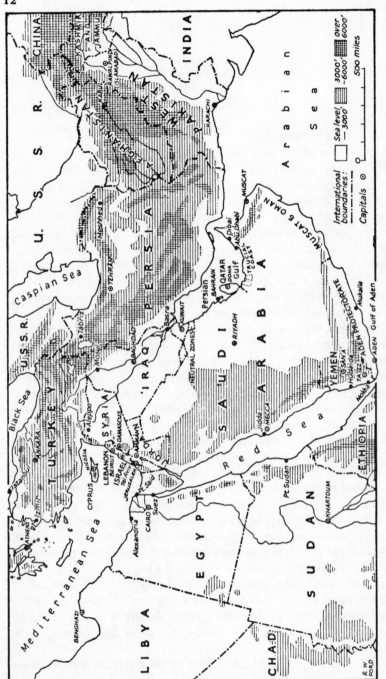

THE MIDDLE EAST: GENERAL

Republics, the Hashimite Kingdom of Jordan, the State of Israel, the Republics of the Lebanon, Syria, Turkey, 'Iraq and Cyprus, the Kingdom of Persia, that of Sa'udi Arabia, and the Imamate (but since September 1962 the Republic) of the Yemen, the small Arab states and shaikhdoms of the Persian Gulf coast, the Sultanate of Muscat and Oman, and the new People's Republic of Southern Yemen. We are covering, therefore, some 3,500,000 square miles of land, and some 140,000,000 of human beings. Of all this, nearly 1,000,000 square miles belong to non-Arab states, with 62,000,000 inhabitants; the rest is Arab country.

The region forms, to the eye of the space-traveller (or map reader), a single roughly quadrilateral land-mass, some 2,200 miles from west to east and 2,000 north to south, pierced by two sharply intruding seas on the south, the Red Sea and Persian Gulf, and one on the west, the Mediterranean. The area falls almost entirely between the lines of longitude 25° E to 62° E, and between latitudes 13° N and 42° N; it is all, therefore, outside the tropics except the southern half of Egypt, all the Sudan, and southern Arabia. Typical mileages, to show the scale of the area, are: from the Nile Delta to Khartum, 1,100 miles; Aleppo to Aden, 1,750; the Aegean to the Caspian, 1,250; Lataqiya to Meshhed, 1,425; Istanbul to south-eastern Arabia, 2,250.

These are formidable distances; the territory is wide. It would be more manageable, and its problems diminished, if the natural blocks or major fragments which compose it were to correspond to its political, or national, pattern. But they are far from doing this. Excepting the island-states of Cyprus and Bahrain, and perhaps the detached sea-and-desert-bounded Sultanate of Oman, no single political unit in the Middle East enjoys the security, or the convenience, of natural boundaries. On the contrary, the geographical blocs or units, such as they are, are all composed of more than a single state. The Nile Valley contains Egypt and the Sudan, an area of Libya and Ethiopia, and part of central Africa. Arabia, a broad spacial unity, adds to the Sa'udi Kingdom the fringe territories of the Yemen, Southern Yemen, Oman, the Gulf statelets and, in its northern extension towards the Fertile Crescent, areas also of Jordan, Syria, and 'Iraq. The Levant coast and hinterland—that is, true geographical Syria—contains Jordan, Israel, the Lebanon, Syria, and the Hatay province of Turkey. In Asia Minor, which contains all Turkey except its small European residue, there are none but the most blurred or arbitrary of boundaries against the U.S.S.R., Persia, 'Iraq and Syria.

The Tigris–Euphrates Valley, all 'Iraqi, is flanked by a quite dissimilar but equally 'Iraqi area of mountainous Kurdistan, and by a Persian province (Khuzistan) which is strictly southern-'Iraqi in character. Persia has no natural frontier on its north-western or north-eastern front, nor on the east; indeed, the land-block of which it forms part includes also Afghanistan and part of Pakistan.

Any who follow today's controversies in the region—Nile waters, Euphrates and Jordan waters, Kurdish unrests and ambitions, Perso-'Iraqi bickering, Persian claims to Bahrain, Sa'udi demands on the Persian Gulf states, and many more—will realize how much happier an area—or possibly less happy, with its most favoured occupation gone?—the Middle East would be if each of its states enjoyed a territory demarkated on something like natural or logical lines; yet nothing could be less likely than the achievement of any such goal.

Looking outward from within the area, one sees how various, and fraught with what implications in war or peace, are its avenues of approach or egress. In the east, Persia lies open to Afghanistan and Pakistan, which are highways to central Asia and the Indian subcontinent; in the extreme north-east, it offers the most open of frontiers to the Soviet Socialist Republic of the Turkmen. In the north-west, beside the Caspian (itself a Russian lake) Persian Azarbaijan looks across no barrier on to the Soviet states of (Russian) Azarbaijan and Armenia, as north-eastern Turkey looks equally at Georgia—these being all territories, south of the Caucasus, which were Persian or Turkish before the Russian conquests of the nineteenth century. The north-western frontier of the Turks is an arbitary, defenceless line as against Bulgaria and Greece and all southeastern Europe behind these. The whole western border of Egypt and the northern Sudan with the Kingdom of Libya is open desert; to the south, the Sudan's neighbours (remote indeed from any Middle Eastern character) are the ex-French independent republics of Chad and Centrafrica (formerly Oubangui-Chari), the ex-Belgian Congo, Uganda, Kenya and Ethiopia. From no one of all these directions have the Middle Eastern peoples, throughout history, failed to derive immigrant elements of their population, culture, or political or dynastic fortunes; and, among the many examples which this consideration, thoughtfully pursued, will evoke—to and from central Asia and India, across the Caucasus, into and out of Europe, up and down the Nile—the sea-ways, and above all those of the

Mediterranean and Aegean, will provide a store not less rich than the routes and bypaths of the mainland.

## 2. Content and Circumstance

Although its formative and dominant features extend beyond it to west and east, a rough classification of our region into three zones is convenient and, since these zones differ so widely in their potential as human habitations, is not uninstructive. The most northerly, a sector of the inter-continental folded zone stretching from the Alps to the Himalayas, covers Asia Minor and Persia; it is marked by long parallel, but sometimes diverging, mountain ranges, whose irregular emergence under powerful pressures of the earth's crust has been further diversified through the ages by more local movements, varying resistances, uneven weathering and other factors. In fact, it is not today a single tidy ridge which reflects in our region these millions of years of geological stresses, with successive earlier and later, stronger and feebler, movements all contributing; it is a wide, deformed and tangled belt of mountainous country, enclosing valleys and lakes, a few rapid unnavigable rivers, depressions rendered salty and repulsive by inward drainage, and high inter-mountain plateaux of which both Turkey and Persia have major examples or of which, indeed, these countries largely consist.

South of this mountain zone lies another, extending from the Sinai peninsula around north Arabia (but south of Taurus) and covering the Euphrates–Tigris lowlands, and the southern shores of the Persian Gulf. Of this area the western flank (Syria, Lebanon, Jordan, Israel) shows faulted, north–south ranges running parallel to the Mediterranean coast; the eastern two-thirds represents the unfolded surviving area of the great Persian Gulf geosyncline deep in the sediments of an ancient sea and modern rivers—and, as we shall see, by far the greatest storehouse of liquid petroleum in the world. This intermediate region is thus less uniform, less clearly characterized, than the other two, yet is more livable and more productive than either.

Our third zone, by far the widest and most uniform, stretching from north and east Africa across almost all Arabia, is that of the African-Arabian Shield. It is characterized by its horizontal masses of ancient and strongly resistant rocks, little disturbed except by the deep (but geologically recent) fissure of the Red Sea, and by volcanic action and lava-flows closely following the fissure line. The

Shield, tilted in Arabia to slope gently downwards towards the east, has been at different geological periods depressed at its edges below sea level, with resulting deposit of sedimentary rocks, not generally comparable in depth with those of synclinal areas but enough to account for Libyan and Algerian oil. The local mountain systems of Oman and the Yemen must be somehow fitted in to the general scheme or schemes of western Asian land-folding, according to the taste of debating geologists.

Partly from these structural differences, partly from others of rock and soil, rainfall and aspect, latitude and temperature, there results in the Middle East an astonishing variety of topographic or land-surface character; the European who has lived in Egypt, or shopped in Beirut, or crossed a desert, or passed months somewhere in an Embassy, cantonment or college, little realizes the widely varied scenic resources, the diversity of settings, which the region can afford. What, and where, are these?

True desert (distinct from lightly-vegetated steppe) is seen by few outsiders, and crossed by fewer. It can be sandy—with or without dunes—or marly, gravelly or stony, for each variety of which local dialects have their word: waterless, or with stretches of salt-marsh: flat or broken or hilly or, as in Sinai, mountainous. Passable always in favourable months by lightly-riding camel-parties, the true desert today offers relatively little resistance to the motor-car, none to aircraft; and one age-long horror is, or need be, no more. Typical middle-eastern deserts, far smaller than the Sahara, are those to east and west of the middle Nile, the Nafud of northern Arabia and the greater Ruba' al-Khali (Empty Quarter) of southern, and the deserts of east-central Persia, the Dasht-i-Kavir and Dasht-i-Lut. Many others would qualify for inclusion. In spite of dust storms and mirage, hideous aridity and wearying surface, the true desert has its attraction, even its beauty; and there are men of quick intelligence and humour to whom it is, if not home, at least familiar and not uncongenial.

The lightest steppe is but one remove from sheer desert, with the basic difference that its scanty, scrubby, thorny, and in rarer places grassy, vegetation can provide, at least in the spring months of a favoured year, some sort of grazing for the camel-herds of the true *badu* who lead in isolation their comfortless, precarious life from waterhole to waterhole. Such steppe country is found, character-istically, on the southern face of the Fertile Crescent, and in partly-vegetated, partly-desertic stretches of Arabia. Less arid but still normally uncultivable steppe is the normal grazing-ground of inlying camel-herds and of the sheep- and goat-owning sections of settled tribes. This is the countryside which, found in southernmost Turkey, western 'Iraq, eastern Syria and Jordan, and wide areas of Persia, can after spring rains turn into a sea of light, ephemeral grass and flowers of wonderful beauty, only to revert weeks later into forbidding brown-grey waste. Steppe life, with all its rigours and poverty, is healthy, strenuous, and full of the tradition and pride of tribalism undebased by the labours of the plough. It is a type of country and of life unknown in western Europe.

Both in utter desert and in all the varieties of steppe-land the oasis is a much-romanticized, yet truly a life-saving, feature. It is marked always by some supply of permanent water, a few dwellings —or in some major settlements, a fair-sized town, as in the oases of central Arabia—probably date-gardens and possibly other limited cultivation, and provision made, by merchant and shopkeeper, for the needs of buying-parties from the steppe-dwelling folk. No country which offers desert or semi-desert areas lacks some examples of oasis life, which modern transport and amenities are daily removing farther from their old remoteness.

A different world is that of the higher, often too the lower, mountain zone with its watered valley cultivation—sometimes immemorially terraced, as in Lebanon or the Yemen—its movement of migratory herdsmen between upper and lower pastures, its clinging hillside villages and intermontane small towns, its planted groves on the lower slopes and the wild scrub or (infrequently) genuine forest on the upper, and in places—the highest peaks of eastern Taurus and of Zagros and Elburz, with Ararat and Demavend outstanding—crowned with perpetual snow. Major stretches of exploitable forest have not, on the whole, survived in the Middle East into the modern age; there is no forest way of life. But otherwise in the wide and wild mountain zones of the region there is room for every type of urban, village, farming and pastoral life, led by peasants, herdsmen and tribes of many races against backgrounds of sometimes grim, sometimes friendly land-surface, at all levels both of physical altitude and of human evolution.

Contrast all this with the lives of the fishing or coast-wise sailing folk of the Black Sea (with its tropical south-eastern shore), or Caspian or Aegean; or the normal Mediterranean seafaring from the delectable villages and port-towns of Syria and Lebanon which face the bluest and clearest of tideless seas; or the reed- and shoal-

and lagoon-fringed Nile Delta, or the featureless sparsely-inhabited shores of the Red and Arabian Seas and the Persian Gulf. No single country of the Middle East lacks a sea-outlet, even 'Iraq with its one river-estuary, even Jordan with only 'Aqaba.

Agriculture, the occupation of far the greater part of Middle Eastern populations, covers in one of its many forms all cultivable areas, tiny percentage as these are of the whole land-surface. Most of western and northern Turkey and part of southern, is agricultural country of a sort, and so is Cyprus, and much of Persia outside the desert regions, and the broad dry-farming lands of the Fertile Crescent as well as the irrigated lands of central and lower 'Iraq, Syria, the Egyptian Delta, the Yemen, and the greater Arabian oases; and later pages of this book may show how various are the scenes and methods, the potentialities of planting and crop-growing in the dozen countries. These are the settled, most favoured areas of many thousands of regionally characteristic villages, locally varying in type, scale, appearance and amenities; of populations sometimes dangerously too dense, sometimes inadequately scanty; of dependence on uncertain rains, or of security assured by irrigation; of primeval method and low yield, or of modern mechanization and pretension. These, in all, are the regions which contain the greatest human activity and wealth production, dull and almost empty as much of them can appear, to the consternation of western visitors, in the seasons when no crops are standing, and where half the land may be fallow. And it is true that few Middle Eastern scenes offer the luxurious greenness of grass and scrub and soft verdant hill and valley, which are the delight of Europe.

These more smiling regions of farmland or easy pasture are those which contain most of the great modern and ancient cities of the Middle East, names too famous to need repeating here; the renowned sites of antiquity, from Persepolis or Babylon to the upper Nile, and the famous still-flourishing shrines of the Islamic and Christian middle ages, from Isfahan and Meshhed to Konya, from Cairo, Damascus and Jerusalem to the Holy Cities of Arabia and 'Iraq.

Of the Middle Eastern landscape, the widest areas present today a picture nearly identical to that of previous centuries, perhaps millennia. Yet a revisiting ghost from antiquity or the Middle Age would still notice changes, not indeed in the face of desert or ocean, but in the course of rivers, the silting at their mouths, the extent of marshes; in human works of drainage, barrage-building, and flood dykes, with irrigation canals and perhaps hydro-electric stations dependent on these. He would see cultivation extended today to limits familiar, perhaps, to our *revenant* from antiquity but far wider than those of the earlier centuries of modern times. He would be shown how thousands of miles of modern roads and railways, with scores of massive river-bridges and hill-cuttings, have shortened distance and sophisticated the scene. A glimpse of seaport installations, giant oil pipelines, industrial workshops, power and telegraph lines crossing desert and mountain, would puzzle and amaze him. In fact, not only in the partly-modernized face of the cities (and hundreds of the villages) has modern effort attacked the whole aspect of the scene, but in the countryside also it is, within limits, ever changing; yet far more is unchangeable, at least until unknown agencies bring about a basic variation of climate. As to this, it has been widely believed that climatic conditions, thought to be cyclical, have varied in the course of human history, and may vary again. Dry water-courses in Arabia, long abandoned, Roman tanks in Jordan, legends of ancient fertility in 'Iraq, and the visible fact of giant canals aligned in now waterless tracts, the imposing scale of steppe-country oases in Persia and Syria, are adduced to prove that, in earlier ages of our race, the Middle East was better watered. This is not proved; it is more probable that the days of greater humidity were those of pre-human ages—the Pleistocene, perhaps; and that, since man's appearance, the phenomena noticed can be well enough explained by a diminished population, a lowered water-table, some deforestation, much soil-erosion and scouring of river-beds, with the abandonment of once-inhabited sites for political or security reasons. In older human times, it rather seems, the conditions of life were substantially as they are today, with the same problems and disabilities, the same balance between agricultural and pastoral life, the same routes and halting-places.

Our region is, almost uniformly, one of hot summers and cold or cool winters, and the range of variation between July–August and January–February is unusually wide. The heat of mid-summer, its severity due to cloudless skies, scanty vegetation and (except near coasts) 'continental' conditions, runs in most Middle Eastern capitals to an average daily maximum in July of 82° to 92° F, but higher—93° to 100°—in Aleppo, Damascus, Teheran, Cairo and Aden, and well beyond 100°, up to extremes little short of 130°, in the cities of 'Iraq, inland southern Persia, and penisular Arabia. In mid-winter, the greatest cold occurs in eastern Asia Minor and parts of northern Persia, where a February average night minimum can be

—15° F, with an extreme of —35° or less. Aden is never less than warm in winter, Egypt cool (45°–50°), 'Iraq cooler (32°–42°), with northern Persia chilly (around 25°), Ankara cold (17°). Snow in winter, habitual in the north and the mountains, is not unknown throughout the region, except in the farthest south. Streams can freeze anywhere north of a line Jerusalem–Basra, and sea-water in the Black Sea. The greatest night–day variations occur far inland, and at high altitudes; here they are a marked feature, and restorative cool nights are the greatest of blessings in scorched 'Iraq and elsewhere. Air humidity is extremely low in 'continental' areas, where great dryness helps the endurance of intense heat; it is greater, or great, in seaside areas—the Mediterranean, Red Sea and Persian Gulf coasts—where, expecially in summer, it is highly uncomfortable. Fog is uncommon, but by no means unknown. The high dust-laden winds of summer, notably in 'Iraq and north Africa (the *sharqi* or *sharji*, and the *khamsin*) are a sore trial during their three or four days' duration; 'Iraq's northerly, date-ripening *shamal* is a corresponding relief.

The whole region would be transformed both in aspect and in economic potential if its rainfall were more plentiful and better distributed. Except in north-eastern Turkey, Caspian Persia, and parts of the Yemen, rain is nearly everywhere inadequate and in most cases gravely deficient. It falls, almost universally, in winter and spring only, with very minor or freakish falls in autumn; but its precise timing, a vital matter to the growth of the rain-dependent spring grains, can vary tragically, and in not infrequent years it can fall to half or less of its normal deposit: that is, well below minimum crop requirements. This does not preclude showers of great violence when they occur, giving, over small areas, an inch of rain in an hour —with effects on traffic which can be imagined. Most of Arabia and Egypt are habitually rainless, the Fertile Crescent and most of Iran ill-supplied with a bare 6 to 14 inches a year, western Turkey and the Levant coast fairly adequately with 20 to 30 inches; but the deficiency of statistics, and the caprices of the weather itself, make precision impossible. Both local and annual variations are extreme, yet of immense importance to immediate human needs.

Are human needs, then, in general well served or not by Middle Eastern conditions? In spite of travellers' tales and some admittedly adverse features, and in so far as one may generalize over so wide and heterogeneous an area, conditions must be pronounced favourable. If temperatures can be extreme, they are never unbearable, and neither physical well-being nor morale need suffer. Cool and clear summer nights are normal. Winds can be high—as they can be in Europe; rains can fail—not in the Middle East alone. Air is pure, often highly invigorating. Every season has its charm, if rarely quite unalloyed. Contrasts of temperature should be welcomed. With a reasonable personal regime and intelligent adaptation to conditions, excellent health can be enjoyed; the indifferent physique of too many Middle Easterners is due mainly to causes other than their natural environment. Indeed, considering the dangers to health consequent on a central position in the world, and numerous centres of thronged pilgrimage, and widely low standards of living, endemic disease is less menacing than might well be expected, and can without great difficulty be almost entirely avoided by the careful and the competent. Malaria is widely prevalent, in its usual haunts, but is easily treated and is being yearly circumscribed. Yellow fever, known in the Sudan, is rare in the Middle East. Typhus occurs epidemically, but is never widespread. Cholera, never endemic, is now uncommon. Dysentery is a known danger to foreigners, but can be kept at bay by due precautions. Bilharzia is common in Egypt and in 'Iraq; hookworm (ankylostomiasis) is similar. Eye diseases, especially trachoma, are common and distressing but, under treatment, now fast diminishing. The same is true of the painless but disfiguring 'Baghdad boil' or 'Aleppo button'. Of all of these and other diseases, dirt, poverty and ignorance are the firm allies, in whose absence they can be, indeed to an encouraging extent are being, overcome. Sheer malnutrition, reflecting a too generally low level of wealth and resources, is by far the greatest enemy of health and vigour, and its progressive correction, significant of all-round improvement in standards of life, must remain the supreme task of governments and peoples.

## 3. *Does it matter?*

This is the moment, perhaps, for pausing to ask and answer two questions which a critical reader may have been formulating. The first is—has this region, upon the many diversities of which we have been insisting, any *unity* at all?—is it authentically a Region? and secondly, is it, or ought it to be, of any genuine or particular *interest* to the present-day citizen of the world?

There is no geological and little topographical unity, racial homogeneity only in a generalized sense, linguistic not at all, political too evidently imperfect. Yet, apart from the sheer propinquity and continuity of the Middle Eastern territories one with another, their over-lapping physical circumstance, and considerable cultural and religious (that is, Islamic) unity, there are also undeniably similar features of character among most of the populations concerned, familar elements of common regional history, not dissimilar phases of national emer-gence and aspiration—and shared antipathies!—and, with all this, much modern inter-territory social admixture, mutual familarity, visiting, intermarriage. It is, on the whole, a Region.

As to its degree of significance to the world outside, it could indeed be, and has been, argued that for some centuries the region has made no first-class, acclaimed contribution to the world's learn-ing, culture or outstanding performance: that it has long fallen away from, and is not yet restored to, the main currents of human progress: that it lacks any broadly based social or intellectual contact with the West. On another plane, it may be felt that the uneasy bickering and inconstancy of its political attitudes, its alleged immaturity or irre-sponsibility in international affairs, its tiresome egocentricities, its failures in democratic government, are neither admirable nor re-assuring. Economically, it is known to possess no single important resource, save only petroleum; it is an area of poverty and want, backward in its traditional agriculture, and but a beginner, and of no more than mediocre promise, in modern industry. These are harsh charges; they are, to be sure, not wholly true nor wholly false; and, either way, there is much more than this to be said.

This region indeed, which seems, by its continuous prominence in the world's headlines, to be thought interesting by mankind at large, has high claims to our close attention, and to our sympathy. In the field of sentiment, it offers a great and often beautiful variety of scene, a persistent survival of the romantic, and the spectacle of societies, themselves most varied, of attractive human beings in many environments and at diverse stages of their evolution from earlier to the most modern phases of development. There are every-where links with the early days of the great religions of Islam, Christianity and Judaism, all of which are still abundantly alive in the area. To the missionary and educator, the field has long been one of outstanding attraction and major effort. To the archaeologist and historian, it is a region of unique appeal for its ancient and medieval civilizations, for the world's earliest recorded ways of life and cities and empires, with all that these involve and offer. To the orientalist it is the greatest of storehouses. And to thousands of families in the West it is the scene of two world wars in our own century, whereby thousands of their kinsmen found graves in 'some corner of a foreign field' within these territories.

In the sphere of economics, the presence in the Middle East of the greatest petroleum deposits in the world must outweigh its comparative lack of other indigenous wealth, and must be of outstanding interest to the producing countries themselves (who own the oil-fields), to the great international companies entrusted by them with operation, and to the world at large whose adequate supply of this most indispensable of substances depends on the Middle Eastern sources. Apart from this, the agriculture, the stock-breeding, and the increasing industry of the territories themselves are, and can be, on a scale by no means unimportant; the populations can offer markets which will inevitably increase in scale; and they call for assistance in the execution of their own development plans, which the nations of the West do not find uninteresting. Nor is the economic future of Middle Eastern countries, on their national scale, other than an engrossing study.

Strategically, this three-continental region has all the importance of its unique central position, its immemorial east–west routes between Europe and Africa and central and southern Asia, its endless available airfields, its almost unavoidable (but nationalistically sacrosanct) inter-continental corridors of air-route. It contains narrow but vital strategic sea-ways—Bosphorus, Dardanelles, Suez Canal, and the straits at the base of the Red Sea and Persian Gulf —and naval bases (actual and potential) of great value. It seems indeed to be recognized that to wage global war without holding at least a favourable position in the Middle East, the wasp-waist of the Old World, would be barely a possibility. Of its value as a counter-attack area against northern enemies there may, in the age of atomic warfare, be less certainty; in a conventional war, it would be at least considerable.

As to the present politics of the region, these, in terms of the internal stresses and intrigues, the personalities and the fragile institutions of each single territory, are a study perhaps fascinating, often depressing, certainly instructive; and if today most of the Middle Eastern countries are of no great moment in the balance of world affairs, some few are of more significance and higher potential, while nearly all offer the far from banal spectacle of political entities yearly developing their public and economic life and passing, as they hope, from backward obscurity into a place and an individuality of their own on the world stage. This aspect, the emergence of communities from colonial or provincial or mandated status into sovereign rank, affords interesting examples of a movement common in twentieth-century Asia and Africa, and among the most significant of our times. Its immediate interest is all the keener since most of the nations concerned, once made members of United Nations, take their place among the officially uncommitted or unaligned, and, linked with sister nations of Africa, can by their votes exercise an influence wholly disproportionate to their own strength, wealth or population.

But this is still not the whole content of their international interest. Because the Middle East contains the sacred homelands of Islam, and the State of Israel, and the birthplace and home of Christianity's Founder, it follows that Muslims, Christians and Jews throughout the world take a keener interest in its vicissitudes, as these affect their religion and their co-religionists there, than in the fortunes of any other region on earth save those of their own residence. Muslims of Indonesia, Pakistan, Morocco, Senegal; Jews in New York, South Africa, London; Christians throughout Europe, America, Australia; all or any of these can be moved by actual or threatened events in the Middle East, and by their own government's attitude towards them, in the direction of political gestures or pressures at home which these governments cannot ignore. Thus Middle Eastern antipathies and hopes can cast their shadow into far-off lands, and can remind distant governments and publics of the unique and too easily dangerous sensitiveness attaching to the region of which we write.

# CHAPTER TWO

# ANTIQUITY

## 1. *Before the Dawn*

DOUBTS as to whether a Social Geography should pay heed to ages of past history in the region concerned can be dispelled by some cogent considerations. The early origins of the inhabitants, most imperfectly ascertainable, may throw but scanty light on their present idiosyncracies, but can hardly be uninteresting; their successive stages of cultural history have all contributed to what they now are, their racial admixtures show at least with what sort of human blends we have to deal, and the mere growth in scale of human groupings—village, canton, city-state, nation—reveals the power or impotence of contemporary society to face new problems. The effect of foreign contacts, by action and reaction, through trade or mere cultural borrowing, can be assessed. The influences of environment on the march of local history can hardly escape the observer, and may sway his present judgments, since they are sure to persist. The occasions of the introduction or evolution of new conceptions and inventions in the region may have significance. And in the recorded, or often enough the invented, achievements of their alleged forebears, a modern nation may find inspiration or political predilection still today operative.

We pass perforce, therefore, to a consideration of the races of men found originally and later in our region, and their early and subsequent history, until we see them in our own century taking form as the familiar nation-states of today.

In terms of population, we are limited to very few original elements. They belong, as do practically all later accretions that we shall note, to the Caucasiform group of humanity: that is, roughly, to the European-like, largely or mainly 'white', wavy-haired, narrow and salient-nosed, thin-lipped part of the human race so classified. The student of Middle Eastern affairs is almost never concerned with Negroes or Mongols, but only with our own main family. And, even within this, many sub-groups have no place on our stage; except for uncertain or slightest admixtures, the scene belongs to Alpine, Mediterranean and Nordic man.

Nordic man does not appear in the Middle East till historical times. He belongs by origin to the great central Asian grass-lands, but with gradual specialization to northern conditions in Asia and then in Europe. The body is slender, extremities long, skull and other bones rugged, face and nose narrow, cheekbones fairly prominent, colour blond. The variations of stature and skull-form (mainly long-shaped) show in historical times much admixture with the original 'pure' type (whenever and wherever evolved and dispersed) of other breeds encountered during millennia of movement.

Primeval Alpine man is of darker colouring, abundant body-hair, lightish eyes, medium height and strong build, with short or roundish head, high curved occiput, short narrow nose, broad face. The special Alpine type which, all agree, has contributed so largely to Middle Eastern populations (especially in Asia Minor, parts of Persia and 'Iraq, and the Syrian mountain-country) is the Armenoid, with a characteristic flat occiput, receding forehead, strong brow-ridges and cheekbones, long face, and a high-bridged nose with depressed tip and curved wings—the so-called 'Jewish' nose. It is likely that these Alpine types were, from some unknown place of origin, very early entrants into western Asia. They have dominated mountain areas ever since, but have penetrated far less into Africa or Arabia.

Mediterranean man is today found (never 'pure', but nearest to purity in Arabia and North Africa) all round the Mediterranean coasts, in non-mountainous 'Iraq and Persia, in Palestine and Egypt. In what is effectively a complex of similar types there is always discernible a dolichocephalic skull and a sallow pigment. In western Asia the type is of generally medium to tall stature, with prominent cheekbones, oval face, narrow skull, and a large, fairly broad nose, straight or convex and placed high on the face. The area in which this extremely prevalent breed, Mediterranean man, may have originated cannot be discovered; indeed, not only the unknown, probably unknowable, provenance of all human families must be emphasized, but the fact also that purity of type had been lost millennia before any race emerged into history; not only are all men mongrels, but they have been so for many thousands of years. It is apparent, however, for our present purpose that the first occupation of our region by *homo sapiens* was at a very remote palaeolithic period, when, after the retreat of the last glaciers, human societies penetrated the area: societies of physical types which, blended and adapted through the centuries to many environments, have in

Europe and Asia persisted and progressed more, in terms of valuable achievement, than other branches of the human family. And the same processes of migration, penetration, settlement, and reblending have, as Middle Eastern history repeatedly illustrates, continued from prehistoric times without interruption to our own.

In the days when the earliest artifacts, as discovered in many parts of the Middle East, were fashioned by fumbling human or near-human fingers, there was already a wide diversity of communities in many settings—hunting, food-gathering, fishing, or busy with the earliest agriculture and animal husbandry—incorporating the basic Alpines and Mediterraneans we have described, and keenly conscious of village, tribal or (later) city identity. Among these, the prehistoric Egyptians of, let us say, 5000 B.C., seem to have been brunette Mediterranean types with almost certainly some darker-skinned admixture from the south, with a strain also of Arabian from across the Red Sea, and probably already some contribution of Alpine immigrants from the Syrian hills. They lived in villages, farmed, fished and hunted, used pots and baskets and flint-knives in neatly-built houses, knew weaving and leatherwork, obeyed half-priestly head-men, worshipped gods. The earliest Syrians were Alpines in the coastal ridges, mixed already with Mediterraneans from the flat Fertile Crescent hinterland where the latter prevailed. These Neolithic folk were, like the Egyptians, very far from savagery; they had their homes, furniture and implements, their way of life varying between steppe, valley and sea-coast. The use of copper came in about 4000 B.C. Cyprus was perhaps first occupied by emigrants from western Asia, with a mixture of very early Aegean settlers. In Asia Minor one would expect Armenoid types, perhaps already diluted by the inward movement of undiscoverable non-Alpine strains from south-east Europe or south Russia by way of the Caucasus. Civilization, well begun by the fourth millennium B.C., varied here as between the fringes of the central plateau, the two plains south of Taurus, and the Aegean-type valleys of western Anatolia; but in them all civilized village life was already developed. Persia, not yet Aryanized, held a diffused, intelligent, village-dwelling Neolithic population, presumably Alpine and Mediterranean. Only in the south, the future Khuzistan, does it seem that some alien strain (just possibly north Indian or Dravidian) had penetrated. It had created the highly developed civilization of Elam, already grouped in large villages or even cities under priest-kingly control, with skilled agriculture, fully articulate religion, and foreign trade.

The same picture holds good for central and southern 'Iraq. The Sumerians, small, dark and round-headed, and speaking an agglutinative language, remain mysterious, but, whoever they were, they had welded aboriginal elements into a new type of community, grouped in highly organized and competitive city-states directed by able, sophisticated men. Elsewhere in 'Iraq, Mediterraneans, with Alpine types in the (later) Kurdish mountains, were dominant. The open plains of northern 'Iraq and eastern Syria had held from remote ages settled and half-settled communities, less advanced than those we have mentioned but already providing the means of communication between Asia Minor, Syria, and the Euphrates Valley. In Arabia the population was probably less impure Mediterranean, but had experienced at some period an incursion of round-headed large-nosed Alpines from the northern mountain-zone to such territory there, in the deep south, as suited them. Arabia indeed, potentially the most isolated of our areas, was no doubt already developing its own migratory and, in the extreme south-west, settled ways: was reaching the limits of population it could sustain, and cradling the original Semitic stock—a population, that is, substantially uniform in type and speaking some basic variety of the later modified and localized Semitic language-family.

All this involves much vagueness and doubt; and even the terms and classifications we use have little enough of precise content. It is certain, however, that the more favoured areas of the region were inhabited by man from his earliest ages, and that he had by 5000 B.C. passed through the stages of acquiring speech and clothing, domestic comfort, settled residence, and relatively advanced notions of social organization, during millennia when his presence is still but faintly discernible to the archaeologist. And of what other area of all the world could this be said with so much confidence?

We proceed next to ask what, after a great leap through centuries, was to be the Middle Eastern picture by—to take a date almost at random—2500 B.C.

## 2. Earliest History

The emergence of our region into a faint light of history was by 2500 B.C. far from complete; we depend still on the archaeology which, in the hands of patient experts of a dozen nations, at scores of buried sites, has in the last century and a half made the Middle East the paradise of the scholar-digger.

But the pace of change was by that date already accelerating far beyond the nearly-static tempo of past millennia. The use of metals —copper, then bronze, then iron—was spreading into the fields of ornament, utensil and weapon; clothing, housing, specialization of function, were all developed and developing. Agriculture, and especially controlled irrigation, the lifeblood of Egypt and 'Iraq, had made strides of progress. Early forms of writing, not yet alphabetic, were in use in Sumer, Babylonia, Elam, Egypt, in the hands of priests, traders and account-book-minded landlords. The arts had reached a high perfection, royal and public building attained unknown levels and used materials brought from far afield. The worship of local (city and tribal) gods was ever more elaborated, and merged with the pretensions of local rulers more and more theocratic. Egyptian sovereigns had from about 3000 B.C. onwards built the greatest of the pyramids, the Sumerians their *ziggurats*, and by both Nile and Euphrates the sciences of measurement, astronomy and mathematics had been much more than initiated. The grouping of villages and the countryside into larger units was in train; the chiefs of Elam successively but ephemerally mastered each other; in 'Iraq the Sumerian cities formed short-lived empires within their world, which was gaining space physically year by year, as it still is, by riverain silt-deposit on the Gulf shores. The title 'Lord of Sumer and Akkad' was claimed by the priest-king of one city after another, with varying fortunes. In Egypt the Nile-side villages were drawn closer together and, after intermediate stages of unifying, the legendary Menes at last created, in the First Dynasty, a single Egyptian Kingdom destined to set the not-always-maintained standard of country-wide unity. What forms, if any, of grouping were in hand elsewhere, in Persia, Anatolia or Syria, we cannot know; but probably some nucleus of consolidated power in Cappadocia was already forming, and some city-king of Cyprus could briefly claim the whole island's allegiance.

Intercommunication between the various territories, highly significant for their later fortunes, was by this time increasing. There are suggestions of an inroad of Asiatic (Syrian or Arabian) tribes into Egypt, perhaps in the third millennium. There was trade and raiding out of Egypt towards Sinai, Syria, Nubia, and intercourse between Syria, Cilicia and 'Iraq. The Tigris–Euphrates Valley was, as ever, exposed to incursions from the surrounding mountain country to the east and north, and this could not remain one-sided. Already the traditional function of hungry Arabia, as a reservoir of potentially emigrant tribesmen, had begun to operate; Semitic-speaking tribes, probably in slow persistent trickles with occasional denser waves, had by 2500 moved into eastern Syria, perhaps abortively down into Egypt, certainly into central and western 'Iraq. Here, the area immediately north of Sumer had become largely Semitized (while retaining or borrowing Sumerian ways) and recently under a great leader 'Sargon of Akkad' had raided far afield into Syria and Lebanon and the Persian hill-country. This was a one-man exploit; Sargon neither founded nor conceived an empire and did not long disturb the balances of city power even in Sumer and Akkad. But from now onwards the Semites were, with great persistence, to repeat their gradual yet pervasive entry, every few centuries, deep into the Fertile Crescent—yet were never to penetrate into Anatolia or Persia or, save briefly, into Egypt. The 'Iraq city-states of this period traded widely with neighbouring lands, enriching their material life and techniques, and their knowledge of the world.

A thousand years later, in 1500 B.C., the picture has changed in a score of ways. Far to the north-west, Greece and the Aegean had begun to receive waves of Nordic Greek-speaking immigrants, and these were developing an amazing civilization based first on Crete and spreading soon to the mainland, to the islands, and to the western approaches of Anatolia. In Asia Minor, associated waves of Nordic immigration, by way of the Bosphorus and possibly the Caucasus, had entered the territory, provided a new dynamism and a ruling class, and fashioned, *inter alia*, the strong continental power of the Kheta, or Hittites of Cappadocia. This by 1500 had gained control of most of Anatolia, had occupied Cilicia and northern Syria and the great trade-routes, and had raided Babylon. At home it evolved an efficient government, as then conceived, with a careful diplomatic service, an established law, a complicated polytheism, and its own social system. The Hittite State, using metals (though not yet iron) and based on a well-adapted agriculture, had already attained a high standard of life under its ruling dynasties and provincial governors.

In Syria, the year 1500 opened upon a scene where an extensive political unity had never been attained; the country, from Sinai to Cilicia, was too open, too vulnerable to stronger neighbours on north, north-east and south. It had developed instead a highly civilized system of city-states, which had by now absorbed and learnt from Semitic invaders of the great Amorite migration-wave, had sustained strong influences from Egypt and from 'Iraq, and was subjected to Hittite aggression from behind the Taurus. The cities of all parts of

Syria had multiplied their mutual and their foreign connections, had corresponded with a score of distant potentates and merchants, and had perfected the system of writing imported from Babylonia. On the coast, the Phoenicians developed on lines of their own, with a wide sea-borne trade and close contacts with other east Mediterranean seafarers; they were wealthy, self-contained, and devoid of imperial ambitions. The Canaanitish amalgam in southern Syria, who consisted of earlier Palestinian stocks with a now dominant Semitic element, still awaited the Hebrew invasion.

Egypt had suffered much and achieved much in the last thousand years. The Pharaonic dynasties had succeeded, with some lapses, in retaining Egyptian unity against the sometimes successful pretensions of regional kinglets and priestly ambition, and with each century had rendered the prevailing theocratic system, with its ancestor-worship, its colossal burial places, its powerful priestly interest, its divine omnipotent Pharaohs, more rigid and conservative. Trading and military and naval expeditions had around the nineteenth century extended Egyptian influence in coastal Syria almost to the point of empire; the aggressive Libyans were kept at bay, Nubia was colonized, lost and reoccupied, the land of Punt (perhaps Somalia) was visited for its tropical products. In the eighteenth to the sixteenth centuries a confused period of dynastic weakness was followed by an Asia invasion and partial occupation, that of the mysterious Hyksos, under whom weakness and regionalism again prevailed. Traditionally 'shepherd kings'—which seems to mean nomadic tribesmen from the Arabian steppes—the Hyksos are thought by other scholars to be some intrusive northern element, or even a mixed force of mercenaries collected in Syria itself. Nobody knows. The eighteenth dynasty, however, arose and expelled the intruders in the mid-sixteenth century, restored Egyptian unity, and reasserted full imperial power over Syria and the upper Nile. This, at home and abroad, was Egypt's greatest period; it began about 1525 B.C.

In 'Iraq the exploits of Sargon of Akkad were followed by an obscure period in which the city-states, under each its dynasty, could preserve their own now complicated and refined manner of life, but suffered also, it seems, from incursions of hill-tribesmen from the east, and even more, from the current waves of ex-Arabian Semitic invasion and immigration. This was operative equally in northern 'Iraq, where it transmuted the old population into a new, Semitized and formidable type—the disciplined, militarist Assyrian devoted to the truculent service of his (Semitic) god, Asshur. In south and central 'Iraq it led to the establishment of the new, dynamic state of Babel or Babylon, in which by 1800 B.C. their great king Hammurabi ('Amraphael, King of Shinar' in the Bible) had fashioned an 'Iraqi empire, raided his neighbours, and gained immortal fame by his code of laws. Babylon, greatest name in ancient 'Iraq, held thenceforth for more than a thousand years a unique status by its wealth, culture and dominion. But for the moment it was to fall, soon after Hammurabi's death, by natural causes and by the effects of a long-range Hittite raid, to the obscurity of a centuries-long occupation by a Kassu (or Kassite) dynasty, imposed, it seems, by tribesmen from the Persian mountains, and capable of acquiring civilization from its new subjects, the Sumerian and Akkadian cities. 'Iraq has little history known to us from 1750 onwards till fully three centuries later. Culturally its ways of life, sciences, writings, and political forms remained remarkably uniform and constant, and closely parallel to those of the contemporary Nile Valley. Elam at this period preserved its independence, and even gave rulers, for a time, to some of the Sumerian cities. A major part of 'Iraq's extreme south formed its own Chaldaean State of 'the Sea-land'.

The Kassu, with all their own mystery, are significant of great events elsewhere. They were in all probability forerunners of a great movement of peoples from the central grasslands of Asia, a movement which was reaching and overspilling the Persian plateau towards the second quarter, or the middle, of the second millennium B.C.—and related, therefore, to the contemporary descent of Nordic peoples into the Aegean world and Anatolia. These people, whose cousins were simultaneously invading India, spoke Aryan or Indo-European languages, were of generally Mediterranean type and, with their vigour and mobility, their fresh conceptions, their new and (for a time) supreme war-machine the chariot, could provide the Middle East with a contribution in blood and character to counterbalance that of the Semites. The first phase of this process was to furnish a ruling caste to widely separated communities in various parts of Persia. In the north and north-west 'Iraq and north-east Syria, around the same period, populous communities hitherto obscure turned into considerable states under dominant Indo-European clans or families; the Hittites (p. 30) were one such, the Hurrians, with their still unlocated capital at Mitanni, were another, while around Lake Van, deep in the mountains, was a third, the little-known State of Urartu.

## 3. Crowded Millennium

The thousand years stretching from 1500 to 500 B.C. were filled with great events in our region—movements of peoples, rise and fall of empires, disruption and coalescence, significant innovation—which have visibly and invisibly marked the course of all later periods. It was an age of large-scale political experiment, of developed international relations, of a new confrontation of Asia and Europe, as well as of scientific and political discovery—of the solar calendar, human records, alphabetic writing, coinage—which we directly inherit. And for every notable event known to history, a score of items were occurring unseen and unrecorded yet integrally part of, and perhaps in aggregate profoundly affecting, the whole march of affairs and the future.

The Egyptian monarchy, with its background of a culturally static population, a privileged priesthood, and strong cross-currents of internal ambition and subversion, failed in these centuries to maintain its imperial position. In spite of repeated military expeditions northwards into Syria, and bloody battles there against confederate Amorite cities and their allies, in spite also of an ever-active diplomacy and royal intermarriages with Hittite rulers and Mitanni, the mastery over Syria—at best a mere overlordship over tributary communities—was weakened, regained, and lost. The strain of control, so far from the homeland and among vigorous and alien city-states, proved too much for the Nilotic power, and this was further weakened in the thirteenth to twelfth centuries by attempted foreign invasion of its own frontiers, on land by incursion of Libyans, and by sea from northern Mediterranean forces, mainly Greek and presumably all-'European'—the Sea Peoples of contemporary inscriptions. These trials were survived; but from 1050 onwards national weakness was more apparent, the kingdom itself was divided and reunited, all military dependence was on mercenaries, the throne fell to Pharaohs of foreign origin, and an occasional expedition despatched into Palestine could do no more than sack a city (as Jerusalem in 930) and return. Egypt with all its immemorial and strangely specialized culture, law-codes, science, medicine, arts, and complete mastery of its unique environment, was no longer a great power. Its rulers were glad to welcome Greek colonies in the Delta, and were forced, in the mid-seventh century, to bow to the invading Assyrian power of Asshur-bani-pal, to pay him tribute and accept his garrisons. A national revival under a new Greek-aided dynasty followed the fall of Assyria, and Egypt could enjoy a century of revived prosperity and a resolute but finally abortive attempt to refound its empire in Asia. But Egyptian forces were defeated by Babylonia (Carchemish, 605), and less than a century later (525) the country fell helplessly to the new, all-conquering, Persian Empire.

In Anatolia, the fortunes of the Hittite State in the seventeenth and sixteenth centuries are unknown to us; thereafter, stronger than ever, it established relations with resurgent Egypt, could interfere decisively in Mitanni affairs, ally itself with rising Assyria, and keep its place in Syria until, after the extinction of the Mitanni principality, it could dominate it. The Hittites absorbed a further incursion of Nordic tribes from the north-east, intrigued and bullied among the Amorite and Phoenician city-states of Syria, and played the role of paramount power in the Levant whenever Egyptian control weakened; Hittite-Egyptian fighting was indecisive, and a régime of formal treaty and royal intermarriage suited both parties better. In Anatolia itself, Hittite predominance did not exclude a number of other independent, if intermittently tributary, states on fringes of the plateau —Lycians, Carians, Lydians and others. The seemingly sudden end of the Hittite State in its own homelands, around 1230 B.C., is best explained by further and stronger Nordic incursions from eastern Europe—perhaps of the Phrygians (who proceeded to found a rich, progressive state in western Anatolia), and certainly as part of the massive restlessness of the Mediterranean-Aegean world in the thirteenth to twelfth centuries. Similar blows were to fall again on the plateaux and valleys of Anatolia in the early seventh century when an invasion of northern tribesmen from the grasslands beyond the Caucasus—fierce, horse-mounted Kimmerians, and Scythians the scourge of the settled populations—poured into the land, and made a place for itself there partly by founding small mountain principalities under their own ruling caste, and partly by slow absorption or dispersal, as one more digested, invisible element in the population. But the Hittite name, and much of its prestige and culture, survived in 'Hittite' cities of north Syria (known as such to the Assyrians and in the Bible) in the ninth and eighth centuries. The Hittite blood and tradition, as of a race of imperial conquerors, were a legacy to successors in Anatolia.

In Syria, political unity was never achieved. The cities of Phoenicia —Ugarit, Byblos, Tyre and Sidon amongst them—persisted in their far-flung maritime trade, were familiar with all parts of the Mediterranean, founded colonies in north Africa (Carthage and Utica) and

Spain (Cadiz), and benefited by the collapse of the Cretan sea-power, about 1400. The strong and highly civilized city-states of the hinterland could sometimes combine—notably but vainly against Egyptian, Hittite or Assyrian pretensions—but more often pursued their bickering separatism even in times of foreign overlordship. Their struggles partly conceal from our sight a major event common to all Syria in this period, the gradual but pervasive incursion of yet another major wave of Semitic-speakers from the eastern and southern steppe-country, this time the Aramaean. The newcomers acquired no empire, the cities founded by them claimed no major place in the teeming political life of the Levant; but within three centuries (fourteenth to eleventh) the Aramaeans not only became full Syrians but, by intermixture and intermarriage, by the almost universal spread of their Aramaic (north-west Semitic) speech—soon to be the *lingua franca* of a great part of the Middle East south of the Taurus—and by merging their culture in that of the pre-existing population, they became easily the dominant element in the territory.

With the rest, they suffered in these centuries the aggression or butchery of Assyrian armies, and found themselves at most times tributary to Nineveh or Babylon. First in the thirteenth and twelfth centuries, and later in the ninth and thereafter, the kings of Assyria with their bloodthirsty armies entered the territory to destroy and loot, and to claim every privilege of ruthless conquest. Not always successful, since their communications were long and the military effort immense, their king could in the eighth and seventh centuries undertake repeatedly the conquest of the Syrian principalities, including those of Palestine and the Hebrews. Esarhaddon's invasion of Egypt, by way of Syria, in 670 was the last appearance of this detested power on the Mediterranean coasts.

In southern Syria—Canaan, or Palestine—the entry of the Hebrew tribes, subject of so much curious legend and later intense world-interest, took place slowly over many decades about the thirteenth century. Overcoming by degrees the resistance of Transjordan tribes and fortresses and those of Canaan itself, the new Hebrew or Israeli community was important in Palestine by the twelfth century, and dominant, though still locally resisted, by the eleventh; its half-anarchic period of 'the Judges' gave way to a central monarchy by 1000 B.C., as recorded in the Bible stories of Saul, David, Solomon and their quarrelsome successors. These rulers, and especially the last-named, were able effectively to create one more among the many petty states of the Levant; they traded widely, organized a close national life, and found peaceful or violent contact with Egypt, Phoenicia and the Amorite and Aramaean cities. They overcame after long struggles their enemies, the doughty yet highly civilized Philistines, a community of European immigrants (p. 33) now settled on the coast of Palestine, and they developed, with sublime poetry and sonorous 'prophecy', the worship of their vengeful tribal god Jahweh, or Jehovah; a religion destined to develop, in the hands and hearts of a gifted race, into a broad monotheism with a moral content rare if not unique in that period, side by side with an exclusive nationalism which prevented its wide diffusion. Meanwhile, the two yet smaller kingdoms into which the Hebrew State divided, those of Israel and Judah, both fell victims, like all their neighbours, to the armies of foreign empires. Both were invaded and became tributary to the Assyrian tyrants. Thousands of Israelis were carried off to captivity in Media in 721, while Assyrian colonists, brought to Palestine, settled and intermarried there to form the Samaritan community. The kingdom of Judah and Jerusalem, after a further century of strain, threat, and invasion, fell in spite of an Egyptian alliance to the arms of revived Babylon (p. 37) in 586, and the 'Babylonish captivity' of its people began. This ended in 538 with the gradual return of part of the exiles, under the Persian Empire; a larger part declined to leave their new homes.

In lower 'Iraq, the supremacy of rich, luxurious, learned Babylon, once freed from its unwanted Kassite rulers (c. 1200), was never in doubt until the end of the period we are reviewing. The old Sumerian states were slowly losing their traditional character and contributing little new; the Sea Lands, like them, were undergoing population changes, probably by Arabian immigration, but managed to keep their near-independence. Babel itself, with a revived vigour and sense of mission, organized its own central area of 'Iraq, raided mountain and desert neighbours, and until 612 maintained with its formidable northern neighbour relations varying from war and mutual destruction to peaceful ceremonial exchanges. This neighbour was, from the fourteenth century onwards, the aggressive and brutal, but efficient and not uncultured state and later Empire of Assyria. With its successive capitals at Asshur, Nimrud, Khorsabad and Nineveh, the Assyrian kings, who included such great names as Tiglath-Pileser, Asshur-Nasir-Pal, Shalmaneser, Sargon, Senna-cherib, Esarhaddon, inspired terror in a wide circle of territories by their military prowess and innovations, which included the use of horse-chariots. Apart from Syrian and Egyptian campaigns, which enforced obedience and tribute, the Assyrian invaded also Asia Minor, outlasted the Mitanni and the Hittites, clashed with King Midas of Phrygia, put an end to Elamite independence, practised long-drawn diplomacy with Pharaoh, and pressed hard on Babylonia. Assyrian merchants settled in north-western Persia, in and beyond the Taurus, in Elam and southern 'Iraq. The state was for five centuries (twelfth to seventh) a major power of the Middle East, and for the last three of these was harshly dominant. When Nineveh, exhausted by incessant warfare, fell in 612 to a newly risen Iranian power, that of the Medes, it left vast records in stone and marble, but little in humanity or the arts of living. The succession fell, as we shall see, first in part to the Medes, in part to Babylon (whose last century of independence under a Sea Land dynasty was one of power, wealth and foreign campaigns), and later all to the Persian Empire.

In Persia the appearance of a great power, emerging from the new country-wide demographic conditions there which followed the Indo-European (or Indo-Iranian) mass immigration (p. 32), was long delayed: partly, no doubt, because this inward flood was a continuing and restless process needing time for absorption, habituation and community-building, and partly also through the jealous power of neighbouring Assyria which was forced, for its own security, to deal hard blows at such hopeful new Iranian groupings—in the Azarbaijan region, for instance (Urartu, p. 32), and in western and southern Iran. But the Aryan ruling caste, which penetrated both throughout Persia (except in certain aboriginal enclaves) and deeply also into Asia Minor, but never into 'Iraq or Arabia, contained newness of thought and potential, and some remarkable characters, one of whom was soon to emerge. We cannot now know the course of alliances, intrigues, expansions or hostilities among malcontent neighbours of Assyria in the twelfth to eighth centuries; but a Median nation, across the Zagros from 'Iraq, came into existence in that period, resisted Assyrian raids, and produced (or was produced by) a strong ruling family. By the end of the seventh century Nineveh was exhausted and degenerate, and the Assyrian power fell in a day and for ever (612 B.C.). Babylon resumed its independent sway in 'Iraq, while the vigorous rising state of Media took the place of Assyria in all the northern and eastern dominions of its empire.

The Median State lasted a bare half-century, time to establish new forms of rule in Iran itself and to press new foreign campaigns, notably against Urartu and the Lydian State in Anatolia. Power then passed to a south Persian nation, of closely similar racial mixture. It was led by Cyrus (or Kurush or Khusrau), of the so-called Achaemenid family. From this followed immediately the world-famed Persian Empire, whose armies in the next few years took Sardis, destroyed Lydia, subdued the Greek cities of the Aegean coast of Asia Minor, overthrew Babylon and absorbed its dominions, lorded it on the Syrian coast and hinterland, and invaded the eastern regions of Persia itself and far beyond them. Later kings, successors of Cyrus (Cambyses, the great Darius, Xerxes, Artaxerxes) invaded and ruled Egypt, visited Nubia or Kush (the Egyptianized, independent kingdom of the middle Nile), and overcame a Greek revolt in Ionia (499).

The life, more than two centuries long, of this immensely extended, highly organized and, at its best and by comparison with previous empires, humanely administered Persian Empire, stretching with close intercommunication between its score of satrapies from central Asia into Europe and Africa, was to witness, along with all the age-long phenomena of royal intrigue, provincial and tribal revolt and racial separatism, great changes also in political and administrative conceptions, with new standards and currents of thought flowing westwards into western Asia. A seriously attempted central control was accompanied, in the Empire's first and best period, by much local freedom, reasonable taxation, fair justice, and willingness to acquire culture and ideas from others. It was an Empire of Indo-European, or Indo-Iranian, leadership in succession to two thousand years of Semitic; and it was destined to be succeeded by other rulers of Indo-European mind and orientation—Greek, Roman, Byzantine —for nine full centuries, until the coming of the Arabs and Islam.

### 4. *Persia, Greece, Rome*

Something approaching the political unity of western Asia was achieved during the two-century period of Persian dominance, thanks to its organization and prestige, its formidable military machine, its sporadic unformidable opponents. The Great King failed, indeed, to subdue by his arms the brilliant, restless Greeks, who at first resolutely held their own but later vied with each other, Greek against Greek, in intrigues with the nearest satrap: Greeks at their most wonderful period of questing intelligence, love of personal freedom, devotion to art, science and philosophy, but cursed with endemic disunion and instability in their politics. The Persians retained Egypt, though with a régime highly unpopular and intermittently rejected. Fragmented Syria took generally the line of nonresistance, and Phoenicia that at first of devotion and valued naval co-operation, followed by a revolt which Artaxerxes bloodily repressed. Asia Minor was for the most part Persian-governed, but increasingly in the fifth and fourth centuries 'native kingdoms', and anarchic tribal groups in the mountainous or coastal fringes, began to re-arise from their now multifarious population elements, and paid minimal regard to the behests of harassed satraps, many of whom schemed themselves for independence. In 'Iraq, the status of a subject province was accepted after initial revolts, and its age-long civilization greatly influenced that of its imperial masters. The Persian homeland, where lay three out of the Great King's four capitals, was habitually unquiet in its open eastern frontier regions and in outlying areas elsewhere, but the régime was generally unthreatened; in spite, however, of the official and general adoption of the worship of the supreme god Ahuramazda (that is, Zoroastrianism) and his vast number of lesser, satellite deities, the loosening of administrative and social standards, with deterioration in the royal family and general corruption and loss of impetus, weakened the Empire more and more from the mid-fifth century onward, until it was bound to fall at the next serious blow.

This came from the west. In twelve years, 334–323, Alexander of Macedon—young, brilliant, impulsive, visionary—conquered Egypt and north Africa and the whole of western and far into central Asia, ostentatiously adopted Persian ways and those of oriental kingship, and installed a rough but comprehensive administration, with dozens of Greek cities, settlements and garrisons, and thousands of Greek officials, traders and colonists.

Almost in a day the whole balance of world civilization (west-east, Greek-oriental) appeared to be shifted; and indeed these conquests, this new Empire, heralded a tremendous influx of Greek or Hellenistic influences, of culture, speech and religion, deep into the Middle East: influences destined to last, though far from uniformly, for nine centuries until displaced by Islam. This penetration was on a scale at least comparable to that which the west again undertook, but this time not militarily, in the nineteenth and twentieth centuries of our era. Two features of post-Alexandrine Middle Eastern Hellenism, which were to continue or increase throughout Roman and Byzantine times, may in passing be indicated: the one, that it was generally limited to urban and educated circles, extending little to the country-

side, the tribes, or the poor; the other, that it was not by any means
uniformly beneficent, since through defects both in itself and in its
vehicles, and through its unselective, too ready acceptance in the
east, what it in the end contributed was far below the best that the
west had (or had had, a century earlier) to offer. This aspect too, it
may be felt, was destined to repeat itself in the Middle East two
millennia later.

Alexander's Empire, after his early death, immediately fell apart
into the hands of his Macedonian generals, the self-appointed
Successors.

In Egypt, the line of Ptolemy managed to maintain itself for three
centuries, though after more than a hundred years of quarrels and
campaigns it lost to its Seleucid rivals most of its Levantine territories and pretensions. Cyprus, which had belonged to Achaemenid
Persia, was lost but later recovered for Ptolemy. Many thousands
of Greeks were settled in Egypt, the city of Ptolemais was founded,
Greek privilege emphasized, and an inevitably re-emerging Egyptian
nationalism was kept in check. The régime of the Successor was in
Egypt on the whole unhappy, 'race relations' distressingly poor,
the ruling house itself divided by faction and intrigue; and in the
first century B.C. the Ptolemaic power could survive only under
Roman patronage. Its end came in 31 B.C., after the lost battle of
Actium and the romantic suicide of Queen Cleopatra. Egypt, by
now a strange cultural and demographic blend of old and new,
Egyptian and Greek, became a Roman province with special status;
Alexandria survived as the greatest centre of contemporary Hellenism
and learning.

Syria, at first divided between the successor-states of Ptolemy
and Seleucus, fell in time solely to the latter. His policy of thorough-
going Hellenization was fairly acceptable in most areas, where indeed
it was no novelty; but in largely Jewish Palestine, despite the willing
modernism of the more evolved classes, it provoked a determined
uprising, that of Judas Maccabaeus and his line, which founded and
maintained an independent state destined, in spite of rival policies
and factions within it, to survive into Roman times. (Its successor
was the Hellenized, or Romanized, puppet state of the Herods, till
A.D. 6). Other areas of Syria and its hopeful city-states assumed at
the same time a near-independence, among them those of the half-
Arab Nabataeans around Petra in southern Transjordan, and the
ancient coastal cities of Phoenicia. The reduced, distracted Seleucid
Empire, at last confined to Syria, with its capital at Antioch, finally

yielded to the power of Rome. In 64 B.C. it was made by Pompey a province, later two provinces, of the Republic: provinces which still contained semi-independent enclaves and privileged local rulers, and strong cross-currents of diverse culture, religion, and temporal interest.

In Asia Minor under the Successors each of the three main claimants strove initially for mastery. But within a century only Seleucid pretensions remained, and these only in the south-east; the central and main block of the territory had split or relapsed into independent kingdoms—those of Cilicia, Cappadocia, Pontus, Paphlagonia and Armenia. Part of the centre had been occupied, about 280, by an irruption—once again!—of northern tribesmen from Europe across the Bosphorus, this time the (Celtic) Galatians, who founded a state around Ancyra (later Angora or Ankara); the west belonged to monarchies of Pergamon, Rhodes, Bithynia, Phrygia and a number of smaller units. In them all the processes of westernization proceeded apace. The advance of the Roman power eastward led first to diplomatic relations, then to invasions and campaigns, then to the creation in 133 of a Roman province of 'Asia', and finally after 63 B.C. to comprehensive settlements in each Anatolian area. These gave provincial, or dependent, or allied, or independent status to successive regions and states, among which those of Pontus (Mithridates) and Armenia (Tigranes or Dikran) were to prove the longest to survive. The whole region now lay open to Greco-Roman penetration, colonization, and influences of every kind, opposed only by Persian counter-influences and coercion.

The latter country and 'Iraq formed the eastern half of the Seleucid inheritance, in which the Indian and central Asian conquests of Alexander soon became independent, the rest treated at first to a resolute régime of Greek and Macedonian colonization and favour to the Greek cities (including a new capital, Seleucia, founded on the middle Tigris), but later, and in spite of this early discrimination, to the ultimate coalescence of most of the native Persian and new Greek populations. No Persian resistance on national lines was encountered, and religious tolerance was practised; nevertheless, the open eastern frontiers were often ill at ease and, as the dynasty declined, outbreaks of sporadic insurgence called for efforts of suppression not always successful. The Seleucid frontiers gradually contracted. Only in the mid-second century B.C. did a major rival appear to the uneasy Seleucid power in the east; it was the increasing strength of a Parthian, that is north-east Persian, or Perso-Scythian, tribe-group or nation, formed by the descendants of one Arsaces, who had begun a slow rise to power a century earlier. This Arsacid or Parthian Empire had by 130 B.C. firmly established itself in eastern, northern and western Persia, and in 'Iraq as far as the Euphrates. 'Iraq as well as Persia was thus lost to the Seleucids. The latter were, moreover, further embarrassed by growing Parthian relations, often those of suzerainty, with the ambitious potentates of eastern Anatolia. The new Empire was, however, never truly robust; tribal and nomadic in origin, its organization was sketchy, its feudal structure unsure, its armies little trained. Adopting Zoroastrianism and a strong strain of Iranian national feeling and anti-western prejudicies, the Arsacids were still far from closing the doors to Hellenic practices, arts, pleasures and influences, though these became politically unfashionable with the ruling class; instead, Persia was being little by little re-persianized. The interesting Greek kingdom of Bactria, a relic of Alexander, was swamped by Scythians in 128 B.C.

The Parthian Empire, such as it was, lasted for four centuries. The succession, after its last feeble decades, fell to a national and nationalist all-Persian dynasty of the Sassanians, true successors, as they could justly claim, of the Achaemenids, and devoted or even fanatical Zoroastrians and traditionalists. The Sassanian period, which endured until the Arab invasion (A.D. 637), was perhaps Persia's most secure and brilliant era, during which it enjoyed a good administration and legal system, a renaissance of its own art and culture, strong priestly influences (now facing the rival claims of Christianity and Manichaeism), and witnessed at the same time the almost total eclipse of Hellenism and the Greek language. Of its foreign relations we shall speak later.

The rest of the Middle East, from Bosphorus and Nile to Euphrates, found itself, as the Christian era opened, under the Empire of the Roman Caesars, an Empire exercised largely by direct provincial rule, partly by a system of subordinate, client states (as for a time in Palestine, and for much longer in eastern Anatolia) and partly by alliances and spheres of influence beyond the frontiers, as in Armenia. The gift of Rome to this eastern world was its Pax Romana, security from outside aggression and from other than temporary and local domestic disorder, and a wide, almost a world-wide, field for its subjects in trade, travel and literary and official ambition. The distinction of Roman or non-Roman became blunted as the centuries paased and the franchise was extended; local and municipal self-government was allowed, when not abused; large numbers of Roman

cities were founded and Roman conceptions of order, the rule of
law, civil dignity and personality had every chance to take root, even
though in practice Roman rule was too often corrupt, oppressive and
disliked. With all its pockets of surviving local devotion and its
shadowy areas of backwardness, the social and public tone of the
Empire was European, Roman-Hellenistic, and later Byzantine. The
west had made, it seemed, a vast inroad into the east, and the distinctions of which Periclean Greece had proclaimed itself so conscious
were out of sight—for ever, a thoughtful contemporary must have
thought! Dozens of the best writers, scholars, and artists of the
Roman and Byzantine worlds (including Christian saints, hermits,
Fathers, heresiarchs) were of Middle Eastern birth; and the rapid
rise and spread of Christianity (the official religion of the Roman
Empire from A.D. 313 onwards), in spite of its own many and bitter
doctrinal disputes, was another welding element between west and
east, another potent force in society—yet was also, because standing
for personal, anti-imperial values, another force added to the revival
of local, nationalistic, foci of loyalty. In these years, save only in
remote regions of mountain or desert, the great majority of the
Middle Eastern population became Christian as well as European.
Judaism had meanwhile sustained a severe blow by the destruction
of Jerusalem by the Romans in A.D. 70, and the diaspora of the
Palestinian Jews.

Externally, the dominant feature of the times was the struggle
between Rome-Byzantium and Arsacid-Sassanian Persia for the
allegiance of the eastern Anatolian states by rival diplomacies of
threat, inducement and fomented internal dissidence, and for possession of the Mesopotamian flat-lands, now Persia's western
province, by direct force of arms. These needless and weakening
struggles, essential to neither Empire and destructive of both, contributed to their later, easy conquest by the Arabs; and it would be
tedious to describe their intricate, swaying fortunes, which involved
the greatest rulers and generals on both sides, and the flower of their
armies, for seven hundred years. They were marked by fierce battles,
and by deep massive raids—to the Mediterranean, into Anatolia,
even into Egypt—and the wholesale removal of captive populations.
Other features were occasional calm interludes, broken treaties, the
encouragement of embarrassing pretenders, and the head-on confrontation of rival religions. But, as the seventh century opened, a
total transformation of the whole Middle Eastern scene was at hand,
from the most unexpected of directions.

## 5. *Some features of Middle Eastern antiquity*

A few moments of reflection, even at this mid-point of history which our survey has now reached, and even after no more than hasty a scramble through four millennia, may be instructive. We have seen the high state of civilization in which certain, very limited, communities (Sumer, Elam, Egypt, Crete) emerged from the darkness of prehistory; civilizations built up by unknown hands at a slow but increasing tempo, and resulting from we know not what changing environments and racial mixtures. And we have noted the, thereafter, comparative rapidity of social and political change, and the ever-growing scale of political units into groups, states, nations, empires. There has been endless movement of peoples into and within the region, each bringing unascertainable contributions of character, technique and habitude; there has been coalescence of the new elements, or their disappearance, or their successful establishment of a ruler or ruling class. There have existed, concurrently, areas of continued aboriginal backwardness, of which parts of Persia and Anatolia furnish examples; areas also of remoteness from, nonparticipation in, the field of Middle Eastern development, such as southern Arabia or the Sudan. With new blood, and often without it, have arrived, repeatedly, new cultures, and the flow of these has been (an aspect now half forgotten) east–west as well as west–east, as is testified by early days in the eastern Mediterranean and by Greek borrowings from Babylonian and Egyptian science. The conception, incidentally, of an 'unchanging East', dear to our own nineteenth century, is revealed as clear absurdity.

The record has shown the effect of a secluded or protected geographical location on the possibilities of early empire-building which, achieved by Assyria, Egypt and Persia, proved impossible to fragmented Greece as also to the Syrian communities on their much-trodden land-bridge; but not even the isolation of Hittites or Iranians or (the most striking case) of Egyptians could in fact protect them finally from invasion and overthrow. (Modern transport and modern armaments have, of course, now destroyed all hope of safety through inaccessibility.) Meanwhile, no profundity of study is likely to reveal, to anything like our satisfaction, why success, power and progress came to one ancient emergent nation rather than to another; varying answers lie somewhere, no doubt, in the field of favouring environment, exceptional leadership, a strong ruling caste, some fortunate blend of aboriginal and immigrant, some timely discovery or import of technique, weapon or concept, or a sudden acquisition of wealth by raid or warfare, or a catastrophe befalling neighbours. Nor are we able to assign reasons for this or that notorious 'national character', if such authentically exists. There is less, or no, mystery about the mere impulse of early rulers to acquire wealth and empire, since it conforms to the deepest and worst instincts of our kind, not least when these are confronted with the familiar dichotomy of 'us' and 'them'—*our* community against the foreigner, Hellene versus barbarian, Jew against the uncircumcized—in which latter-day conceptions of European and Asiatic, or white and coloured, have come to take their maleficent place. Nor indeed is there much mysterious about the inability of early empires to endure; this is easily traceable to their uneasy heterogeneity, to the normal lack of intelligent loyalty to the imperial centre, to failure by the latter in sympathetic devolution or even in acceptable tolerance, and to the great distances which must be destructive of control, because beyond the range (in spite of Achaemenid and Roman improvements in communication) of contemporary transport.

At all periods we have had occasion to observe the strong influence of religion, ranging from ceremonially worshipped city-gods and deified rulers to—to us more acceptable—monotheisms. This influence was rarely beneficent; it created, at least in its public manifestations, a lust for divinely approved conquest (as in Assyria), or a jealous nationalism (as in Israel), or an anti-social privileged class (as in Zoroastrian Persia, and in Egypt), far more than it inspired to morality or gentleness.

One more feature, prominent in later history, had already shown itself in these pre-Islamic times: the eager adoption of national legends as emotional rallying-points. Based often on more than half-mythical figures of heroic dimensions, as in Greece or Sassanid Persia, or on alleged divine discrimination, as in Hebrew history, such legends could too easily be a powerful force inspiring peoples to self-glorification and aggression.

# CHAPTER THREE

# NINE CENTURIES OF ISLAM

## 1. The Impact

THE Prophet Muhammad, son of 'Abdullah, was born about A.D. 570 and bred in a leading family of Mecca, then a considerable and highly civilized city, caravan centre, and sanctuary of western Arabia. He passed there most of his life of trading, meditating and preaching, lawgiving and organizing; and his new creed of Islam was finally adopted, thanks to its own force and content and to his burning sincerity, by nearly all the townsfolk of Mecca and Medina and by most of the primitive and chronically lawless and divided tribesmen of Arabia, before his early and sudden death in 632.

The faith of Islam, which means 'submission' (to the will of Allah), however rigid and positive in its monotheism, was yet with no great difficulty livable in terms of contemporary Arabian life, by reason of its easy intelligibility, its attractive concessions and promises, and its wise adaptation to Arabian conditions: conditions which themselves, climate and terrain apart, reflected a centuries-long past of earlier civilization in the west (and particularly the fertile, settled south-west) of the peninsula, adopted in varying degrees by its quick-witted, impatient, unstable sons in city and desert. The religion as it took form in the utterances of Muhammad—he was illiterate—and even more in the later-compiled Qur'an (Koran) and the collections of his Sayings, was not, like Judaism, that of a nationalistic community, but had universal appeal. Developing monotheistic ideas which (a fact often under-emphasized) were endemic in Arabia, and drawing, often naïvely and with imperfect understanding, on Christian and Jewish sources available in many Arabian communities as well as in Syria, Islam as it took independent shape insisted above all on the uniqueness and the eternal, universal power —but also the lofty compassion—of Allah; on the status of Allah's Prophet as that solely of a man and a messenger, the last and best of a long line of prophets but without personal claim to divinity; on belief in angels and devils and the Last Judgment; on the holy books of previous revelations and the new divinely-dictated Law, on public prayer, fasting and almsgiving, and the annual Mecca pil-

grimage; on Holy War against the pagan; and on certain rigidly
defined improprieties, such as the use of wine and pork, usury and
gambling, and images which might lead to misplaced worship.
Slavery and polygamy were both accepted as natural institutions,
but with a new emphasis on the duty of restraint and kindly treatment. Many pre-Islamic elements of custom and ritual, and some of
belief, were indulgently incorporated. It is, indeed, idle to look in the
Qur'an or the Traditions for a developed, satisfying system of
theology; what was offered, and is offered today, was a single, complete law and guide to human life, claimed as divinely revealed, as
adequate to every activity and situation, and as the sole pathway to
eternal bliss.

No close series of historical events in the Middle East has ever
produced results so immediate, yet so profound and lasting, as those
which followed the unbelievably rapid, unexpected and complete
conquest by the earliest Muslims, under the first Successors (or
Caliphs) of the Prophet, of practically all the territories of western
Asia (except Anatolia) and of north Africa. These conquests, dating
from the fourth decade of the seventh century of the Christian era,
represented in one, but a quite incomplete, sense another great out-
pouring from the human reservoir of Arabia; they proved final and
irreversible, yet were orderly, unmarked by ruin or massacre, and
were preliminary not to a violent but rather to a peaceful revolution,
visible and invisible, in society and policies and men's minds throughout the region, and far beyond it. The changes which henceforth
supervened in these ex-Roman and Persian provinces led them, as
we now see, from antiquity to the Middle Ages, and introduced
modes of living and thinking which were viewed for centuries as
those which most distinguished Asiatic from European societies.
The substantial reorientation of the whole Middle East gave new
importance to hitherto neglected regions, notably Arabia itself; it
obliterated long-standing boundaries, and made the Arabs for
centuries the most considered people in the region, instead of
the least. The social structures within each conquered territory
changed overnight, with a new aristocracy and plutocracy, new
land-ownership, new privileges which incoming and settling Arab
Muslims were in no hurry to share with the growing crowds of
converts.

From the camps and settlements, and soon from the cities, spread
the new, Arabian fashions in dress, speech, manners and private and
public way of life; and this, the highly characteristic, dignified, self-

contained Muslim fashion of living, was accompanied, as it spread more widely, by the general adoption of Muslim conceptions of society and the universe. Conversely, the early Muslim material contribution to wealth or economics was negligible, unless in the form of an abrupt redistribution of possessions.

The Muslim reconquest or restabilization of Arabia, necessitated by the death of the Prophet, was complete by 634; the invasion and occupation of 'Iraq, Persia, Egypt and Syria were achieved within the next decade. These truly remarkable victories and permanent acquisitions were carried out by sparse, ill-equipped and untrained 'troops', under commanders hitherto unknown and untried. Reasons for this ease of conquest lay in the exhaustion of the Sassanid and Byzantine Empires, the scanty loyalties they had inspired, the divisions caused by heresy, and the general resentment at oppression and over-taxation. Nevertheless, every detail of the campaigns, every episode and leader, every authentic or imagined conversation, became thenceforward part of the basic Arab, and Muslim, tradition and heritage; with the Prophet's own life, it was their heroic age, their lasting inspiration; and, leading back to the speech and words, the poetry and fable, of pre-Islamic ages in Arabia, it helped to seal the close and persisting, yet not easily definable, bond between the Arabs and Islam.

The wide territories thus acquired for Islam and Arabism had been strangers hitherto to Arabian cultural or spiritual influences, even though receptive at times, as we have seen, of mass immigration from the peninsula. Arabic soon became the official language and predominant tongue in all but Persia, Persian becoming largely Arabic in vocabulary; Islamic in religion, through gradual, un-forced, progressive adoption of that faith by populations little devoted to their corrupted or worldly Byzantine Christianity or to the national creed of Persia, and eager to qualify for the social as well as fiscal benefits reserved for Muslims; and sharers in the prestige, the sense of compact superiority found in the single, highly conscious Muslim community which was at once a nation and a supernational social and religious entity, and which was held firmly together as such, in spite of all dynastic or doctrinal quarrels, how-ever bitter, by the bonds of the sacred Law and the Tradition, and the shared sense of prized distinctness from all non-Muslim com-munities. The time required to render the conquered territories substantially Islamic varied locally from a few decades to three centuries; some pockets of resistance—often recognizable as the

1. Pipelines crossing the hills in the Agha Jari area, Persia

2. Abadan refinery and the Shatt al-'Arab

3. Tabriz: new and old bridge across the Aji Chai river

4. Digging their fields near Isfahan.

5. The great Square in Isfahan

6. Southern Zagros: oil-field country

7. Teheran: a side street

8. Mount Demavend in the Elburz

Christian minorities of later days—declined Islamization, and were
tolerated without oppression. The Islamic conquests were never
ethnic, since the numbers involved, even including the later immigrants who for centuries thereafter moved up in small or greater
bodies from Arabia, were never such as obviously to modify existing
physical types; all were absorbed, as later arrivals in the area (Turks,
Mongols, Tartars) were in due course to be absorbed. Some departments in culture, in trade and craftsmanship, in government itself,
remained for centuries as unresentedly non-Muslim. Indeed, a
great part of the governmental systems of the occupied countries
—not including, of course, the courts of justice, or law-codes, or
military establishments—stayed for a considerable time unmodified,
with administration in the hands of the former officials and with the
old currencies and taxation and irrigation systems still in operation.
Central and western Anatolia, against which with its Byzantine
emperors and armies, its high level of cultured development and
prosperity, the Muslims matched themselves in vain, resisted Islamization for more than four centuries, and in the end were never
Arabized.

Apart from this latter territory, to which Islam penetrated only
from the later eleventh century onwards, the strength of the hold
of the new Faith, and (as we shall see) the local dilutions or admixtures
which it was to undergo, varied widely; it produced everywhere,
however, a specifically Islamic civilization with much in common
which was outwardly apparent and much that was inwardly fundamental, while it was subject also to the strong influences of pre-
existing populations, environments and cultures. It followed that
Muslim society differed perceptibly though unessentially in Egypt,
Arabia, Syria and 'Iraq, though all were Arabic-speaking and in
close intercommunication. In Persia the Arabic language failed, in
the end, to displace the Persian, and Persian national pride and
idiosyncracy, art and subtlety, so far prevailed over the incoming
Arab contribution that, two or more centuries after the conquest,
Persia, though deeply Islamized in its own heterodox fashion, had
still its language and its culture intact.

## 2. Golden Age

The six centuries of the western Asian record, from A.D. 632 to
1258, were those of the early, the mature, and the final periods of
medieval Islamic civilization. They formed the era of the Caliphate

at its greatest (indeed its only) reality, and witnessed the succession of phases of power and decline, state-building and invasion, among the Middle Eastern peoples which gradually moved towards the setting of the stage, in the wasteful, disorderly fashion of human history, for the groupings and nations of our own time.

The political history of the period, detail of which cannot be included in these pages, falls into stages which it is possible to delimit only by over-simplifying the course of events and ignoring a world of activity, intrigue and disorder which produced them. The succession of the first, the 'well-directed' Caliphs, four in number, lasted for a bare generation (632–661) after the death of the Prophet; strife and jealousy were already stirring, and the third and fourth Caliphs were both murdered. Then while Islamic—at this stage Arab—rule was settling down in the new-conquered provinces, the Empire's centre of gravity shifted in 661 from the Hijaz to Syria, and for a century the Caliph, deriving now from another branch the Prophet's own tribe, the Quraish, ruled from Damascus by his viceroys and governors a still expanding Empire. The dominion of these Umayyid Caliphs was firm, efficient, worldly; but even their greatest rulers—Mu'awiya, 'Abdul Malik, al-Walid—are today little remembered by the world at large. A second major shift of power, from Syria to 'Iraq, marked the replacement of the Umayyid by the 'Abbasid dynasty when the supreme power was seized by descendants of the Prophet's uncle, al-'Abbas. These retained it, in changing and sadly diminishing form, from 750 until 1258, based still on the new capital of the Islamic world, Baghdad, founded by them in 762. This was the ever-famous Caliphate of the 'Abbasids, the earlier period of which, in the eighth and ninth centuries of our era, was by far its finest in practical, as distinct from cultural, achievement. The long line of these Caliphs, succeeding always by family claim to an Empire which in temporal terms was later to diminish almost to vanishing point, contained great names—al-Mansur the founder of Baghdad, Harun al-Rashid, al-Ma'mun—as well as a host of obscure sanctified puppets. The political unity of the Empire was broken increasingly and beyond hope of repair, from the mid-ninth century onwards, by the establishment of a score of effectively independent states within nominally Caliphate territory; these offered the Commander of the Faithful a merely formal allegiance or none at all, while of many temporal dynasties, from the tenth century onwards, he was, otherwise than in Islamic prestige, the mere dependant. With the extinction of the 'Abbasids by Mongol hordes in 1258 ends, save in Egypt and Syria, most of what still remained of the glories of medieval Islam.

Certain features of this six-century period need little emphasis here, though they fill its long-drawn record with pages of intrigue, violence, and bloodshed. Such were the bitter quarrels between individuals and families, with high office—and the Caliphate itself —as the prize, followed by war and the execution, or the mere murder, often of persons with high claims to Islamic reverence; these included the Prophet's own son-in-law, 'Ali, his grandson Husain, many of his staunchest original supporters, and many later Caliphs. Strife between pretenders to power, between rival dynasts, against ambitious provincial rulers, against seceding or aggressive mobs turned into fighting forces (Carmathians and Kharijite heretics, rebellious slave-armies, or the followings of upstart 'prophets'), was exemplified in every decade; and for the first four centuries of the period large-scale and reprisal-provoking expeditions against the still Christian-held territories of 'Rum' (Asia Minor) were almost annual events, and caused a ruinous drain of blood and treasure.

The Caliphate itself, an institution never closely formulated but conceived as rather constitutional and temporal than spiritual, changed essentially during the period. From being, as it was at first, entrusted to the fittest person in age, piety, efficacy and general acceptability to act as official head of the Islamic world (and therefore as chief enforcer of the sacred Law), the position became an object of keen temporal rivalry and soon, as the Umayyids and early 'Abbasids had made it, a hereditary kingship of almost normal oriental type. This status was modified again when in Baghdad the Caliph's own mercenary bodyguard could exercise a tyrannous and humiliating control, and even drive him from his capital or take his life; and again, when with the Abode of Peace occupied by the thrones and armies of upstart Persian or Turkish princes (p. 54), the 'Abbasid was no more than their outwardly venerated pensioner, and giver of empty, formal recognition to their authority.

The Arab Empire of the early Caliphs lasted as a single sphere of government, with minor but serious local usurpations, for three centuries. During this period the Arab ruling class saw itself decreasingly differentiated from the upper strata, and then the main body, of the Caliph's multi-racial subjects, as indeed were, with passing years, the further incoming contingents of Arab tribesmen from the far south. In the administration of the Empire, Arabs played first little, then a limited, and finally a large part as they acquired the needed experience and skills; Arabic became the official language of government, Arab coins were minted, and Arab conceptions of law, conduct and justice prevailed, while in the fields of finance, diplomacy and economy they made their contribution even though the far more sophisticated and adapted methods of Constantinople and of Persia, familiarized by long usage in the now occupied territories, were generally adopted in more or less Arabized form. Thus, variously derived, a full provincial and central administration for the Empire was evolved and, with some admitted inconsistency and discontinuity, applied.

Even in the early-middle ninth century, however, the slightness of Arab control in Persia began to appear, where that country's own national life was still vigorous though in part concealed; and Persian influence in Baghdad itself was, from the beginning of the century, considerable. Henceforward, officers of the Caliphate government, members of outstanding local or transplanted Arab families, successful generals, or scions of central Asian noble families, managed to found dynasties of their own in different areas of Persia and to transmit power to their sons and grandsons. Such were the Tahirids (820–874), Dulafids (825–896), 'Alids (864–1032) and Saffarids (867–903), and these were partly contemporary with, partly succeeded by, the more formidable states of the Samanids (874–999) of eastern Persia and Turkistan, and then by the various branches of the Buyids or Buwaihids (932–1062), one of which entered Baghdad itself, occupied most of 'Iraq, and deprived the Caliph of all but his prestige. Nor was this all; lesser Persian statelets continued to form—Ziyarids (928–1042), Hasanwaihids (959–1015), Kakwaihids (1007–1051), and in 'Iraq itself and to the westward, tribally-based Arab dynasties had arisen, each for a brief life of sovereignty. Such were the Hamdanids (929–1003), 'Uqailids (996–1096), Mirdasids (1028–1079), Mazyadids (961–1150), and the Kurdish Marwanids (990–1096). At the same period in Egypt, and with it usually most of Syria, after more than two centuries of resented and resisted rule by the viceroys of the 'Abbasids, effectively independent dynasties founded by ex-Caliphate officers had flourished for a generation or more (Tulunids 865–905, Ikhshidids 935–969) before the more formidable and longer-lasting State of the Fatimids moved in from North Africa in 969, and founded Cairo. They were to remain in unchallenged dominion for two centuries, a period of wealth, luxury, and cultural achievement, some pretensions to empire (in Syria and Arabia), frequent warfare with Byzantium, and wide trading relations with Europe. In Arabia, the shift of Islamic power to the north—to Damascus, then to Baghdad—led to a world of disgruntled Hijazi intrigue and armed reaction, with violent interruptions of Caliphate rule. The extravagant impieties of the Carmathian sectarians were especially outrageous in and around Mecca, until the Fatimid power could restore tolerable conditions. Later, at the end of the tenth century, families of Sharifs (descended, therefore, from the Prophet) managed to conduct a precarious government in Mecca, while in the Yemen a succession of similar city-dynasties maintained an isolated independence, theocratic in tone and heedless of the far-off Caliph.

The Arab Empire was thus already fragmented before as well as after its capital had been occupied by secular, and mostly non-Arab, forces and rulers; the Middle East had become once again—though now with the important new element of a shared religion, law and sense of community—a group of independent though similar states. Of the latter, it is noticeable that they could emerge from very different origins, racial, social and personal; no suggestion of nationality as a basis for unity or separation existed, while the notion of rule by the consent of the subjects, or even of their welfare, was inconceivable; and even adherence to a heterodox form of Islam seemed to matter little, since both Buwaihids and Fatimids were Shi'i. Rule, while it lasted, was transmitted from father to son, the Caliph's formal brevet being usually but not always asked and forthcoming. The princes issued their own coinages, though their scale of empire varied from a few valleys to a considerable state, and their effective authority differed correspondingly. A single family or clan often split dynastically into branches, each assuming rule in a separate province or city or area; their natural enemies and probable successors were each other, or some new local aspirant like themselves, or the jealous relations of the ruler himself, or the resentful Caliph. The type of government provided by these now forgotten medieval Muslim states, which covered so great areas of time and territory, was, if one can generalize, formal and orderly, studiously Islamic in law and conduct, and often favourable to art and culture.

## 3. *Turks and Moguls*

The second millennium of the Christian era opened, then, with the Caliphate helpless if tolerated and by some revered, Persian and Arab secular dynasties lording it from central Asia to the Mediterranean, Arabia governed precariously under petty if holy city-

princes, sayids or sharifs, or by the new Shi'i masters of Egypt—or
enjoying congenial anarchy. Egypt, with most of Syria, was ruled
from Cairo by the Fatimids. Muslim conquest and government, so
early divorced from the Baghdad Caliphate, had long since been
carried beyond Middle Eastern frontiers into Central Asia and
northern India, along the north African littoral as far as the Atlantic,
and into Spain and Sicily. Eastern and south-eastern Anatolia was
Muslim under Hamdanids and Buwaihids; its western marches were
still part of the dominions of Rum under its Byzantine emperors,
often invaded but never conquered.

But a moment of major change was at hand; a new character was
to enter upon the western Asian scene, in the guise of an eager
immigrant and conqueror, but with new gifts and qualities: the
Turk.

The words Turk or Turkish stand, ethnically, for no definite
human type or group. The term is linguistic, covering the speakers of
Turkish dialects, and is racial only as a vague designation of interconnected groups who emerged from central Asia as nomadic tribes
in the early Middle Ages; these represent steppe peoples not unlike
the earlier Aryan-speaking communities of similar provenance,
except in their different language-structure and their greater measure
of contact, in blood and culture, with Mongol stocks farther east.
The Turks were also, as compared with the Aryan-speakers, in
general more warlike and enduring, less artistic and intellectual.

The Seljuq Turks (so called from the name of an earlier chief)
entered the Middle Eastern world from inner Asia at a time with the
Caliphate was fragmented and decadent, Islam itself no longer simple
or uniform, the Byzantine Empire intact and still capable of aggression, and western Europe soon to launch the Crusades. An advance-
guard of Turks was indeed already known, since the early ninth
century, in Persia, 'Iraq and farther west as slaves, mercenaries, and
hired officers of the Caliphate. The Seljuq incursion, that of whole
communities recently converted to orthodox Islam and led by virile
and ambitious chiefs, entered Persia in the first years of the eleventh
century, swept away the power in that territory of the doughty
Ghaznavid State of Afghanistan and north India—and with it some
lesser Persian statelets—unified its own community and command,
and assumed rule in all parts of Persia. Tughril Beg after occupying
Hamadan, Rayh, and Isfahan in 1041 entered Baghdad (1055), dismissed the last Buwaihid, re-established Sunni orthodoxy and
'protected' the Caliph, and died (1063) sole master of a loosely united

Seljuq Empire stretching from east Persia to the fringes of Syria and the Taurus. The original invaders were thereafter reinforced periodically by fresh Turkish contingents from the east, in sufficient force to impress that language and character on wide areas of the Middle East, notably Azarbaijan and northern 'Iraq (and later, obviously, Anatolia), as well as profoundly to affect its political history. The Arab states of the Fertile Crescent did not long survive the Seljuq flood, though Fatimid Egypt, with much of Syria, could still maintain itself secure and prosperous.

A nominal though always imperfectly unified Seljuq Empire continued in being until the mid-twelfth century. Its great rulers were Alp Arslan (1063–1072), Malik Shah (1072–1092), and Sinjar (1117–1157); but, as ever, local offshoots ruled by sons and nephews managed to establish, in the twelfth century, separate if connected dynasties in Persia, Syria, 'Iraq and Kurdistan. A further, yet largely contemporary, phase was reached in the appearance, all over the Middle Eastern map, of dynasties founded by ex-slaves or captains or ministers of these Seljuq princes. These were the Atabegs, and such dynasties, with varying lives and fortunes, flourished from the early twelfth to the mid-thirteenth century in northern 'Iraq (Baghdad, Mosul, Arbil) and the Jazira (Diyarbakr, Mardin, Sinjar), in northern Syria (Aleppo), and in Armenia and Persia (Azarbaijan, Fars, Luristan, Kirman). They fell in the end, one by one, to ambitious rivals, or to each other, or to one of those major thirteenth-century cataclysms shortly to be mentioned. Some pockets of local, pre-Seljuq, power—notably that of the heretical, dreaded Assassins of Alamut in the north Persian mountains—managed to survive till Mongol times. The epoch of the Seljuq emperors and their diverse, widespread Turkish successors, in spite of its full share of violence and egotistical brutality, gave the Middle East two centuries of relatively stable, unprogressive Islamic rule, and contributed much to the substance, and to later conceptions, of medieval Muslim life.

The 'Abbasid Caliph survived in the teeming, immensely wealthy and cultured city of Baghdad, still bestower of the formal brevets of princedom, still titular head of the whole Islamic community. In Arabia, one princely or sanctified family after another ruled the few cities of the Hijaz and Yemen, with occasional acknowledgment, to suit their purposes, of the overlordship of Cairo or Baghdad; the Arabian tribes were as ever ungoverned save by their own customs and some diluted Islamic notions. South-eastern Arabia (Oman) became a semi-heretical Imamate of the 'Ibadi sect, in almost complete isolation. In Egypt, Fatimid rule after two centuries gave way in 1169 to that of the famous Kurdish-born Saladin (Salah al-Din), an outstanding officer of the Zangid Atabeg of Syria. He died in 1193. His dynasty of the Ayyubids, orthodox Muslims unlike the Fatimids, held power in Egypt, with most of Syria and part of western Arabia, for a century; he himself is best remembered for his powerful but chivalrous opposition to, and reconquest of, the Crusader-founded Latin Kingdom of Jerusalem (1099–1187), in campaigns of which the earlier phases (in the First Crusade, 1097–1100 and the Second, 1147–1149) had witnessed the Islamic prowess of the Syrian Atabegs. The whole episode of the Crusades, abounding in picturesque if not always edifying episode, and still to Muslims an example of western 'unprovoked aggression', left finally no more than minimal effects on the contemporary society or policies of the Middle East, and bequeathed, even to Syria, and even after so close a confrontation, almost nothing of western thought or achievement.

The impact of the Seljuq Turks, profoundly important throughout the Middle East, was in no direction more decisive than in Anatolia, where it entirely altered a position and frontiers uneasily maintained, between the Cross and the Crescent, for more than four centuries. As part of almost the first phase of the Seljuq onslaught, forces and, with them, considerable civil population elements, swept by order of Tughril Beg, about 1050, from the northern Jazira deep into Asia Minor. In 1071 at the fateful battle of Manzikert the Roman Emperor was defeated and captured, Seljuq Turks spread over wide areas of Anatolia and could establish a considerable state in the central and some western areas. Its capital was for a time at Nicaea (Iznik) and it soon assumed a degree of paramouncy over the other Turkish prince-doms which formed, such as the Danishmendids of Sivas (Sebastia) and Kayseri (Caesarea). Throughout the twelfth century and there-after, more and more miscellaneous Turkish or Turkoman bands and parties, armed and unarmed, entered Asia Minor, nomadic and predatory in habit, feudal in organization, innocent of culture, crude and ill-instructed in their Islam. The first-born state, that of 'Seljuqs of Rum', was forced to retire from much of its western territory after its defeat by the First Crusade at Dorylaeum (1097). Western Anatolia was to be a bone of contention between the Greeks and the Turks for a century more. But on the Anatolian plateau, with their capital at Konya (Iconium), the Seljuks, profiting from the weakness of the forces and statecraft of Byzantium, extended their power to the south-east: a move accompanied by the ruin of the countryside, the retrogression of government and civilized tranquillity, and the loss of much, or nearly all, of the long-collected heritage of Greece and Rome. But they had come to stay, and on their own destructive terms.

A catastrophe more sudden and far more bloody than the Seljuq invasion of the mid-eleventh century was now to ensue in the mid-thirteenth. Mongol hordes, moving from the farther East early in the twelfth century, first consolidated a wide empire of many peoples in central Asia under the single rule of Chinghiz Khan, then destroyed the power of the Shahs of Khwarizm (or Khiva)—a power centred at Khiva but extending, in the first quarter of the thirteenth century, over nearly all Persia and 'Iraq—then entered north Persia with Azarbaijan and Transcaucasia. Chinghiz Khan, proverbial for ruthlessness, died in 1227. His vast empire did not long remain united, collapsing into several portions (each a major state in its own right) in the 1260's. But his dreaded armies still had, after his death, a generation of havoc to wreak in the Middle East; the 1240's saw the crushing of the Seljuq realm in Anatolia (later followed by its reduction to a state of vassalage to the Mongols), and in the 1250's the famed and feared grandson of Chinghiz, Hulagu, swept over the rest of Persia, took and sacked Baghdad, destroyed all that was destructible in 'Iraq (including its priceless canal-system), and advanced as far as Syria. Only a surprising defeat at the battle of 'Ayn Jalut (1260) prevented these greatest of barbarians from subjugating all Western Asia. Hulagu, paying faint feudal homage to his suzerain the far-off Great Khan in China, ruled from India to the Black Sea and almost to the Mediterranean. The Caliphate, except for an obscure 'Abbasid pensioner maintained at the court of Cairo, was no more; the states and dynasties of Persia, or 'Iraq and the Jazira—Turkish, Persian, Arab—had gone for ever. And even in the Egyptian-Syrian State, where the Mongols met their match and made no headway, a change of rule had preceded, by a few years, the Mongol inrush; the Ayyubids, founded by Saladin, had given way in 1250 to a dynasty of Turkish or Circassian ex-slaves, or Mamluks, whose origins were in the picked bodyguards and fief-holding officers of the Ayyubid rulers.

## 4. Darkest Age

The period of two centuries and a half which separates the Mongol invasion under Hulagu from the establishment of the Ottoman Turks as the paramount power of western Asia is among the darkest known to our region. Subjected to despotic, warring rulers of no more than ephemeral interest, under overlords without local roots or devotion, without aspiration to progress or enlightenment save in rarest individuals, and suffering materially from the destruction wrought by the Mongols and the resulting poverty or despair, the populations were helpless witnesses or victims of strangers' struggles for power. In the provision either of new racial elements or of practical or cultural contributions the Mongol-Tartar period was far inferior to that of the Seljuqs and their Atabegs (1037–1258). At best it permitted, by its very miseries, the slow regrowth in Persia of a national spirit never wholly extinguished, and, in the Arabic-speaking countries, the assurance of no more than a feeble resistance to the powerful imperialism from without which was, early in the sixteenth century, to submerge them all.

Persia and 'Iraq were in this period governed for seventy years after the death of Hulagu (1265–1335) by his descendants in the Il Khan dynasty, with its centre at Tabriz. Its frontiers marched with those of the central Asian Mongol Empire, those of the Egypto-Syrian State of the Mamluks, and, until 1453, those of the shrunken dominions of the eastern Roman emperors. A dozen Il Khan rulers succeeded Hulagu, in a now Muslim government undistinguished and alien but no longer barbarous, until the usual processes of intrigue and violence destroyed it. Three lesser principalities succeeded: that of the Jal'airs in 'Iraq and north-western Persia (1336–1411), the Mudhaffarids in Fars and Kirman (1313–1393), and the Sarbadarids in Khurasan (1337–1381). The latter two fell at the end of the fourteenth century to the forces of Timur the Lame, the Jal'airs to those of a dynasty of Turkoman chieftains of the Black Sheep tribe-group who from 1378 to 1469 managed, with interruptions due to Timur's irresistible raids, to maintain a state stretching from Armenia and Azarbaijan to southern 'Iraq. The Black Sheep, who were of Shi'i faith, gave way in turn, about 1470, to the similar Turkoman dynasty of the White Sheep, who were Sunni; their centres of power were in Azarbaijan and the Jazira.

A far more imposing figure and shaper of eastern destinies was Timur, a high-born relation of Chinghiz Khan. Timur, from his base in central Asia, launched from 1380 onwards a series of campaigns which conquered all Persia with a ferocity rare even in the Mongol-Tartar world. He took and sacked Baghdad in 1393, overran 'Iraq and the Jazira, invaded Asia Minor to defeat and capture the

Ottoman Sultan (p. 60) in 1401–1402, and after brilliant successes in Syria received formal homage (but nothing more) from the Mamluk ruler. He died in 1405. The Timurid Empire, for a few years extraordinarily extensive, could not endure; many of Timur's conquests were revealed as little more than destructive raids which bequeathed not empire but anarchy. This empire maintained itself, under the great Shahrukh and his successors in Persia, for a century of decreasing power. (The Timurid dynasty of Babar, which became that of the Moghul emperors of India, does not here concern us.) In Asia Minor and Syria the Timurid tide swiftly retreated, and soon little or nothing of Mongol power remained. In 'Iraq and Kurdistan, Azarbaijan and the Jazira, the principalities of Black Sheep and White regained their thrones, and the last-named was still in power when in 1502 the great national revival of Safawi Persia swept it away.

The history of Asia Minor in this period moved fast, and to significant ends. The first Mongol incursion (1243) and the subsequent overlordship of the Il Khans, destroyed most of what remained of Seljuq power; this made it the easier for a dozen, if not a score, of local small-scale principalities to establish themselves in the ex-Seljuq territories, and beyond them. Their rulers, mostly ex-vassals of the Seljuq but with loyal heterogeneous followings of their own, were by race Turks or Turkomans, Greeks, Kurds, Armenians, or a variety of mixtures; their power dated from around 1300, by which date the Seljuq rulers were far gone in enfeeblement, but was precarious and unequal. One amongst them, established as a separate unit located near the Byzantine frontier at about that date, and led by a succession of outstanding chieftains, now rapidly expanded. It absorbed its nearer neighbours, occupied Bursa (Brusa), sent forces across into Europe, and by 1370, under a great ruler, Murad I, had conquered wide areas of Balkan territory. Such was the genesis and youth of the Ottoman (Osmanli) Turks, named from Osman their founder; though the Turkish, or Turkoman, element among them physically was in fact minimal, it was to this constituent in their leaders and population that their pride and consciousness were directed. Indeed, Asia Minor had by now long ceased to be Greek; it had become a racial and cultural amalgam known as 'Turkish', speaking that language and proud of its far-off half-mystical origins.

The Ottoman power, on varying terms—but at least those of equals—with Constantinople and the minor states of south-east Europe, and pushing its conquests far into Thessaly and northern

Greece, had by 1400 absorbed most of the post-Seljuq amirates of Asia Minor. The invasion of Timur inflicted a severe set-back, from which however in a dozen years recovery was complete. The Anatolian amirs restored by Timur were again dethroned; a widespread rebellion was put down. Europe was next raided or conquered to the Danube; and in 1453 Constantinople itself, greatest of all prizes, fell to Ottoman arms and became their capital: a capital which later history was to show as fatally misplaced for a power whose roots and strength were in truth Asiatic. Wars with Serbia, Hungary and Venice continued, the Empire grew fast; a new power not only by Middle Eastern but by world standards had arrived, and was fast developing its own novel institutions and seeking new frontiers. Its Islam, or that at least of its rulers, was orthodox, its ambition and sense of destiny immense, its superiority complex limitless; and its hereditary monarchy was still producing great rulers. The upper strata in Ottoman-Turkish society, including its rulers, had by now widely intermarried with Anatolian and European Greeks, and was already composite in its culture and far from its barbarous origins. So opened the sixteenth century.

The island of Cyprus, ruled from Constantinople from the year 400 onwards with only brief interruptions by Arab invaders after 650, passed in 1192, after short interludes of other rule—Richard I of England seized it from the Greeks in 1191 and sold it to the Knights Templars, who resold it to Guy de Lusignan—to French ex-Crusader kings. These were to hold it for three centuries, with but one (Genoese) interruption. It fell next to the Venetians, in 1498, and was so held for a further eighty years, till the Ottoman conquest.

The Mamluk dynasties of Egypt—these were two, the Bahri (1250–1390), and the Burji (1382–1517)—in spite of periods of murderous violence among themselves which led to short uneasy reigns, were destined to pass their power from master to slave, or father to son, for more than 250 years. On the whole they provided Egypt, and normally most of Syria, with an effective if restless government, distinguished by its achievements in art and, mainly religious, architecture. The Mamluks could boast also in Baibars, Qala'un, Nasir, and half a dozen more of their slave-kings, some rulers of outstanding merit, who performed doughty services to Islam in arms not only against the last remnants of the Crusaders, but in resistance also to the Mongol hordes of Timur himself. They little expected, as the sixteenth century opened, the quarter from which their end as rulers would come.

## 5. *Islamic Civilization*

Since this over-compressed and doubtless distorted narrative has now reached a period less than a half-millennium from our own, and since the main contribution of Islam to Middle Eastern (as well as much wider) society had by now been made—a contribution of transcendent and lasting significance—a page may well be devoted at this stage to assessing something of the nature of the Islamic civilization and communities from which is so directly derived the modern Middle East, in many countries of which this medieval period (both the true and the idealized) is the pride and boast of their modern nationalism.

Racially, no profound change occurred in the content of the Middle Eastern populations between A.D. 600 and 1500; when there were internal population movements, or such from outside the region, they were in general soon absorbed and contributed little (though considerably more than nothing) to existing racial composition. The single-community pretension of Islam, and a single dominant language, encouraged far more internal migration—by Persians, for example, or North Africans, or, later, by European Muslims—within Dar al-Islam than that of previous centuries, and many families of such migrants were to be known in new homes by a reminiscent surname. More Arab tribes moved from Arabia into the Fertile Crescent and into and beyond Egypt—and, exceptionally, into Persia—and with these, encouraged by Islamic usage, more negro slaves. At the same time an increase in nomadism was to turn back to grazing lands where settled populations had long dwelt, as in 'Iraq between the rivers and in north Syria. The infiltration, then the large-scale incursion, of central Asian Turks—pre-Seljuq, Seljuq and post-Seljuq—involved a more significant addition, which left some visible influences everywhere, with enclaves of Turkish-speaking population in a few localities; and, as we have seen, it transformed completely the culture and very life of Anatolia.

The Mongol or Tartar contribution, politically of the highest distinctive importance, was racially as well as culturally almost negligible, so small were the population elements of Mongolian type left behind when their warriors withdrew. The contribution of the infinitely mixed, Greek-speaking hotch-potch which was the Anatolian population when this first became accessible to Islam, was at first limited to Asia Minor itself (so soon to become Turkey-in-Asia),

until Ottoman dominance of nearly the whole Middle East brought
Anatolians, now Turks, in hundreds, as soldiers and officials, to
every subject territory.

The Muslim civilization of these centuries was, with all its pal-
pable unity, both complex and variegated. If differed obviously, as
between the great cities and royal or viceregal courts, and the open
country. In the latter, it is safe to imagine, life was but little altered
in most essentials from that of earlier, pre-Islamic, ages, and a replacement of the old language and tax-gatherers with new could scarcely
modify a hard and changeless environment. Indeed rural life, as
that also of the great nomadic tribes (unchanged in every respect
since the Times of Ignorance), received little from Islam and contributed little to it; and even the traditional picture of high fertility,
marvellous gardens and abundant crop-yields in the fabulous days
of the Caliphs owe, it is probable, as much to legend and idealization
as to fact.

The true and indeed glorious Islamic civilization of the cities
varied as between different regions. The incoming Muslim Arabs
were few in number, and brought with them no more than a scanty
and scarcely transplantable civilization of their own, above all in the
material and artistic fields; it was inevitable, therefore, that the
mixed culture which developed in Egypt, or Syria, or Persia should
incorporate much, in tone and feature, of what these countries had
already long since achieved, accepted and lived. Differences between
countries in dress, dialect, social usage or taboo resulted, and such
are still observable today. It may be asked, indeed, how these few
Arabs of Arabia, so poor and inexperienced, could impose themselves at all upon far more populous and extensive, richer, more
sophisticated territories so as to justify the phrase 'an Arab civilization'. Yet the term is not unjustified; the Arab Muslims brought rare
gifts and qualities, their initial simplicities were of short duration,
and, intellectually and culturally, they could soon hold their own
with any. They brought from Arabia, and it kept them united amid
diverse peoples, their own conscious solidarity, a fresh, confident
approach, a burning enthusiasm for the Faith, and that Faith's drive
and restraints. They brought the language of the Prophet himself,
his Qur'an and Traditions, the divinely-given Law, and the pride
and the folk-tales of the Prophet's own country and age-long way of
life. In Islam, for centuries the focal point of all thought, law and
living, Arabic was the sole, and the divine, key to knowledge and
acceptable doctrine, of which the earliest exponents were Arabs to a

man. It followed that in medieval Islam the Arab enjoyed a scarcely contested moral superiority.

But the contributions from other sources to their evolving and evolved civilization were essential to it, and made it what it became. That of Persia, where indeed the masses were never deeply Arabized, was subtle and pervasive in all fields of literature, science, theology —and luxurious living; not their own national myths or claims, but their *finesse*, their metaphysical teaching, their artistic and literary gifts, their craftsmanship, left a deep imprint in Baghdad and other great cities of and beyond the Caliphate. From the west and north came, into the cultural pool, a major contribution of Byzantine art and architecture, governmental procedure, coinage, and (as from Persia also) words into the Arabic tongue. From such direct contacts with Europe as existed—through traders to and from Egypt and Syria, Holy Land pilgrims, frontier neighbours with Greek-held territory in Asia Minor, scholars, war captives, Crusaders at work and play—came glimpses of a wide, impious, unknown world beyond Islam. From or through the Christian communities, from Egypt to Persia, came conceptions and usages which reflected not only Christian, and not only Judaic, thought and speculation and custom, but the whole body of Hellenistic literature and learning with which Islam had somehow to come to terms: and behind that, the classic philosophers, scientists, and doctors of old, with Plato and Aristotle at their head.

The 'Arab civilization', which, after its first post-conquest decades of acclimatization and acquisition, took gradually from the ninth century onwards a characteristic and a dynamic form, was indeed a remarkable phenomenon. Imposing in appearance, great in achievement, rich in the products—which became and are still the legacies —of hand and mind, it can claim, in spite of all political distractions, to have contributed one of the great periods of human history. Not only in or near the seat of the Caliphate, but in cities throughout the Middle East as well as north Africa, Spain, central Asia and India, it produced orderly and gracious cities, mosques and palaces, barracks and offices, caravanserais, libraries, public baths, pools and fountains. Many or most of these were of unusual, sometimes outstanding, architectural beauty, both of outline and in each meticulous detail. Delightful gardens abounded, bridges and streets were maintained, paved and cleaned, water supplies were provided, security was assured (doubtless with no infrequent lapses) for residents, pilgrims and travellers. A comprehensive civil service saw to the conduct of government, markets were regulated, craftsmen multiplied, trade flowed across every frontier. The Law was upheld and administered, and justice the first objective of the better rulers. Taxation, in normal conditions, was moderate, great works of irrigation and flood-protection were carried out.

Benevolence towards art, study and literature was rather the rule than the exception among Muslim princes, and these activities could not but flourish in conditions which provided wealth and leisure, and inexhaustible human and cultural material both religious and secular, in a region-wide society which blended, as we have seen, many diverse contributions and racial and environmental varieties. From Egypt and Syria to the Hijaz and farthest Persia the period from the mid-ninth century onwards produced artistic work which was, within the fairly narrow Islamic limits, of high merit in textiles and brocades, carpets, glassware, leather and woodwork, jewellery, metalwork, paper-making and illumination, tilework and design. The period produced an abundant literary output—some reflecting an Arab, some a Persian, some a Hellenistic background, and much that was blended from varied sources—in poetry, music, history, philosophy, geography; in physical science and medicine, astronomy and mathematics; and in the wide field of religious, religio-legal, and metaphysical speculation or exposition. In these few lines we must dismiss, reluctantly, a copious and remarkable literature, which included also, with profound results on human cultural history, the translation (and thereby, for centuries, the rescue) of works of the greatest Greek thinkers.

Islam itself, as a religion and way of life, underwent profound changes in these centuries, changes whose course and ramifications cannot be followed in detail here. As the size and the geographic, racial and historical variety of the region precluded the possibility that the Caliphate could long survive as a single state, so the same features—and with them the restless individualism of minds, and pre-existing religious-philosophical tendencies—were bound to destroy much of the unity of Islam itself, and admit deep clefts and varieties within it. Primitive Islam was too simple, too little thought-out, too vulnerable to survive unmodified and undeveloped; and, with far subtler Hellenic and Hellenistic strands of thought entering the Islamic world, and Zoroastrian elements from Persia, and Christian and Jewish contributions (not unknown, already, in the Qur'an itself, though unadmitted as such) brought in by eager converts, and relics of animism or ancient local beliefs from many quarters, there

The Golden Horn, Istanbul (*above*)

The Place de la Nation, Ankara (*top right*)

General view of Ankara (*right*)

The tombs of Osman and Orkhan, Brusa (*below*)

Turkey:

13. Camel convoy with reed mats

14. Village transport, with olive trees

15. Turkish village market

16. Antalya, Northern Turkey: small boat harbour

17. Open space and market, Kayseri, Turkey

18. City and castle: Mardin, Turkey

19. Haifa, the harbour area

20. Agricultural colony, Nahariya, Israel

was copious material for speculation and new thinking, or for sheer heresy, within Islam. Differing religious interpretations—of the rights of succession to the Caliphate, for instance—were soon adduced as political and dynastic arguments, and led to the great split between the Sunna (traditional orthodoxy) and Shi'a, the sect of the followers (almost the deifiers) of 'Ali. Repeatedly a movement of political or popular secession or rebellion was presented as a religious issue, by the Carmathians, the Kharijis or the Assassins; the names of highly unspiritual leaders became those of major sects of Islam; and a new regional religious attitude, for example in western Arabia, could be determined by its political misfortunes. The adoption by this or that Caliph or prince of a new pseudo-Islamic conception could instantly affect his friends and foes in the dynastic or political field.

The picture of an Islam divided by walls of mutual disapprobation, perhaps hostility, between communities was much intensified, from the tenth century onwards, by the proliferation of the new Ways of a host of variously orientated Sufi or mystic sects, varying from the unorthodox to the heretical or barely Islamic, and led by thinkers, saints or mystics, or charlatans to whom, and to whose followers, orthodox Islam had ceased to appeal. These Sufi orders, often incorporating emotional non-Islamic conceptions and devoted to individual teachers, shrines, incantations, and ceremonies, became a major element in the body of Islam; an element which departed far, very far, from the Prophet's teaching, but which attracted and held within its Faith thousands of the simple, the impressionable, the deprived. At the opposite end of the Islamic range stood, and stand, the Men of Learning (the *ulama*) of sober, traditional, established Sunni orthodoxy, rigid guardians of the Faith unpolluted.

# CHAPTER FOUR

# MODERN TIMES

## 1. Sultan and Shah

THE story of the world-famous Ottoman Empire, from its half-concealed, intrusive, gallant beginnings to its shabby and help-less decline is, in outline, well known. Since it covered, with various degrees of effectiveness, all the Middle East which is here our subject, except Persia and the farthest fringes of Arabia, and since Turkish influence on Arab society thus imposed was and remains profound, the story closely concerns us; but it can be told only in briefest outline.

The main eastward and south-eastward expansion of Ottoman power occurred half a century after the fall of Constantinople to their arms (1453), and their completion of the conquest of the Balkans and south Russia. It was Salim I—the Grim!—who, now secure in the possession of all Asia Minor, including the territories of a Greek survival in Trabzon (Trebizond), those of the White Sheep, and those of minor Anatolian valley-dynasties, led his army eastward, met and beat at Chadiran (1514) the forces of newly-arisen Safawi Persia (pp. 59, 69), acquired Kurdistan and Cilicia, and effectively parried the danger of Persian (and therefore Shi'i) westward penetration. The Grim Sultan proceeded next to defeat the Mamluks of Egypt, make the Nile Valley an Ottoman province, acquire the Hijaz and its Holy Cities, and take with him from Cairo to Istanbul (as Constantinople had now become) the robes and trinkets of the 'Abbasid Caliph, which honorific rank the Sultan was later to assume. His yet greater son, Sultan Sulaiman Qanuni (the Lawgiver, called in Europe the Mag-nificent) (1520–1566), took Erzurum, suppressed serious sectarian troubles in Anatolia, and in rapid campaigns added Tabriz (tempo-rarily) and then Baghdad, with most of 'Iraq, to the Empire. Repeated wars with Persia ended with a peace treaty in 1555; Baghdad and much more was retained, Tabriz was surrendered. Turkish fleets dominated the Mediterranean, and in the Red Sea established foot-holds in the Yemen. Cyprus was acquired from the Venetians in 1571, the year of Lepanto.

The sixteenth century in Turkey was one in which external

triumphs (not unaccompanied, however, by reverses) were mixed with much internal disorder created by lawless nomadic elements—the old, essential Turks—by extremists' and heretics' religious movements, by revolts of provincial Pashas and ambitious robber-barons, and by the gross indiscipline of the Turkish soldiery, notably the famous Janissaries. These conditions made possible the Persian recovery of Azarbaijan and 'Iraq, where Baghdad fell to them in 1623. The position was outwardly restored by the prowess of Sultan Murad IV, who disciplined the provinces and sects of Asia Minor, punished the Janissaries and purged the civil service. He then strongly engaged the Persian power, recovered Azarbaijan, 'Iraq and Kurdistan, and by the Treaty of Qasr-i-Shirin (1639) established an eastern boundary (which left, Tabriz and Azarbaijan to Persia) nearly identical to that of today.

From 1640 onwards, after three centuries of success, began three more of humiliating decline. Except for the addition of Crete (1645) no new territory was to fall to Ottoman arms, while the loss of province after province, especially in Europe, marked the ensuing years. The well-known Turkish system of recruiting both their fighting forces and their whole civil service from trained and devoted ex-Christian slave-boys, of many Asiatic and European races, had worked well, by Turkish standards, for two centuries; but from the eighteenth century onwards it was an obsessive anachronism, and was finally abandoned. No progress, because no new conception capable of shaking an almost morbid conservatism, could be achieved in the body politic. Corruption and venality spread to the point of universality. Control and security fell to the lowest levels and the remoter provinces and their governors rendered an ever diminishing obedience to the Padishah and his viziers. High office was everywhere for sale, the purchase price recoverable from the public. The Islamic religion, retained with full rigid orthodoxy by the Sultanate and the 'Ulama, who provided almost the only Muslim educated class, was throughout much of the Empire defiled with all sorts of heresy and barely-Muslim contamination. The administration of the provinces was capricious and venal, habitually combining truculence with weakness, injustice with high pretension. By any standards the rule of Law, even of the Shari'a Law to which there was conceived neither rival nor replacement, did not prevail. Taxation was oppressive and monstrously ill-regulated. No economic conceptions existed save those dictated by immediate, blind self-interest. The important Christian and Jewish minority communities, in part self-governing under the *millet* system, were, while still regarded as politically innocuous, treated with tolerance; commerce and nearly all foreign social contacts (at least until the late eighteenth century) were the near-monopoly of these non-Muslims. Turkish Muslim society was ceremonious, ultra-polite, archaically stratified, strongly tinged with religiosity. The political or military power of the Sultan-Caliph ceased to be the terror and, in spite of the enormous popular prestige of his throne within Turkey and the fabled luxury of his Court, was later to be the scorn, of Europe and the world. The line of rulers themselves, once outstandingly able, was too often corrupted by extravagance, vice and harem influences into ignominy. The defeat of Turkish arms in Europe at St. Gothard (1664), Choczim (1673), and Lemberg (1675), the fatal siege of Vienna (1682), the fiasco at Mohácz and loss of all Hungary, the invasions of Turkish territory by Austrians and Venetians, the battle of Zenta (1697) and treaties of Carlovitz (1699) and Passarovitz (1718), were followed by successful Russian counter-invasions from 1736 onwards. By the end of the eighteenth century the Ottoman Empire was far gone in humiliation, feebleness and misery.

Egypt in the same period passed through three centuries of disorderly government, little as this, one may suppose, affected nine-tenths of the public. The Sultan's viceroys could not for long prevail over the entrenched local authority, and the far stronger forces, of the Mamluk beys; insubordination, murder and massacre, overt rebellion and large-scale armed quarrels between Mamluk cliques and candidates for power not only reduced Ottoman authority to a flickering shadow but involved the self-made rulers, or irremovable officials, in Syria also. Egyptian Islamic civilization, by now a peculiar blend of Nilotic, Mediterranean, Arab and Turkish, remained highly distinctive and by no means without attraction.

Western Arabia, claimed as belonging to the Ottoman dominions, increased its (largely involuntary) contacts with the western world; Portuguese, English, Dutch and French shipping and traders intermittently appeared on its coasts. The attempts of Istanbul to exert authority, whether in the Hijaz or the Yemen, were successful only locally, temporarily, intermittently; the indigenous lines of sharifs and amirs, with their wealth of local contacts and intrigues, could more than hold their own. It resulted that the Hijaz for short, and the Yemen for long, periods were left alone by their nominal overlord the Sultan-Caliph; of Turkish direct administration, and indeed of social or cultural influence, there was little or none. So passed three centuries of intense, sophisticated, self-seeking intrigue in the historic and holy Arabian cities, surrounded by purest non-government in the tribes and oases. In central Arabia the Wahhabi movement, a strong puritan Muslim revival, arose in one of the small Najdi amirates about 1740; its founder and adherents gained converts and strength, raided and conquered, carried terror into 'Iraq and the Hijaz, alarmed the Sharifs of Mecca, and was reported to Istanbul as a new threat or indignity; and indeed of these Wahhabis, and of their original backers of the House of Sa'ud, much was later to be heard. Eastern Arabia—Oman and the Trucial Coast, Bahrain and the al-Hasa coast-strip—had little visible history; its contacts were with the Gulf itself and India, its isolation from the Ottoman power complete, while its fierce local struggles for power, from one of which a new (the present) dynasty arose in Oman in 1741, mattered nothing to the world outside. The tiny state of Kuwait was founded about 1750 by a party of 'Aniza tribesmen from the desert hinterland.

'Iraq and Syria, Arab countries but nominally Turkish since the sixteenth century, endured as best they could the long Ottoman domination and all the characteristic features of its provincial administration. Their distaste at an oppressive, alien and incalculable government was tempered in some measure by its not inconsiderable short-term shrewdness, its prowess in 'divide and rule', and the unique prestige, felt by every Sunni, of the Sultan-Caliph. Local despots and dynasties could rise and fall in the Kurdish mountains, the deserts and marshes of lower 'Iraq, the coasts of southern Syria, the deep valleys of Lebanon; governors-general and their elaborate entourages, military commanders and judges, could come and go; the Sultan's government somehow survived, with all its weaknesses, shame and absurdities. The constant seventeenth- and eighteenth-century wars with the rulers of rival and incompatible Persia disrupted it no more than did its own habitual impotence to impose its will, keep order among its tribes, or guarantee an ordinary bestowal or use or continuity of power. The society and manners of the period were of medieval-Islamic type, artistic or cultural output was negligible, security poor or non-existent, poverty extreme.

Persia herself, a few years before the great eastward Ottoman expansion, produced suddenly a unifying, all-Persian, Shi'a-inspired revival, conceived and led by a religious aristocrat, Isma'il Shah the Safawi (or, to our Elizabethans, the Sophy) who inspired and rallied his country, exalted the Shi'i branch of Islam, and posed at least potentially a major threat to the Turks. The Safawi dynasty, at its

height a match for the Ottoman power, ruled Persia without a rival
for 225 years, built and adorned cities, notably Isfahan, and treated
and traded with the powers of Europe. Shah 'Abbas the Great was its
outstanding figure (1587–1629). Afghanistan broke off from the
Safawi Empire in 1747, under a separate Sunni dynasty, and has
never been reunited. The Safawis were succeeded by a brief Afghan
usurpation (1722), and then, after a decade of anarchy, by the
dominant figure of Turkish-descended Nadir Shah (1736–1747) the
Afshari—statesman, great soldier and conqueror, but brutal despot—
and after him by the mild and civilized rule of Karim Khan Zend
(1750–1779), with the capital at Shiraz. This too-short phase ended
with the enthronement of the bloodthirsty tyrant Agha Muhammad
(1779), first of the Qajar dynasty, of Turkish tribal origins. He was
succeeded in 1797 by Fath 'Ali Shah. Persia throughout these three
centuries was politically independent and reasonably secure. Notably
backward in conceptions of government, it was polished and sophisticated in social forms, highly cultured on traditional lines of art and
writing in its small educated élite, yet in the country at large almost
untouched by modern or western influences; the lot of the poorer
worker, villager or herdsman had changed little since antiquity.

## 2. The Nineteenth Century

Immense, yet almost nowhere spectacular, changes occurred in
Middle Eastern society and policies between 1800 and 1914. These
were at their least in Arabia and Persia, at their most striking in
Turkey and its provinces.

The Ottoman Empire with its Sultan-Caliph remained in existence
until World War One, but lost most of its territory in Europe—Greece
(1830), Rumania (1866), Serbia, Montenegro, Bulgaria, Thessaly,
Bosnia, Herzegovina (all in 1878) and, in 1912, almost all the rest
north-west of Marmara—and in Africa (Algeria 1830, Tunis 1881,
Libya 1912). In Asia the Sultan lost Cyprus to Great Britain in 1878
and an area of eastern Anatolia, to Russia, in the same year. Everywhere else, though with widely varying degrees of real control, or
intermittent interference, or merely nominal suzerainty, the Ottoman
power persisted, its progressively modified—and, in general, improved—governmental machine somehow operated, its peculiar
social and religious mystique prevailed. Except in Arabia and Egypt,
for reasons which will appear, the discontinuous half-hearted
struggles of the Ottoman power to modernize and revivify itself, to

catch up with the nineteenth century, to gain the respect or at least the tolerance of Europe without losing that of its own subjects, were visible in every province, from Basra or Sinai to the Bosphorus.

The reforming movement, deeply important both socially and governmentally, began with well-meant but abortive projects late in the eighteenth century (Salim III, 1789–1807), and had more to show under Mahmud II (1808–1839), to whom was due the destruction of the Janissaries, the formation of a new Prussian-trained army, schools and medical and military academies, increased foreign trade, and the multiplication (for better or worse) of resident foreigners in Istanbul and elsewhere. In the period 1839–1876 two major attempts at fundamental constitutional-legal reform were made (1839 and 1856), largely under European pressure; both produced considerable though inadequate results, both were followed by a wave of educational, administrative, economic, and even, within limits, political development, only to give place again to the thirty-year absolutism, secretive, corrupt, obscurantist, despotic, of 'Abdul Hamid II: a ruler who, detested by all progressive elements, and known in Europe as the butcher of the Armenians, was sincerely lamented, as an exemplary Muslim and as Caliph, by millions in his shabby and backward Empire. As the climax of a long-maturing plan by progressive army officers with wide backing, the Sultan was dethroned and replaced, by a complacent nonentity, in 1909. In the period 1909–1914 Turkey, with a restored but little respected parliamentary constitution, was in practice run by a clique of officers devoted, in foreign affairs, to Panturanianism and to Germany, and in internal policy to single-party power—that of its own Committee of Union and Progress—to a purging of the administration, and to insistence on national unity as Turks, even though three-fifths of the Empire was in fact linguistically and self-consciously Arab. The years immediately preceding 1914 were scarcely less unhappy and distracted than former decades; but by dint of nearly a century of attempted reform, and by greatly increased foreign contacts through improved land and sea communications, international posts and telegraphs, a railway network in Anatolia, foreign missions, increasing travel to and from Europe, the foundation of schools and colleges, modernized law codes and procedures, the beginnings of industrial development, the presence of European military and naval experts, the Turkish scene and urban society at all its higher levels—and, scarcely less, that of the 'Iraqi and Syrian cities—was far removed from its aspect of a century earlier. However superficially, indiscriminately, imperfectly, long stages of modernization had been some-how accomplished, new and irreversible conceptions had been admitted.

In the 'Arab provinces' the aspect of life in the cities was not dissimilar from that of Asia Minor; in the tribes and villages it was still traditional in form and spirit, except in new-fashioned official nomenclature and system and in greater signs of governmental activity. In 'Iraq—that is, the three *vilayets* of Mosul, Baghdad and Basra, later to become 'Iraq—the new era began in 1830 with the fall of the century-old dynasty of slave-Pashas, followed by the pro-gressive introduction of all that could substantially or nominally be made available of the codes and departments, the troops and police, the modern communications (roads, bridges, railways, river-steamers), the attempts at land-settlement, and, in general, standards and procedures less archaic than those of earlier days. And in society, urban or tribal alike, new ideas, a new awareness of the world outside, some suggestions of western manners and fashions, had become gradually visible. In Syria—that is, the *vilayets* of Aleppo, Damascus and Beirut and their sub-districts, with the two 'independent sanjaqs' of Dair al-Zaur (Deir ez Zor) and Jerusalem and the tiny internationally guaranteed 'autonomous Lebanon' dating from 1861 —the case was similar or perhaps indeed more marked as foreign (notably French and American) contacts were closer. The short-lived emergence of local, almost independent rulers—Ahmad al-Jazzar of Acre and Damascus, the Amir Bashir of Lebanon—and the Egyptian viceroyalty of Syria for a decade, belong to the earlier years of the century, as do the Maronite-Druze clashes to the middle; the last half-century of our period, in Syria as in 'Iraq, was mostly peaceful and (except for the Hamidian stagnation) not wholly unprogressive. In both territories an Arab nationalist or home-rule movement came, slowly and uncertainly, into existence with its tentative, but later bolder, propaganda and its secret societies and conferences; but it failed to make much headway against either the jealous autocracy of 'Abdul Hamid or Young Turk intransigence. Some small-scale but interesting colonies of European (mainly Russian) Jews in these years were being founded, with 'Zionist' as well as pre-Zionist funds and initiative, in the south Syrian *sanjaqs* of 'Akka (Acre), Nablus and al-Quds (Jerusalem).

Egypt, invaded and evacuated by Napoleon in 1798–1801, and thereafter subject to the increasing and finally dominant authority of Muhammad 'Ali Pasha, an Albanian captain, emerged at the end of

the first decade of the nineteenth century from bitter and bloody struggles for power involving Turks, Albanians, Mamluk Begs and foreign (French and British) armies, to find itself destined to be governed for the next thirty years by Muhammad 'Ali, under a merely nominal Turkish suzerainty. The Pasha, after restoring order and massacring almost the whole body of the Mamluks, sent forces on his suzerain's behalf to Arabia to deal with the Wahhabis, conquered and occupied most of the Sudan, and created an Egyptian fleet and army. His establishment of local industries was generally a failure, his brutal use of forced labour was deplorable, his fiscal oppression almost intolerable; nevertheless, he introduced cotton cultivation, carried out large irrigation works, and after his armies' successful campaigns in Asia Minor and Syria he could count his rule as permanent and hereditary—as it proved to be. Under his successors, considerable progress achieved in modernized public services, and the opening of the Suez Canal (1869), was accompanied by foolish extravagance and reckless borrowing. This led, on behalf of the European lenders, to an enforced Anglo-French control of Egyptian expenditure. A nationalist or anti-dynastic revolt, that of Ahmad 'Arabi in 1882, led next to British armed intervention to support the Khedive, and thereafter to an effective British occupation and government of Egypt, whereby, in the event, an immensely improved administration and a reasonable financial régime were by degrees achieved. The Sudan, grossly misgoverned for half a century, was the scene in 1882 of the fanatical Mahdist rebellion; this led to the total loss of Egyptian control, chaotic conditions and general depopulation for sixteen years, until its reconquest by Kitchener (1898) and the establishment of an enlightened administration in the formal guise of an Anglo-Egyptian condominium. The government and people of Egypt entered the twentieth century nationally solvent, intelligently governed, forward-looking, prosperous; but they were still faced by serious problems and among the intelligentsia and the politicians were, ever increasingly, resentful at their effectively subordinate status in their own country. The territory contained great potentialities, a small upper class conspicuous for their wealth and culture, a mass of peasantry in great poverty, and all the attractions of a vast tourist centre.

In western Arabia, officially the *vilayets* of Hijaz and the Yemen, the intermittent, half-hearted yet bitter struggle between Turkish pretension and local independence continued; one or other branch of the Sharifian family in Mecca, and the Zaidi (dissident Shi'i)

Imamate of San'a in the Yemen highlands, claimed and could for long periods exercise substantial autonomy; but, in the nineteenth century, first Egyptian and then Turkish governors did their best to diminish this and to assert imperial authority. This clash involved constant, fluctuating trouble—intrigues, interventions, expulsions, violence, and decades of treacherous diplomacy—while the Yemen in particular became the dreaded graveyard of Turkish armies. From the mid-century, Ottoman rule became somewhat more real, though still interrupted by frequent revolts; the Yemen highlands were penetrated, and a new small state of 'Asir, north of the Imamate, was recognized under a ruling family of Sayids. In 1908 was completed, as far south as Medina, the Hijaz Railway from Damascus, intended to serve pilgrims and to endear the Sultan-Caliph; but the Prophet-descended Sharif of Mecca abated none of his pretensions. On the Arabian south coast Great Britain occupied Aden in 1839, Perim Island in 1857, and began to exercise a vague protectorate (under the government of Bombay) over the Hadhramaut hinterland, the future Aden Protectorate.

The British were active also in eastern Arabia. Here they discouraged and finally suppressed piracy, the slave-trade and gun-running, kept political watch over the area, charted the Gulf waters and entered into agreements and 'truces' with the ruler of Muscat and Oman (then as now an independent state) and with the small and weak coastal shaikhdoms of the so-called Trucial Coast, and Qatar, Bahrain and Kuwait. None of these was colonized, all under their own shaikhly dynasties were protected. Kuwait was, like most of Arabia, the subject of a Turkish claim to suzerainty, which existed solely on paper. Central Arabia, meanwhile, saw in the early years of the nineteenth century the further expansion of the Wahhabi power under the Sa'ud family; this was followed, however, by its almost complete suppression by a military expedition ordered by Istanbul but executed by the Pasha of Egypt (1817–1819). The Sa'udi power later revived, showed aggression by raids and tax-collecting forays towards the east and south-east of the peninsula, but was again diminished by a Turkish-fostered rival Amirate, that of Ha'il in the Jabal Shammar, and by a brief Turkish occupation (1870–1913) of the al-Hasa coast of the Gulf. The Najdi amir of the Wahhabis, however, after a period of defeat and banishment (from 1891) re-occupied his homeland and oases in 1901 and, regaining al-Hasa in 1913, re-established his government of the Najd deserts while submitting, as 'Wali of Najd', to a purely nominal Turkish suzerainty.

Arabia as a whole began during the nineteenth century to attract the interest of the West; much of it was penetrated and described by successive European travellers, diplomats and scholars.

Persia in this century fared but poorly. Campaigns with Russia in the early years, ending in 1828 with the Treaty of Turkoman Chai, deprived her of a wide Transcaucasian area and secured privileges for the Russians. Wars with Afghanistan, in one case involving a brief British intervention (1856), followed in mid-century. Russian expansion in central Asia menaced the Shah, but a safe frontier was established in 1884. Throughout the century, and not least during the long reign (1848–1896) of Nasir al-Din Shah, the society and economics of the country were stagnant and medieval, its government despotic and illiberal, the Shah extravagant and greedy, the small but would-be progressive western-educated intelligentsia unheeded. Districts of Persia remote from the capital (Teheran, since 1788) enjoyed no government worth the name, or were the tacitly admitted private empires of land-owning notables or tribal princelings; insecurity was general, corruption universal, progress in any direction nugatory. Only in 1906 did popular discontent and mob action succeed in obtaining the grant of a constitution; but, opposed by the Shah, it was barely operative, disorder continued widespread, Russian penetration was resolute and, in north Persia, authoritarian and threatening. Spheres of permissible economic activity in Persia were delimited as between Russia and Great Britain by the 1907 agreement, the text of which emphasized the intention of both (sincere as far as regarded Great Britain) to respect the independence and integrity of the country. Oil was discovered in the Khuzistan province of south-western Persia by a British concessionary company in 1907, and was at once developed; it was destined to become Persia's greatest single asset. The export of oil began in 1912.

## 3. The last half-century

The half-century after the first world war saw striking alterations in the political map of the Middle East. It saw the emergence of new sovereign states from the shrinkage of the Ottoman domain, and the enhanced status of once subordinate territories. Of the states which today (1969) constitute the Middle East, very few correspond in their geographical boundaries or their international status with their counterparts of the period before the First World War; such few, indeed, include no more than Persia, the Sultanate of Oman,

Southern Yemen, and some Arabian shaikhdoms. The territory of historic and geographic Syria—three provinces of the Ottoman Empire (p. 72)—was divided into four states; those of the restricted Syrian Republic, of an enlarged artificial Great Lebanon, of southern Syria now to be known as Palestine and later as Israel, and of the desertic region east of Jordan, to be known at first as Transjordan, later as the Kingdom of Jordan. The three *vilayets* of the Tigris-Euphrates Valley became the Kingdom, later the Republic, of 'Iraq. The mid-desert Wahhabi principality of the House of Sa'ud became a kingdom stretching from the Red Sea to the Persian Gulf. Egypt attained full independence as a sultanate, then a kingdom, then a republic. Cyprus emerged in 1960 as a bi-racial sovereign republic. In Turkey itself the ancient monarchy made way for a modern-type republic, ruling, however, less than half of the former Turkish territory.

Nor, for the rest, do even these visible changes of name or status or frontiers equal in importance the profounder movement in social and governmental conceptions and progress in these countries, and in their material development. The whole region has in our day assumed a new importance from a variety of aspects (p. 21 ff), and occupies a place of greatly enhanced significance in the world. If the famous Eastern Question of Victorian times (which concerned the impending demise of the decrepit Ottoman Empire, and aspirants to its succession) has been settled by the then unforeseeable course of history, the new Middle Eastern Question, or questions, remain with us for solution; they concern the stability, viability and attitudes of the new states in the region, and their interrelations and foreign policies. The pages here following can attempt no more than to give, in the fewest words, a sketch of the stages by which the present-day political map came to be drawn; other aspects of the territories in their new form will occupy subsequent chapters of this book.

TURKEY, left defeated and apparently prostrated after the War of 1914–1918, yet emerged from its astonishing aftermath, by her own efforts, more united, compact and progressive than ever before. If her condition late in 1918 appeared desperate, in the subsequent six years her statesmen, with Mustafa Kamal Pasha (later Kemal Atatürk) towering above them, defied the Allies, successfully resisted the imposed partition of his country, evicted the invading Greeks from Asia Minor, rejected the damaging Treaty of Sèvres, and renounced for ever the Arab provinces of the Empire. Kemal after brilliant successes established a republic, dethroned the Sultan, and inaugurated a remarkable series of modernizing, westernizing, laicizing reforms. The capital was moved from Istanbul to Ankara in the heart of Anatolia. Islam was disestablished, its religious schools and brotherhoods repressed. European clothes (and hats) were *de rigueur*, Roman script was substituted for Arabic, new codes of law were introduced and a republican constitution proclaimed, and the administration was overhauled and amended at every level. The new régime and most of its frontiers were internationally established by the Treaty of Lausanne (July 1923); Turkey, now relatively small and for the first time mainly homogeneous, had turned into a modern, constitutional state. It was free thereafter to press on with reform, to suppress its rebellious Kurds, to extend education (including adult education), to experiment cautiously with party and parliamentary systems, to fix its frontiers—accepting the loss of the Mosul *vilayet* to 'Iraq in 1926, but acquiring Alexandretta-Antioch from Syria in 1939—and to join the League of Nations (1932).

Kemal died in 1938. Throughout the Second War the country, courted by both sides, preserved its neutrality. After it, Turkey was a founder of United Nations, successfully resisted Russian pressure, ranged itself openly with the West, joined NATO, and enjoyed copious western material aid for its never robust economy and its armed forces. Its internal politics have been uneasy, but with a trend towards the acceptance of democracy. In 1950 the party of Atatürk peacefully surrendered power after the country's first free elections. The next decade saw the rule of the Democratic Party, with economic advance but a gradual regression from political freedom, until in 1960 the military seized power. But this *coup*, unlike others in the Middle East, has seemingly resulted in a strengthening of democracy; having promulgated a new constitution and destroyed the Democratic Party, the soldiers returned power to the civilians. Since then two relatively free elections have been held (1961 and 1965), civilian ministries have accepted their results, and prospects for stable parliamentary government seem good.

CYPRUS, declared a British Crown colony in August 1914, remained as such with a normal colonial administration until the establishment in 1960 of the Republic of Cyprus, which was accepted as a member of United Nations; the intervening half-century had been filled, intermittently in the 1930s but continuously after 1945, with a violent campaign by Greek Cypriots in favour of Enosis, or union of the island with Greece. This was led after 1950 by Archbishop Makarios, but opposed no less whole-heartedly by the Turkish element, and by the Turkish Government.

The campaign, conducted with great bitterness, violence and bloodshed, ended, after many tragic episodes, with an Anglo-Greeko-Turkish agreement (1959) for full Cypriot independence (not, after all, Enosis), which, with the establishment of a bi-national Republic of Cyprus, accepted in 1961 as a member of the British Commonwealth, permitted the retention of a British military base on the island. However, the 1960's were to see continued communal tension between Greek and Turk on the island rather than its abatement. In 1963 the participation of Turkish Cypriots in the government came to an end after a series of constitutional disputes. Guerrilla warfare between the two communities began in the same year, leading to the establishment of a United Nations Peace-Keeping Force in Cyprus early in 1964. Minimal interaction, periodic skirmishing, and near-war between Greece and Turkey (in 1963–1964 and 1967) have been the troubled lot of the Republic since its independence.

Unlike those former provinces of the Turkish Empire which are now sovereign states, PERSIA, for all the complications and abiding problems of her existence, had by the 'sixties changed little in fundamentals since 1914. During the First War her condition was highly confused and almost anarchic, with warlike operations waged on her soil by Russian, Turkish, British and (her own) tribal forces, followed by an abortive Anglo-Persian treaty in 1919 designed to assist her in rehabilitation and government, and by a Russo-Persian treaty in 1921. The rise to ministerial power, and then in 1925 to the throne of Persia, of the uneducated but ruthlessly capable army officer who became Riza Shah Pahlavi, in supercession of the effete Qajar dynasty, inaugurated a half-generation of despotic government and sweeping reforms. The tribes and local rulers were disciplined as never before, communications and government-initiated industry were vastly extended, rough but effective government intruded actively in every sphere. The state finances were re-established with enforced taxation and wide-stretching government monopolies, local crafts were fostered, new law-codes adopted. The representatives of old-fashioned religion were terrorized, women (in law and regulation at least) were emancipated and social manners in the cities increasingly westernized. But the avarice and cruelty of the ruler destroyed his popularity, and his obstinately Germanophile policies, in the early days of the Second War, led to his abdication in 1941. Trans-Persian routes to aid Russia were thereafter widely used by the Allies, including the United States, in 1941–1944. After the War, determined Russian attempts to penetrate and dominate Persia were with difficulty—and incompletely—

frustrated by the Persian Government, with western help. In its postwar internal history, three periods may be distinguished: the Musaddiq era of the early 1950's, falsely hopeful and ultimately destructive, with its needless and suicidal battle against that demon of the Persian psyche, the Anglo-Iranian Oil Company; a full decade of groping thereafter (1954–1963), filled with shortlived ministries, failures to create a 'loyal opposition', and stifled political *coups*; and the 'White Revolution' since 1963, in which Muhammad Riza Shah Pahlavi has led with much apparent success the attack on the near-medieval economic and social order. Formally, Persia is (under its long-lived Constitution of 1906, since amended) a constitutional monarchy with a 200-member Majlis (National Assembly) and a part-nominated Senate of sixty. But serious problems remain, government by decree has been far from uncommon, and may well recur.

The 'IRAQI and the LEVANTINE provinces of the old Sultan's Empire entered, after the First War, a wholly new phase of their existence; from being shabby and neglected dependencies, they became sovereign countries central to, and highly important in, the new Middle Eastern picture. Liberated from the Turks in 1914–1918 by British forces, and entirely divorced from Turkish authority, they became in the post-war settlement the separate governments of 'Iraq, Syria, the Lebanon, Palestine, and Transjordan. All of these were in 1920 recognized by the principal Allied Powers, with the later confirmation of the League of Nations, as potentially independent states in need, temporarily, of assistance. They were accordingly placed under Mandate—the new form of international trusteeship, well described as 'imperialism in reverse', designed to meet such cases: 'Iraq, Palestine and Transjordan under Great Britain, Syria and Lebanon under France. Their history from 1921 onwards was one of territories under Mandate, until the Mandatory Powers, responsible as they were to the League of Nations, in due (or undue) course surrendered their trusteeship powers, and the territories became fully sovereign states.

'IRAQ, where King Faisal, of the revered Sharifian family of Mecca, was installed as constitutional ruler in 1921, made immense progress towards modernization, good government and stability under British guidance until 1932. At that date the Mandate was surrendered, the country becoming a fully independent member of the League of Nations; its frontiers had been stabilized, its security and public services developed, its officials and army trained, its legal and constitutional systems installed and operative. Once 'free', the government of 'Iraq was afflicted between 1932 and 1941 by a series of military *coups d'état*. The Second War period was one of stress and wartime difficulties, but peaceful except for one brief, abortive Nazi-favouring military movement; and from 1945 to 1958 policies and administration of normal Middle Eastern type continued, with the new oil-wealth (p. 254) making possible great projects and improvements. The era of stable growth ended abruptly in 'Iraq in July 1958, when a military revolution destroyed the monarchy and declared a republic. In the decade following 'Iraq has seen three more such *coups*, bringing to power either weak and unstable, or strong but arbitrary, military régimes. The proclaimed goals of these 'revolutionaries' have been Arab unity and socialism; but nothing has been achieved in the former field, while the latter has brought, on near-Marxist lines, the redistribution of land with state direction, or confiscation, of industry, banking and insurance. These extremist politics, and the inability to pacify the discontent of 'Iraq's Kurdish population (p. 119), have hampered orderly development, and marked the suspension of all free political life.

Geographical SYRIA was after 1918 detached permanently from Turkey and divided, as we have indicated, into four separate states. The French Mandate covered the thenceforward restricted Syria as one unit, and an enlarged LEBANON (the old mainly Christian autonomous sanjaq of Mount Lebanon of 1861, but with the addition of important Muslim districts) as another. The mandatory régime, to which France devoted much effort and expense, lasted from 1920 till its somewhat inglorious end in 1943–1945. During its course, important benefits accrued to both territories in the fields of administration, law, the armed forces, communications and the public services, and much was done visibly and invisibly to prepare the two states for an ultimate independent constitutional and international life of their own. The political aspects of the period were less happy, and French handling of the important minorities, and of impatient nationalist aspirations, was often so far ill-judged as to lead to seriously impaired security and to widespread (never universal) political discontent, which was increased by French reluctance to terminate the Mandate and depart. The problems of society and government in the two republics, since their achievement of sovereignty at the end of the Second War, have been quite different. Lebanon since 1946 has been repeatedly torn by intercommunity (mainly Muslim-Christian) as well as by normal political faction, and passed through a brief civil war in 1958; thereafter, it resumed its 'confessional' form of government under its elected President, its unicameral legislature, and its cabinets composed of ministers representing the communities in strict proportion. Syria was in 1949-1954 subjected to successive military régimes, and from 1954 to 1958 returned to uneasy party competition and shortlived, unstable ministries. In early 1958 the seeming collapse into chaos of the political system led (on Syrian initiative) to its union with Egypt in the United Arab Republic; but excessive Egyptian control, and the application to Syria of measures more suited to Egypt, led to the former's secession in late 1961. Early in 1963, power in Syria was seized by the Ba'th Party, long the leading advocate of 'Arab socialism'; it promptly declared Syria a 'democratic, popular, socialist republic' and began a series of radical economic reforms to realize its socialism, if not its democracy. In 1966 the party's yet-more extremist wing seized power, since when Syria has been the most ideologically-oriented and 'revolutionary' of all the Arab states and perhaps, for the time, the least promising in either its political or economic prospects.

The southern districts of the Turkish *vilayet* of Damascus east of Jordan—those of Hawran (in part) and Karak—were, in the early post-war days of 1919-1921, a no-man's-land of rudimentary government, under vague British control. In the latter year the territory, restyled as the Amirate of TRANSJORDAN, was entrusted, under a British Mandate separate from that of Palestine, to the Amir 'Abdullah, son of King Husain of the Hijaz and brother of Faisal of 'Iraq. Its history from 1921 to 1946 was generally peaceful and, on a humble scale, progressive, with minimum and acceptable British guidance. In 1946 the country, already a member of the Arab League, became independent, and in 1948, renamed the Hashimite Kingdom of JORDAN, acceded to full sovereignty and membership of United Nations. The parts of Palestine not occupied in 1948 by the forces of Israel (p. 134) were incorporated in Jordan, in which also much of the evicted and fugitive Palestinian Arab population took the refuge of homeless and hungry exiles. King 'Abdullah was assassinated in July 1951. He was succeeded by his mentally afflicted son Tallal, and a year later by his grandson Husain. The largely desertic and barely (or non-) viable kingdom since then has been subjected to both internal and external tensions which have several times made its collapse appear inevitable. Such were the endemic dissatisfaction—and rioting—of its ex-Palestinian majority against the King's moderate attitude towards Israel; propaganda attacks by the more revolutionary Arab states; and a series of military clashes with Israel, culminating with the Israeli occupation of Jerusalem and the West Bank in June 1967. The régime in Jordan is that of a constitutional monarchy with a two-chamber parliament, one house elected, the other nominated, and a cabinet responsible to the lower house. In practice, the Royal power is paramount.

No phenomenon in the modern Middle East, indeed in the world, is more remarkable than that of the establishment of the State of ISRAEL. An undertaking was given by the British Government in 1917 to a leading Jewish personality to 'view with favour the establishment in Palestine of a National Home for the Jewish people . . . it being clearly understood that nothing shall be done which may prejudice the civil and religious rights of existing non-Jewish communities in Palestine . . .'. This undertaking, seized with eagerness by a world Jewry in which political Zionism had constantly gained ground, was incorporated (with the same specific safeguards for the Arab population) in the British Mandate for Palestine, and, with the installation there of a Jewish Agency, was the charter for large-scale but still controlled Jewish immigration in the period 1920–1947. This movement, alarming to the Arabs of Palestine (a 90 per cent majority of the population in 1920), and to Arabs everywhere, could not but lead, with the dynamism of the Jewish minority and the background of powerful Jewish influences in the world outside, to the disappearance of all possibility of self-determination for the Palestinian population. Frequent disorder marked the years 1919–1946; conferences, missions, restatements and counter-statements of policy, and representations made by Arab states, all equally failed to find a solution for the dilemma as between immigrant Jew and native Arab—a solution which, as long as the safeguards prescribed in the Balfour Declaration and the Mandate were in practice ignored, not only did not, but could not, exist. The abominable treatment of European Jewry by Hitler's Germany during the Second War greatly increased Jewish pressures to be admitted to Palestine; the government of the United States, for whatever reasons, adopted a powerful pro-Zionist attitude in 1945–1948; and British abandonment of the Mandate, in despair of an agreed 'solution', was followed by the proclamation at Tel Aviv of the state of Israel in May 1948. The state so established is a single-chamber parliamentary republic. Its vigorous multi-party system has made coalition governments the rule. Internally, the past twenty years have seen the emergence of a dynamic, modern, progressive state, augmented in population by a continuing Jewish immigration and in resources by massive financial assistance from abroad. Its foreign policy has been marked by a militant defence of its sovereignty and nationhood; a willingness to reach accord with its Arab neighbours only on the basis of the *status quo*; a steady intransigence towards the claims for recompense of the Palestinian Arabs whom its creation displaced—and a grim determination to meet Arab threats with preventive war. Two such wars have been waged by Israel in its short history; in 1956 when its Sinai campaign destroyed Egypt's newly-acquired military machine, and in 1967 when Egypt, Jordan and Syria were defeated and Israel in the process occupied significant tracts of each.

EGYPT, on the outbreak of war in 1914, was immediately and for ever severed from her long but now meaningless Turkish connection, and became a Sultanate under declared British protection, a status which Egyptian politicians strongly resented. After the war period, in which Egypt served as an important Allied base and entrepôt, its future status became in 1919–1922 a burning question which led to a series of demands and refusals, demonstrations and imprisonments, diplomatic missions and outbreaks of violence. Finally in 1922 a unilateral declaration by Great Britain confirmed the country's formal independence, as a constitutional monarchy; but four 'reserved subjects', as between Egypt and Great Britain, remained for solution later. Fourteen uneasy but (with sad lapses) non-violent years followed, in which the problem of Anglo-Egyptian relations, viewed from two widely different angles, remained uncomfortable and seemingly unsoluble; in 1936, however, under threat of Italian aggression in East Africa, a Treaty was concluded whereunder Britain retained only minimal rights, in the fields of defence and communications. The internal struggles between a corrupt and reactionary Palace and successive Prime Ministers continued, as it was destined to do, till 1952. In the Second World War Egypt took no part save that, again, of Allied base, a role which, in self-defence, compelled the British (King Faruq being, like his father, Italophile) to a measure of interference in Egyptian affairs. After the war Anglo-Egyptian negotiations for an improved Treaty were renewed, to be constantly broken off—usually on the Sudan issue, or that of the Suez base—and once more restarted, with uniformly unproductive results. Finally, the 1936 Treaty itself was unilaterally abrogated by the Egyptian parliament in 1951, and the integral union of the Sudan with Egypt under a single crown was proclaimed. The British-occupied Canal Zone, the subject already of prolonged negotiations, became now a scene of active hostilities, and serious riots took place in Cairo (January 1952).

The Egyptian revolution of July 1952 overthrew the long-detested monarchy and (in 1953) instituted a republic. Since then constitutions and ministries have come and gone, but real power remains in the hands of the leader of the revolution, President Gamal 'Abdul Nasir—the 'Nasser' of western publics. After a first few shaky years of consolidating power and the undertaking of some mild reforms in the areas of law, agriculture, and social policy, it was the régime's conduct of foreign affairs in 1955–1956 which by rapid steps led Egypt—and its leader—to primacy in the Arab world, marked by an agreed British evacuation of the Canal Zone in 1954, the achievement of a position of independence from the west with the negotiation of an arms deal with the Soviet bloc in 1955, and finally the dramatic nationalisation of the Suez Canal, the resistance to 'imperialist' pressures against that action, and a diplomatic (though not a military) victory over Anglo-French-Israeli invasion in 1956. The Suez episode made 'Abdul Nasir the outstanding hero of an Arab world which had been for so long dominated by the west, and the years following saw the zenith of Egyptian influence in the Arab world, with the agreed union of Syria and Egypt in the United Arab Republic in 1958 as a visible manifestation of that influence. Against this, Syria's abrupt secession in 1961 was a serious setback, and the pan-Arabist hopes of 'Abdul Nasir and his followers in later years suffered a series of further blows. Such were the emergence of other radical reformist régimes which have challenged 'Nasserism' on its own ground, a prolonged involvement in a Yemeni civil war militarily unsuccessful and morally debilitating, and the internal difficulties of Egypt in the economic sphere, difficulties which not even the adoption of 'Arab socialism' (an egalitarian étatism preaching social solidarity, rather than a class struggle, as the path to modernization) from 1961 onwards has been able to correct. Coupled with the crushing defeat by Israel in 1967, the United Arab Republic in the late 1960's has the appearance of a weary régime whose greatest achievements lie behind it in its creation of a truly independent state and, within this, a reorientation towards social justice. Constitutionally, the state is a democratic socialist republic with a dominant (indeed, ubiquitous) Presidency and a 350-member National Assembly elected from the only permitted political party, the Arab Socialist Union.

The Anglo-Egyptian SUDAN in the last half-century passed through a period of constitutional reform, fair internal stability, and sound development. The British administration, frankly paternalistic, and (except latterly with the small Sudanese political class and the Egyptian co-dominus) generally acceptable, made way after the War to self-governing institutions. After prolonged negotiations with Sudanese representatives grouped in articulate but discordant political parties and with the government of Egypt, a régime of subordination to Egypt was convincingly rejected and the independent parliamentary Republic of the Sudan was proclaimed in January 1956. But late in 1958, surprisingly, parliament and all political parties were suppressed by an army revolution. The military ruled the Sudan until 1964, when—truly an anomaly in the modern world—popular riots returned the civilians to power. From 1964 to 1969, the Sudan witnessed vigorous but generally peaceful inter-party competition, free elections and coalition government. In May 1969, however, the army—this time led by younger, more radical elements—again seized power in a new *coup*.

The ARABIAN peninsula has changed in half a century less than any Middle Eastern area: socially and culturally little, economically much (by reason of oil development), and in politics more apparently than profoundly. The Najdi, central Arabian, Wahhabi state of the Sa'udis, after preserving its neutrality during 1914–1918, managed to suppress its rival in Jabal Shammar (p. 74) in 1921, to evict the Sharifian rulers of Mecca and the Hijaz four years later, and to add all western Arabia including 'Asir (p. 74) to their empire, which in 1932 was renamed by its outstanding ruler and creator, King 'Abdul 'Aziz ibn Sa'ud, as the Kingdom of SA'UDI ARABIA. A member of the Arab League and United Nations since the second World War, and without rival in the peninsula, Sa'udi Arabia is politically primitive—a theocratic, despotic state into which some trappings of modern government have been lately introduced but, even so, with no little doubt as to their ineffectiveness. King Faisal ibn 'Abdul 'Aziz, who succeeded in 1964 after deposing his brother, serves also as head of the Council of Ministers. He is a traditionalist and religious but not unenlightened ruler. There is no constitution or national assembly, although elected District Councils and a state Budget are steps towards governmental formalisation.

The YEMEN, freed from Turkish overlordship by the 1914–1918 war, maintained an isolated uneasy, backward but internationally recognized independence under its archaic Imamate; this, and the territory's separate existence, were magnanimously spared by ibn Sa'ud in 1934, when he defeated the Yemeni forces. The Imam's internal affairs appeared disordered and unprogressive; in the international world the Yemen was, though a member of United Nations and the Arab League, unqualified to play any appreciable part. From 1955 onwards some signs of internal dissidence appeared; there were Yemenis who had had enough of the Middle Ages. They struck in September 1962, upon the death of the Imam Ahmad; a military *coup* seized the capital and a republic was declared. But the issue was not to be so simple; tribal forces loyal to the Imamate refused to submit, and from late 1962 the Yemen was wracked by a civil war brutal in its conduct, inflated by the involvement of outside Arab powers (Egypt on the republican side, Sa'udi Arabia on the royalist), and by 1969 not fully resolved. The republicans controlled the most fertile portions of the country and the principal cities, and enjoyed recognition from most foreign countries. The royalists, with mainly tribal support, dominated much of the mountain terrain. The departure of the very large Egyptian 'expeditionary force' took place in 1967–1968, leaving the Yemen to its own dubious fate.

The People's Republic of SOUTHERN YEMEN, created in November 1967 out of the former British Colony and Protectorate of Aden, is the Middle East's newest, and probably its least viable, independent state. Its birth was the product more of imperial weariness and shaikhly incompetence than of revolutionary vigour, and the resulting state unites two widely disparate elements—the bustling city of Aden and its suburbs, and twenty-three more or less primitive shaikhdoms and amirates—in what must at present seem an unhopeful experiment. A year after independence it had no constitution or assembly, a self-styled general of the National Liberation Front still exercising precarious power.

The Sultanate of MUSCAT AND OMAN has given up little of its isolation; admittedly independent and sovereign, it is a member of no international body, has only rudimentary and autocratic governmental institution imperfect control of its own territory (especially in the mountainous and persistently insubordinate hinterland), and, except for recent oil discoveries, minimal resources. Only in the late 1960s, under the impetus of the impending British withdrawal from the Persian Gulf, and of oil-wealth, has it begun, but hesitantly, to move towards a more developed administration and services and its own armed forces, and even to some association with its immediate neighbours to the north-east.

The small Arab shaikhdoms of the TRUCIAL COAST, under despotic rule internally and British protection externally, had little history in the first half of this century other than *inter se* boundary quarrels, fears of Sa'udi acquisitiveness, and hopes of oil discovery. But the winds of change blow even on the Gulf; the 1950's saw the establishment of a shaikhly discussion-group and a joint military force, while the 1960's have witnessed the discovery of oil in the territory of two of the shaikhdoms, and the creation of a co-operative Development organisation. BAHRAIN Island has a recent history of oil success, of good administration, and of economic and social progress, but none of serious political advance: the family of Al Khalifa declines at present to share power. The QATAR peninsula is equally patriarchal; it has little history other than strictly internal, with the peaceful succession of its shaikhs, quarrels with the ruler of Bahrain, and, since 1950, great wealth due to oil. Nevertheless, the British decision to withdraw its military forces from the Persian Gulf by 1971 must affect all these statelets, and in 1968 planning for a future 'Federation of Arabian Amirates' was begun towards a joint constitution, shared diplomatic representation, and a federal capital. The disparities of economic circumstance and the historic enmities of the nine shaikhdoms lead, however, to serious doubts about the establishment of any valid or viable federal, still less a unitary, state.

KUWAIT, free of all Turkish claims since 1914, passed thereafter through phases of varying relations with Sa'udi Arabia and 'Iraq, and maintained its sovereign status. The oil-wealth of the state, first exploited in 1946, has been on a fantastic scale. In 1961 the Anglo-Kuwait Treaty, whereby the territory was (externally) protected by the British, was annulled, and Kuwait became fully independent. The Amirate then survived, thanks to British assistance, an immediate 'Iraqi attempt to annexe it, joined the Arab League, and in 1963 the United Nations. Internally, the last two decades have seen a rapid increase in population, the blossoming of an opulent welfare society and limited political progress, with the promulgation of a constitution in 1962, elections for a national assembly, and the gradual institutionalisation of 'moderate' ministerial government in co-operation with the royal family, which however remains dominant.

# CHAPTER FIVE

# PEOPLES AND LANGUAGES

## 1. *Territories and Citizens*

SOME account has now been given of the past fortunes of the countries of our region, and their accession to the modern statehood which they enjoy today. We proceed next to deal in outline with the populations which constitute these Middle Eastern states. And, to begin with, it has appeared abundantly that no ethnically pure 'races' can be expected to people them—or indeed any other territories in the world. The extent to which one human accretion after another has, since the dawn of history, diluted or modified original stocks—whatever they were!—has been shown by many examples; and since this phenomenon has been region-wide and has in no way comformed to, or created, present-day political boundaries (which have instead been established by any and every blind chance of warfare, resistance, apathy or caprice), it follows not only that all the populations are deeply mixed and composite from a score of ingredients, but that significant differences in human physique between them are, in the end, not easily perceptible. Any attempt to differentiate, one from another, the average or prevailing human type found in Arab or Turkish or Persian city or countryside must usually fail; the criteria of physical distinction commonly employed give here hopelessly mixed and inconclusive results. Only in a small percentage of cases will there be found a visible survival of some feature held to be characteristic of identifiable 'race'; the small-boned fineness of a Najdi Arab, the flat head-back of an Anatolian Armenian, the (very rare) Mongoloid eyes of a Turk, the recognizable Arab-Berber-Negro mixture in some Egyptians. To these generalizations some keen and possibly over-subtle ethnologist will demur, claiming to find in this or that valley or tribe—or in whole countries —physical types, or single features, which recall a specific, determinable origin; but in four-fifths or more of cases no mere spectator, and probably no expert, could tell by his physique alone a Turk or a Kurd, taken at random, from a settled Arab or a Persian. Except where obvious negro strains are present—and these are found here to a considerable, there to a minimal extent—the dark-white pigmentation, the brown-to-black hair, the brown or grey eyes, the Caucasian features prevalent throughout the Middle East are scarcely to be differentiated by sub-regions. There are, however, perceptible differences in apparent pigmentation between those whose life is passed in the open air—cultivator, herdsman, transport worker—in the hotter countries, and the city-dwelling office workers; the dark hue of the former type, indeed, often leads uninstructed Europeans to exaggerate the duskiness of these populations. And skin-colour can in many cases be lighter in any of the northern countries of our region, among the upper class whose family is more likely to have received, by recent intermarriage, infusions of blood from western Turkey or Europe. But all the races of which we shall speak, except the Sudanis, are 'white races'.

The basis of a claim to belong to this or that national group in western Asia is as elsewhere *prima facie* the passport carried; but this basis is insufficient and can be misleading. It is obvious that Egyptian papers could be produced by a long-domiciled Greek or Italian in Egypt, without such resident being Egyptian in more than a formal sense. The same applies to Greeks in Turkey, as it does to Persians in 'Iraq, or Circassians in Jordan. There are, moreover, cases of more massive minorities of one race, or culture-group, domiciled permanently in the territory of another, and forming a considerable proportion of its population. Such is the extensive Turkoman population—'Turks' in a truer sense, probably, than most Anatolians—in north-western Persia, or the Persian and 'Iraqi Kurds, or the Arab tribes on the (Persian) Karun. If we aspire to identify race with nation, as would no doubt be ideally desirable—and as is demanded by one of the principal bases of the modern concept of nationality—we shall find these racially-linguistically heterogeneous enclaves within other people's frontiers an embarrassment and anomaly; but they exist.

For political and administrative purposes the passport should determine its bearer's obedience; but on the level of the deeper sense of belonging, the loyalty of the member of this or that group is established by other criteria. What makes an Arab, or a Turk? It is the sense of inherited, habitual attachment, even in exile, to the group so named, and this seems to rest on certain unchanging elements. The first is common language, which normally provides the strongest of all single bonds between individuals and peoples; the language of their childhood and maturity, of their shared press and cinema and broadcasts, of their business and society. And a common language opens up, with strong community of feeling, the past glories (real or mythical) of earlier speakers of that tongue, with all their heroic deeds, conquests, and cultural achievements. Add to common language habitual residence in (or at least near) the present-day national territory; in a claim to be accepted as a Persian or a Kurd, one's own or one's ancestors' residence in Persia or Kurdistan or on their fringes must be an appreciable factor. Add again to these a conscious participation in a characteristic way and tempo of life, shown in domestic or public manners, forms of speech, preferences and prejudices, and religion. All these amount to much; but the final criterion which makes a man a true adherent to this or that group—Arab, Greek-Cypriot, or Israeli—is his own essential desire and *claim* so to be. This claim—how difficult, if it is there, for the foreign observer to gainsay!—cannot by itself produce a passport, may be politically thwarted, and may lead to helpless irridentism. Moreover, all the elements basic to such a claim may be present, yet it may never be made; the Turkomans of Azarbaijan, or those of northern 'Iraq, are far from unanimous aspirants to Turkish citizenship, while many Jews scattered throughout the Middle East abhor the idea of Israeli citizenship. Nevertheless, the three bases for what in the Middle East passes for 'racial' grouping must be reckoned as language, present or past habitual residence, and a common emotional devotion to the mystique and heritage of the group.

In none of these nations is the country's population, except in the communities of the Arabian peninsula, limited to a single race or culture-group. Turkey, Persia, the non-peninsular Arab states, Israel: all contain important minorities. And in almost every case there are also groups resident beyond the frontiers which can yet profess more or less valid claims to 'belong'. These are phenomena not less familiar in Europe and elsewhere, and so is the circumstance of a specifically bi-national state such as Cyprus.

It emerges from all this that the racial or culture-group picture of the Middle East is, as we should expect, very much less simple than the political map; the hatching or colouring meant to designate cultural or linguistic groups, whether politically self-conscious or otherwise, splashes capriciously across frontiers in blocks or fragments. The chapters of this book later to be devoted to each territory in turn will try *inter alia* to answer the specific question 'Of what elements does the population of *this* country consist, and in what proportions?' At the present stage it is intended to say something of these elements themselves, wherever they occur; first, however, dealing with the great religion common to most of them, and a constant element in their lives.

## 2. Islam today

No one is ignorant that Islam, in one or another of its sects, is the religion of western Asia, all of which (except Cyprus and Israel) belongs, accordingly, to the House of Islam. It has been shown, moreover, in these pages, first, that the faith of the Prophet included in its original form no more than certain fundamental propositions and demands, and that for these it claimed universal application and validity; and next, that Islam had in the Middle Ages been vastly complicated and divided by rival doctrines, sects and communities many of which stood and stand far apart from the orthodoxy of early times. It is now to be asked, in what forms does Islam survive in our own day, and how far is it an element of continuing force in the private and public lives of its adherents?.

It could be a matter of surprise that, in spite of its comparative rigidity and lack of imaginative popular appeal, the Sunni, strictly traditionalist, element in the Faith (p. 65) not only survived, but has prevailed as a powerful majority up to and into our own age. This has been due to its fidelity to its principles, the high authority it can quote for these, the impressive formulation of the Shari'a Law so central to Islamic communities (and the greatest of bonds between them), the distinguished characters who have upheld the Tradition throughout the centuries, and the support given for half a millennium by the Sunni orthodox monarchy of Turkey, with its immense prestige, patronage and endowments. It has resulted that western Asian Islam is today predominantly of the Sunni branch, though there is, among Muslims, as all know, no centralized Church or priesthood. The outward observances of the Sunni faith—though not its degrees of governmental establishment—are uniform throughout the House of Islam, and its theological background, the result of centuries of controversy and cautious absorption in the Middle Ages, is stable and everywhere accepted. It offers the most moderate, reasoned, and (to a western mind) acceptable version of the faith and law of the Prophet, and undoubtedly the nearest to his own conceptions. The four schools of the Shari'a Law, which are admitted by all Sunnis as unexceptionable, differ between themselves in no very serious respect, and even so in specific provisions rather than basic doctrine. All four were founded, and their codes formulated, by eminent medieval jurists, from whom they are still named. The Hanafi school prevails among the Sunni Turks and, through Turkish influences of yesterday, has followers also in 'Iraq and Syria; the Shafi'i is dominant in lower Egypt, 'Iraq, Jordan, Syria, and part of the Yemen; the Maliki, in upper Egypt and the northern and central Sudan; and the less widely accepted Hanbali, in Wahhabi Arabia only. These adherences determine the school to which the *qadhis* appointed to the religious courts of the country shall belong; but they make to the general public no difference at all, and their variations can be ignored here. The earliest of Islamic seceding sects, the Khariji, retained the full Sunni doctrine, and left the main community solely on the point of practical application, about which they allowed no compromise. Their survivors, known as Ibadis, are found today only (within the Middle East) in the Oman Sultanate, where Ibadism is the official religion.

Of the numerous Sufi fraternities earlier mentioned (p. 65) as within, yet standing clearly apart from, the main Sunni community —groups or coteries and often institutions with widespread branches, of great vitality and emotional attractiveness, but ill regarded by the traditionalist Sunni *'ulama*—a number survive and still play their part; to many indeed (but fewer, perhaps, in western Asia than in other regions of Dar al-Islam) they represent the most living and attractive forms that Islam has to offer. The Sufi sects vary greatly in their material organization, as they do doctrinally between near-Orthodoxy (as in the famous and ancient Qadiriya order, with its venerated headquarters in Baghdad), through different degrees of Islamic (or scarcely Islamic) mysticism to others with more objectionable rituals. Such, for instance, characterized the followers of the great Bektashi order in Ottoman Turkey, long identified with the Janissaries but today no longer there since the revolutionary suppression of the religious orders by Atatürk in 1925; and such also the Mawlawi (or Mevleviya) sect known in Europe from its 'dancing dervishes' but now banished from modern Turkey to a few refuges in Syria. The Sufi or darwish (dervish) orders in Egypt— Badawiya, Bayyumi, Dasuqi—are still important and mean much to their faithful members. The same is true of an almost opposite form of the Faith, as remote as could be conceived from Sufism or any 'fancy religion'; that is, the rigid, unalterably established code of the dour Wahhabis of Najd, who permit no accretion to, or latter-day interpretation of, the Book—and despise the laxity of Sunni and Shi'i alike.

The Shi'i communities (p. 65), which form a large minority in the Middle East, derive politically from the original rejection by the partisans of 'Ali of the claims of all Caliphs subsequent to him, while doctrinally they draw from many elements imported from non-Arab, mainly Persian, sources in the first and second century of Islam; indeed, the fragmentation of the Faith's original ultra-simplicity was an inevitable result of the diversity of countries, communities and minds which Islamic conquests soon brought within its fold, including peoples far more mentally sophisticated than the Arabs of Arabia. To this factor may be added tribal, racial and personal rivalries which could not but arise, and which partly were the causes of combat on the spiritual and theological front as well as the political, and partly used the former as a ready weapon in the latter. Shi'ism, at any rate, had every occasion to grow apart from the Tradition, to gain ground (particularly in non-Arab territory), and to flourish in its various forms. The Shi'i communities, besides their rejection of the Caliphs from the fifth onwards, are united positively also in attributing to a true Caliph or Imam (as they term him) wide spiritual powers and a personal infallibility and authority quite foreign to Sunni conceptions, and in postulating a mystical interpretation of the Qur'an itself, a body of secret knowledge, and a unique relationship between the family of 'Ali and the Creator. The line of Shi'i Imams—valid successors, in their eyes, of 'Ali and the Prophet, as are the Umayyid and 'Abbasid Caliphs in Sunni—is, after the first six, itself in dispute between differing Shi'i sects. The majority (the Ja'fari) sect is dominant and official in Persia, is heavily represented in central and southern 'Iraq, and is fairly numerous in the southern Lebanon, western intermontane Syria, and Bahrain Island. These Shi'is hold that the line of the Imams, after the first eleven, ended with the mysterious disappearance of the twelfth and last incumbent (A.D. 873), who will one day reappear. The Ja'fari branch of the Shi'a has, with considerable background differences from the Sunna, much also in common with it, and may be held to keep the essentials of the Faith intact; but the variations are so far emotional, and have been given so much weight in controversy, that attempts to effect a reunion, and to recognize a fifth orthodoxy school of Law (the Imami), have always failed.

Of other varieties of Shi'ism, the Zaidi sect is free from metaphysical or emotional extravagances, attributes no divine qualities to the Imams, and differs from the Sunna upon relative unessentials; it is the official religion of the monarchy and the highland districts (though not of the coastal areas) in the Yemen. The Isma'ili sect is more widely diffused; its founders left the main body of the Shi'a in the eighth century on a question of the succession to the sixth Imam, and later on matters of mystic theology which carried them to the very fringes—or beyond them—of Islamic tolerance. Isma'ilis are found, in the Middle East, only in small compact communities in Syria and Persia and in the Najran district of south-west Arabia; nothing is left today of earlier sub-sects of the Isma'ilis, whose place in history is that of the Carmathian (Qarmati) rebels of the Middle Ages, of the Fatimid State and Caliphate of Cairo (p. 52), and of the infamous Assassins in their north Persian stronghold (p. 55). The head of the Isma'ili Shi'is in the modern world is the Agha Khan; their main present strength is in India and East Africa. The Druzes (Duruz) of the southern Lebanon, of the mountain named after them in the Syrian Republic, and of northern Israel can be regarded as, in religion, a yet more heretical offshoot of the Isma'ilis, formed in the eleventh century into a separate sect; it was based upon the deification of the Fatimid ruler Hakim—himself apparently a lunatic—and on various mystical and concealed non-Islamic beliefs. The Druzes form, socially and at times politically, a bloc clearly distinct from all their neighbours; their claim to be Muslims at all can, indeed, only with difficulty be accepted, though they seem, in their own secret and graded hierarchies, to accept the main elements of Isma'ili belief. The same may be true of the Nusairis (or 'Alawis) of the west Syrian mountains, an ancient indigenous community whose mixture of local pre-Islamic or non-Islamic beliefs with extreme forms of Shi'ism, and even with Christian observances, has produced a peculiar blend not easily qualifying for inclusion in the Muslim world.

The religion of a fair proportion, possibly 15 per cent, of the Turkish peasantry—notably the Yuruks or semi-nomadic tribes—of Anatolia, is widely regarded as a heterodox, impure form of Islam, and resembles that of the Nusairis in their incorporation of primitive elements from ancient times. Without these Turkey, in spite of Atatürk's destruction of institutionalized religion, would be a uniformly Sunni country. One more scattered, nowhere compact or formidable, minority, found in Persia and in Israel, is that of the Baha'is, founded by a Persian would-be reformer in the eighteen-forties. His syncretic religion, later distracted by schism and always detested by all good Muslims, is in some measure an offshoot of Isma'ili Shi'ism, mixed with ingredients from other faiths. The

Baha'is are of more account and better tolerated in America than in their native Middle East, where normal Islamic tolerance has failed to protect them from the rancour, at times the violence, of the public.

This sketch of the varieties of belief within Middle Eastern Islam, and the representation of these in often antagonistic communities, may lead too readily to the conclusion that the power of the Faith is thereby gravely weakened, or even has ceased to count. It is true that its old unity as the single social-religious body envisaged by the Prophet is no more, and that the initial conquering force of an aggressive creed has long disappeared. Moreover, the contrast between the successes and advances of the non-Muslim societies of the West —the Christian sovereign states of Europe—and the relative backwardness of the House of Islam has discredited the latter in the eyes of some, in addition to the clearly rising or risen tide of world-wide secularism which has gone far in diminishing the power of all supernatural religions. In many évolué Muslim circles their religion is considered by the young and sceptical as something for the older generation, most respected among the least progressive; the outstanding practical reformers of our century—Kemal Atatürk, Riza Shah Pahlevi—were irreligious; and the legislatures of the most modernizing Muslim states, Turkey and Egypt, have replaced Islamic with secular codes even in the hitherto reserved field of family matters. The ideal of many, almost certainly most, young politicians and publicists in the Middle East is now not a specifically Islamic state but one of western-type secular efficiency. All these are facts; is it, then, true that Islam today can claim none but a humble place as a current social and political force, to animate or to restrain?

Such a conclusion would be over-hasty. It can be urged, on the contrary, that major movements in recent history have been profoundly Islam-inspired; such have been, among others, the Wahhabi movement itself, of which the force is not yet spent: that of Ahmad al-Idris (d. 1837) who, with the sanctity gained by founding a new Sunni 'way' which borrowed Sufi techniques, gained a principality in 'Asir on the Red Sea; that of the Sunusi (Senussi) family now on the throne of Libya by way of a similar religious and reforming movement in north Africa; that of the Amir Ghani (Mirghani) family in the Sudan, whose piety and religious-social movement left behind it, in the influential Khatmiya sect, a power in Sudan politics; and indeed the rising and usurpation, also in the Sudan, of the fanatical Mahdi himself, Muhammad Ahmad (p. 86). These examples prove that an effective relation between religion and politics can, or could recently, still exist. And other phenomena support this. One is the clear distinction in a Muslim's feeling towards a co-religionist as against a non-Muslim fellow-citizen (a Copt in Egypt, a Christian in Lebanon, an Armenian anywhere), in times of stress; a distinction no doubt deplorable, but significant of Islamic self-consciousness. Another sign is the force, in any mob street-demonstration, of an emotional appeal to Islamic fervour; and another, the continued basing of political parties—the Muslim Brotherhood in Egypt and Syria, the Fida'iyin i-Islam in Persia, and others in Indonesia and Malaya—on a programme of Islamic revival; and yet another, the visible success of Islam in making far more converts from paganism, in west Africa today, than Christian missionaries can achieve. And, within Islam's most responsible and devoted circles, the effort continues to find ways to restate the Faith in forms less rigid and dry-as-dust, more attractive to the young and westernized, than the time-honoured, almost static expositions of the traditional Islamic apologists.

These are all signs that Islam is alive, has convinced, intelligent and numerous upholders, can be a force in public affairs. To millions throughout the Middle East it is still the Faith by which their daily lives would claim to be guided; though its future may be one of gradually lessening appeal in our rationalizing age, and though its force may be less than that of a century—far more, five centuries —ago, yet in any of its diverse forms it is still precious to millions, colours their lives, and, to some unascertainable extent, may direct their actions.

Meanwhile, the Muslim of any but the least polite, or the most emancipated, society still shows constantly the influence on social behaviour of his Islamic background and community tradition. It is revealed in his conversation as a familiar element in his thought, and the tempo of his actions is traditionally that of dignity—since haste is of the Devil. In spite of all the inroads of cynical modernism, the social observances of daily prayers, the mosque on Fridays, the fast in Ramadhan, and the great Muslim festivals, are still widely alive. The great annual pilgrimage to Mecca, pilgrimages also to Meshhed in Persia, to Karbala and Najf in 'Iraq, and to a dozen other shrines, tell the same story. In most countries a qadhi in every town administers the Shari'a Law within its now restricted sphere, and a mufti gives rulings on religious issues. Mosques are maintained, with their salaried staffs, the mu'adhdhin (muezzin) calls, sermons are delivered, mosque and saintly-tomb revenues (often very considerable) are allotted to charitable purposes, scandals are few, government supervision (a recent feature) is close. Except in Turkey, where its use is much restricted, the garb of religion is seen everywhere; the religious 'establishment' goes on, with dignity and, let us hope, true devotion. There is explicit respect for high Islamic lineage, that of the Prophet's own family, for instance, or of some famed divine such as 'Abdul Qadir al-Gilani. The Shi'i *mujtadhis*, doctors and interpreters of the Law, have still high authority, though no official countenance, in Persia and 'Iraq; dynastic claims, like those of the Sa'udis or the Sunusi, can be based upon it, or, like that of the Moroccan royal family, be enhanced by it. A reputation for Islamic saintliness, even in wild Kurdish hills, brings fame and reverence.

The tolerance traditionally extended to non-Muslim 'people of the Book' (that is, of a revealed religion: the Christians and Jews)—a tolerance which, viewed throughout history, far exceeds the best that Christian history can show—covers also, not without human lapses, the aberrant forms of Islam itself, provided that the essentials of the faith are intact. To pagans alone such forebearance is not owed.

## 3. *The Arabs*

The Arab-speaking people or peoples of western Asia and northeast Africa (Egypt and the Sudan) form, as all know, the great majority of the population of the Middle East as we have defined it. They number approximately 72,000,000 souls, and are divided into ten sovereign states which are members of the United Nations ('Iraq, Jordan, Kuwait, Lebanon, Sa'udi Arabia, Southern Yemen, the Sudan, Syria, the United Arab Republic, and Yemen) and ten minor but independent units which are not (Bahrain, the Sultanate of Muscat and Oman, Qatar, and the seven Trucial shaikhdoms). There are also sizable Arab populations in south-west Persia (the province of Khuzistan, formerly known as Arabistan), the southern fringe of Turkey, and Israel—with the Arab population under the control of the last-named numbering well over one million after the war of mid-1967. In passing, two points affecting Arab territory in western Asia are of interest. The first is that, except in the Yemen and (scantily) in Oman, and in a small area of Syria-Lebanon, Arabs are invariably people of the flat-lands; the process of Arabization by invaders failed to penetrate into the highlands of Persia or of Turkey. The second is that, in all the range of the (eastern) Arab countries (excluding, therefore, the southern Sudan) the sole considerable enclaves of non-Arab-speaking peoples are those of the north 'Iraqi Kurds and Turkomans, the recently-intruded Jews of Israel, and, at the extreme south-western fringe, the partly-Arab bilingual grazing tribes of the central Sudan, the African-type Nubas of Kordofan, and the Nubians of the middle-Nile banks. Elsewhere Arabic speech and consciousness is practically universal.

The vast majority of these Arabs are not so called by virtue of belonging to an ethnically distinct race; they are, as we have seen, except for the central Arabian folk, an amalgam, or rather a variety of different amalgams, of many original races including some, such as the black Africans, far removed from one's normal conception of Arabs. But these peoples have been Arabized, for centuries, to a point where their claim to this classification cannot be disputed if our already suggested criteria (language, residence, cultural devotion, personal claim) are applied. The acceptance, or indeed the proud declaration, of their Arabism by the vast majority of the group throughout the region, is not invalidated by the few cases, hereafter to be mentioned, where such acceptance is doubtful, or is rightly or wrongly rejected by outside observers. The dominating elements of unity throughout the group are many. The strength of these will be apparent when we pass, now, to examine them; and the same scrutiny will reveal considerations detracting, here and there, from their potency. We shall examine elsewhere (p. 197) a field, that of politics, in which Arab unity is notably far from realization.

The claim of the entire block of Arab populations to form a single Community, and to be heard with the greater respect by reason of this fraternal unity, is indeed, in the case of a people divided as they are into self-conscious independent states, a unique phenomenon in the modern world. The Anglo-Saxon nations, the Slav group, the Scandinavians, black Africa: none of these approximate to the educated Arab's conception of his overall singleness transcending national diversity. The uniformly Catholic, ex-Spanish, miscegenated, geographically contiguous states of Latin America offer the nearest approach, yet, for good reasons, do not come near to the Arab sense of unity and mutual belonging and are far from regarding themselves, as do Arabs, as in fact a single *gaum* (folk or people). The nearest parallel to modern Arabism, in this respect, is perhaps the shared and eagerly boasted common Hellenism of the politically detached, independent Greek cities scattered through the Mediterranean world in the seventh to fourth centuries B.C., with their superiority complex as against 'the barbarian', their immense pride in language and tradition, their unique right of entry to the Greek holy places and panhellenic ceremonies—and the Games. This is a far cry; yet the likeness is more than an accident of history, since there are similarities of character and attitude, between Arabs and Hellenes, which have helped to create the parallel.

The Arab countries can, at the outset, claim to form geographically a single block from the confines of Persia to the Atlantic and Indian Oceans. This would by itself imply but a slight and perhaps unreal contribution to unity unless it were accompanied, as among Arabs it is, by the constant intercourse of familiar age-long neighbours, between country and country. The Arabs have in fact for centuries travelled, traded and sojourned in each other's countries, established common enterprises, married each other's daughters, participated as privileged kinsmen in their neighbours' society, and shared in a rich common treasure of history and myth.

The community of language which, above all else, makes this possible is, as everywhere, the greatest of bonds. The Arabic language, almost without qualification that of all Arabs everywhere, is, far more than with most tongues and their speakers, a source of conscious pride and interest; and indeed the language of the Qur'an, of pre-Islamic poetry, and of a vast medieval and modern literature is in itself a rich, flexible instrument in which to indulge the age-long, especial pleasure of Arabs in speech and writing. But is it still a single language, everywhere mutually intelligible? The answer is Yes, to a surprising extent. Historically, the separate emergence of modern Arabic from among a dozen closely-allied Semitic languages seems to date from the fourth to sixth centuries A.D.; it appeared by the latter date in a single, elaborate, closely-developed form, in which its flexibility and curiously delicate mechanism of expression were already evolved (though the script, originally inadequate, was later improved) and which has changed extraordinarily little in the last thousand years—or indeed since the recording of the Qur'an itself. The latter, which made its form of speech a sacred though never a hierarchic language, has been of course a considerable element in establishing it. Since then a large number of words from Persian and Greek have been introduced, to meet administrative, artistic and scientific needs for which the Prophet's vocabulary was unequipped; grammar and accidence were codified by the labours of Arab grammarians, chiefly in 'Iraq in the seventh to ninth centuries; and the more severe and elaborate features of earlier written Arabic have, in the modern language, been allowed to lapse out of use in favour of simpler and handier usages. The Arabic of the present-day press, letter-writing and literature in all Arab countries is, therefore, a remarkably constant international language, not merely intelligible from 'Iraq to Morocco, but substantially identical throughout. In the spoken tongue there are greater differences, due to the absorption of local words from other languages—Persian, Turkish, Greek, Italian, African—and to other factors, and to regional preferences also in pronunciation (for instance, the hard G in Egypt, and the dropping of Q there and in Syria); but even these are not difficult for the traveller or newcomer rapidly to appreciate, and a 'higher colloquial' based on current press-writing is today a *lingua franca* among literate people, even though the speech of some outlying, usually tribal, communities (notably in the Sudan) has departed perceptibly, to say the least, from normal Arabic. It emerges, therefore, that the substantial unity of modern Arabic is even more an effectively unifying factor than could well be expected; and with it goes the press, of which the acceptability knows no inter-Arab frontiers, and the cinema, and, with great importance, broadcasting.

The Arabic language has been, obviously, the vehicle whereby has been preserved the remarkable singleness of the Arab inheritance: that of awareness and pride in Arab past achievement—hailed as such, in spite of sometimes dominant contributions thereto by Persian or Byzantine—in literature, art, architecture, public works; in military and political achievement, whether in fact truly Arab-led or not; in the shared sense of a consciously single social community, widespread over much of the known world, and enduring for centuries—the one Arab Nation, within an even wider House of Islam; in the common awareness of the peculiarly privileged place of Arabs and Arabism in Islam itself; in legend, myth, household story, early and later poetry, anecdote and proverb, and all the background of a people as acquired in childhood and maturity. To this sharing of and pride in the Arab inheritance is due, more than to anything else, the justified claim of its possessors to 'be Arab'. And if one must judge that such claim is less than entirely universal among Arab-speakers, the exceptions are worth mentioning, in passing. They consist of those who, while appreciative of the Arab legacy and unwilling to be excluded from it, yet give first place in their hearts to some other loyalty—that of a local, westward-looking, Phoenician

Lebanon, for instance, or that of an Egypt of the Pharaohs and the Nile, rather than of Arabs and western Asia; indeed, the self-realization of the Egyptians as Arabs, which is substantially complete today, was imperfect (or in some circles non-existent) a generation ago. Such non-Arab localisms are sometimes emphasized by European observers, as discrediting the full unity of Arab sentiment; and indeed they do so, but within narrow, mainly political, and broadly unrepresentative limits. The same is in general true of Arabic-speaking communities who, for reasons implicit in their own histories, have an intense and inward-looking loyalty of their own which doubtless transcends any which they can offer to the main stream of Arabism. This may be the case of the Druzes of Syria and Lebanon (p. 94), the Mandaeans of lower 'Iraq (p. 107), Arabic-speaking Jews everywhere, perhaps the heretical Nusairis of the Syrian coastal ranges (p. 94) and even some, at some periods, of the Christian minorities later to be described (pp. 103–109).

The contribution of religion to Arab or pan-Arab community feeling—the Islamic religion, that of nineteen-twentieths or more of Arabs—may be variously assessed, but cannot be ignored. Something has been said already of the cleavages and sects within Islam, which divide the Arab Nation rather than unify it; but they do not, at their deepest and bitterest, obliterate the boundary which, in the vast majority of Muslim minds and communities, divides Muslim from non-Muslim. There is in the unquestioned essentials of the Faith enough of spiritual and emotional content to make certain that shared adherences to any form of Islam must be a powerful bond between all Muslims—and, for our present purpose, all Arabs; even though non-Muslim Arabs have, in times and places, contributed notably to modern Arabism in the fields of literature, business, politics, society, for each of which it would be easy to quote examples in plenty from Egypt, Palestine, Syria, Lebanon, 'Iraq.

The religious bond in Arab international society may be less obvious to the interested traveller than another feature in their communities which not so much creates as reflects their essential unity: that of the shared way of life which dominates the Arab scene in every region. Here, like must be compared to like; nomad to nomad, tribe to tribe, village and city to their equivalents elsewhere. With this proviso, one can emphasize the close similarity between the form, manner, tempo and social observances of Arab society everywhere in homes, coffee-shops, offices and streets. These differ extraordinarily little, class by class and age-group by age-group, from

Basra to Aleppo or Upper Egypt; and even allowing for elements
that are universal in the modern world, and those common to the
whole of Dar al-Islam, there remains something appreciably Arab in
the forms of courtesy and conversation, the social approaches and
reactions, the domestic arrangements and communal institutions
which have persisted throughout centuries.

There exists, therefore, an Arab World, of which the states and
units in the Middle East which have been mentioned (p. 97) form
part. Within this world there are, it is clear, factors of disruption as
well as of unity. Is there also such a thing as Arab character? It would
be the line of safety, or of pedantry, to deny it; 'national characters'
are notoriously dangerous ground. Nevertheless, certain generalities
seem to be permissible, in the full knowledge that these are open to
countless individual exceptions. Arabs, members of the international
Arabic-speaking bloc, are beyond doubt less, or less efficiently,
warlike than Turks, less artistic or mystical than Persians. They are
courteous according to their code, curious of the unknown, proverb-
ially hospitable, instinctively generous. They are by any standards
highly intelligent, quick in apprehension, witty and humorous, eager
and accomplished formulators of their thoughts in speech; indeed,
facility and fluency can here be their dangers, since these can too
easily be unrelated to facts or to wisdom. Arabs learn quickly and
remember well, but are less disposed to patient inconspicuous research. They are rapid and habitually extreme in judgment and, in
this field, not free from caprice and prejudice. They are freedom-
loving, uncompromising, strongly individualistic, at their worst
egoistic, poor at team-work, reluctant to accept unwelcome decisions
or to subordinate their own wishes to those of a majority or of
superior authority.

4. *Some Arab-world minorities*

We have glanced at certain differences of doctrine, leading often
also to difference of social and political grouping, within Middle
Eastern Islam; and no more than a mention need be made here of
such other Muslim groups within the area, but essentially strangers
in it, as the considerable Somali element in the Aden population and
that of Oman; or the small settlements of Caucasians—Sunni
Cherkes or Circassians and Shi'i Chechens—planted by Sultan
'Abdul Hamid on the eastern borderlands of settled Syria, including
present-day Jordan, to form a stable element among wayward tribes-

men. One may add to these the Pakistanis who, mixed with Indians, are found trading in coastal districts of Oman, the Persian Gulf and Red Sea; or the West African Muslims who pass years, sometimes, in the Sudan or the Hijaz or both in the long course of their pilgrimage to Mecca. And here also we may refer to two other groups of Muslims who, while not Arabic-speaking, are yet, as far as their stage of evolution allows, within the sphere of Arab culture. These are the tiny tribal communities of south-eastern Arabia which speak (Semitic) languages of their own, remote from Arabic; and the part-Arab, part-African graziers of the central Sudan with their Islamic faith, cattle-breeding tribal way of life, but African physique and Hamitic or Nilotic languages. Nor would it be difficult to find other, but in the general picture unimportant, Muslim or indeed non-Muslim communities in the Middle East marked off from the surrounding majorities in their countries by language, type, or alien community consciousness. Such for example would be the long-enduring yet significant community of the Zoroastrians in the Persian provinces of Kirman, Yazd, and Teheran; they are some 12,000 strong, known as good traders and outstanding gardeners, and close kinsmen of the rich, progressive Parsees of western India.

Far more important numerically, politically, and in terms of area occupied, is an element not indeed of Islam nor truly of the Middle East, yet today politically included within it as forming part of the Sudan Republic: that is, the black-African inhabitants, perhaps four millions strong, of the three southernmost provinces, and a large enclave also, that of the Nuba Mountains, in the province of Kordofan. Here we enter an essentially African world, far removed in every respect save the topographical—that is, in physique, evolution, conceptions and beliefs, way of life, languages, social organization—from everything characteristic of the Middle East: the world of the Nilotic Dinka, the Shilluk and Nuer peoples, the Nilo-Hamites of Equatoria, the agricultural Zande and other peoples of the Ironstone Plateau. Of all these, fascinating to the anthropologist (and embarrassing to the present Sudani administration) the present work will say little more; they are no essential part of a Social Geography of the Middle East.

Returning, therefore, to the Arab world, we glance next at some minority elements of which the social importance far outweighs the smallness of their numbers; and indeed the continued existence of these Arab-Christian communities, in an area so long and deeply Islamized, calls attention once more to the geographical and historical forces which have produced or sheltered them. Such are the half-isolated topographical enclaves which have, in times of trouble, been their salvation; the successive waves of conquest and penetration which have introduced new and partly unassimilable minorities, seeking and finding new homes; the long and slow communications which have kept central government action away; and the resulting localism and pride in separateness. In the matter of religion, a separate faith is often the surviving outward sign of a distinct but unascertainable racial or tribal origin, or of an old political secession, and the number of these shows the readiness of Middle Eastern groups to cling to religious beliefs or to evolve new ones of their own: examples, the Yazidis or the Maronites. At the same time, the dispersal of some once compact communities shows the effect of former persecutions (as in the case of the Armenians, or Assyrians), or sometimes reflects their own wide-ranging commercial abilities and quest of opportunity. The recent history of the Christian minorities, at least since the sixteenth century, owes much to good sense and toleration on the part of an authority not often praised: the Ottoman Government. Onwards from the first occupation of Istanbul (1453) the Turks allowed the community cohesion of the Christians (and the Jews also), sect by sect, to form recognized and internally autonomous *millets*, under their own elected heads, with separate representation on local councils, and freedom in matters of religion, personal status, schools, properties and churches, and their community life. The *millets* thus, with exceptions only when the unwise and sometimes fatal patronage of European powers, or their own indiscreet nationalistic ambitions, aroused suspicion and ill will, retained their own individuality and enjoyed a treatment by the public and government which left them little cause for complaint, and which permitted them to advance in education and knowledge of the modern world notably faster than the Muslim majority; a feature tending, however, to diminish, through jealousy and suspicion, their popularity *vis-à-vis* their Muslim fellow-citizens, and perhaps to weaken, as time went on, their own sense of intimate old-fashioned Christian community ties.

Today it is normal for Middle Eastern governments, except those of peninsular Arabia, to declare their entire tolerance of religious differences, with full equality before the law and freedom of opportunity in public and private life; and some of the present-day constitutions are indeed explicit in this sense. Nevertheless, except in the Lebanon, where the Christians in their various communities are approximately half of the population (though each is by itself a minority), and except (until our own day) among the impeccably Egyptian and usually nationalistic Copts of Egypt, the non-Muslim elements in the Middle Eastern states have been and are viewed not without suspicion as being less than true citizens; less than entirely loyal: a suspicion by no means always mistaken, and the more likely to be justified the more the local government employs Islamic slogans to rally mass loyalty, or shows itself crudely chauvinistic and hostile to the (Christian) West. It follows that the Christians are today in general less regarded and less comfortable than in most periods of the Turkish or Safawi empires; they remain, nevertheless, an integral part of these new nations, and a part full of ability, experience and progressiveness, which they ask only to be allowed to use on equal terms in the interest of the country—since they have no other. The host countries seem scarcely to realize the extent to which they, or their governments, may be judged abroad by the degree of reasonableness and humanity with which they treat their minorities, whom too often they regard, in troubled times, as a fair target for nationalistic rancour.

Of the Christian communities, the first we consider is the Greek Orthodox: that is, groups of Arabic or Turkish language in the Middle East subject to one of the Eastern Patriarchs of Antioch, Jerusalem, Alexandria, and Istanbul. The doctrinal differences of these from Rome or from Protestantism need not here concern us; there are variations also of ritual and of discipline (for instance, married priests) of organization and of personnel—the superior priesthood being in Turkey all Greek, in Syria and in Egypt only partly so. The Orthodox communities in each centre, other than in Turkey, tend to stand nearer to the Muslim and nationalistic majority than do the Uniate Churches (p. 107). They are strongest in Turkey (that is, in Istanbul and Smyrna), in Syria-Lebanon and in Egypt, and number between half and three-quarters of a million in all the Middle East. The Greek Orthodox are usually townsmen, and contain many rich and prominent citizens in all walks of life.

The Nestorians (or, today, Assyrians) are a poor remnant of the powerful and widespread Church of that name in medieval times. They number perhaps 125,000 in all, whose rescue from the Turks in 1915–1918 and subsequent settlement in new homes have been tasks of extraordinary difficulty. Using a Syriac liturgy, and served by a rustic priesthood, their ecclesiastical organization is all their own. It is headed by a Patriarch, the Mar Shamun. The Assyrians are

largely farmers, but some thousands have adopted town life. Many
served in 'Iraq (1921–1952) with great credit in the armed forces.
Those of the Urmia (Riza'iyeh) district of Persia were able in part to
re-establish themselves after the cataclysm of 1915–1918; those of
'Iraq, now scattered in villages of the Mosul hill-country, have had
many a sad adventure since that period, and owe their lives and livelihoods solely to British care. Those now in north-eastern Syria are an
offshoot of the 'Iraqi settlements, made under violent stress in 1933
and onwards.

The Copts, with their Monophysite doctrine and their allegiance to
the Patriarch of Alexandria (at Cairo), are almost confined to Egypt
and the Sudan, to whose people they have always and integrally
belonged while refusing conversion to Islam. Their total number may
be of the order of 2,000,000. More is to be said of this interesting community in a later chapter (p. 143). The Syrian Orthodox
(or Jacobite) Church has its Patriarch at Homs (formerly at Mardin)
and, like the Copts, is Monophysite in doctrine, using a Syriac
liturgy. They are found, as townsmen and villagers, in Syria and
Lebanon, 'Iraq and Egypt, to the number of perhaps 100,000.

More significant than these, but equally Monophysite, are the
Armenians, today scattered all over the Middle East—indeed, all
over the world—far from their own historic, but now Kurdo-
Turkish, Armenia. They preserve, physically, evident traits of the
ancient Anatolian population; they retain their national culture,
Aryan language and tradition, their schools, charities, national
Church, and close sense of community and ancient nationhood; and
they exercise in almost every Middle Eastern country their genius
for commerce, finance and craftsmanship. Not infrequently suspected
of tepid loyalty, or worse, to their countries of residence, and shame-
fully butchered by the Turks from 1895 to 1916, they have at times
held high office in all these countries and are capable of being economically as well as socially an element of high value. Their main
concentrations today are in Turkey (particularly Istanbul), in northern Syria and around Beirut, in Egypt and Persia (with important
concentrations around Tabriz in Azarbaijan, and at Julfa, a suburb
of Isfahan), with lesser numbers in 'Iraq and the Sudan. Only in
Persia are the Armenians still, save exceptionally, rural cultivators.
There are in the vicinity of half a million Armenians, of their own
Orthodox Gregorian Church, in the Middle East. (The Armenian
Soviet Republic, in Trans-Caucasian Russia, does not here concern
us, except in so far as it provides a main centre of their Church and

culture; it has, moreover, since 1945 drawn some thousands of Armenians, mostly from Turkey and Lebanon, to reside there.)

These then are the main non-Catholic Christian groups which concern us, to whom can be added the small Protestant congregations (Anglican, Presbyterian, etc.) created in most Middle Eastern countries by missionary work in recent years. One can add also, if dubiously, the small and harmless riverside Sabaean, or Mandaean, community of lower 'Iraq, perhaps 150,000 strong, with their famous skill as silver-smiths and their Christianity (if such indeed it is) mingled with a variety of other elements.

The Catholic Church itself is represented in our region in three ways, and on a major scale. First the Latin-rite Catholics, directly and solely subordinate to Rome, form a scattered community of not more than a few thousand souls, under a Patriarch of Jerusalem. Second, the Maronite Church in the Lebanon, with its compact community of perhaps 650,000 souls (over one quarter of Lebanon's total population), and with lesser groups in Egypt, Syria and elsewhere, is the most important of the 'Uniate' Churches—that is, Churches in communion with Rome and under Papal supremacy— but is also autonomous under its extremely influential Patriarch. It has its peculiar privileges, such as the marriage of the lower priest-hood, and its own Syriac liturgy. The urban Maronites are progressive, virile, intelligent, French-educated folk, the peasants and villagers are hardworking, resolute types, mostly literate; they were from 1860 onwards the heart of the old Independent Sanjaq of Lebanon. They invariably supply the President as well as many ministers and officials to the Lebanese Republic, are prominent in every sphere, and form perhaps the most westward-looking element in all the Middle East.

Thirdly, the six other Uniate Churches represent Catholicized off-shoots of the parent, non-Catholic Churches already mentioned. The Greek Catholics, converted from Greek Orthodox and still using a Greek liturgy, are found in all these countries to the extent of a few thousands, with their Patriarch at Cairo; they are a rich and progressive community. The Syrian Catholics, with their headquarters and Patriarch (today a Cardinal) at Beirut, and with important groups also in Syria, 'Iraq and Egypt, are a no less advanced and dynamic community, numbering in all perhaps 150,000. The Chaldaeans, chiefly found in northern and central 'Iraq, with a few in Syria, are converts from Nestorianism, and at present have far outdone the surviving 'Assyrians' in education, wealth, and social position; with a

total of possibly 100,000, they are mainly townsmen, but also good
cultivators in the Mosul plain; and they were, for a century, good
crews on the Tigris river-steamers. Their Patriarch ('of Babylon')
lives at Mosul. The Coptic Catholics are relatively few, and almost
all in Egypt; their liturgy is in Arabic. The Armenian Catholics,
widely spread but with their main centres around Beirut, follow a
Patriarch of their own (named 'of Constantinople'). All of these
Churches, like the parent bodies from which, largely through Catholic missionary effort, they seceded, have their substantial religious
and community independence, their own pride and exclusiveness,
their schools, orphanages and other charities. There is limited intermarriage between them—and none with Muslims.

Of all these minority communities a feature strange at first sight
to European newcomers is their complete, millennary habituation to
life in the midst of a majority public and government of an entirely
distinct and alien culture, and their normally cordial and familar
terms with friends outside their community—yet the extent also to
which the latter holds, by kinship, tradition, religion, shared techniques of living, and sometimes shared fears, their truest loyalty and
sense of belonging. Nor are these communities immobile: thousands
of Syrians and Lebanese have moved, since the early nineteenth
century, to Egypt and the Sudan, there to excel in journalism, literature and commerce. The interesting group of German (Württemberg)
'Templars', settled in Palestine in the mid-nineteenth century in
and near Haifa, Jaffa and Jerusalem, is now no more, having failed
to survive the Second War. Violence has repeatedly moved, and
decimated, the Armenians and Assyrians, and in the Jazira province
of Syria today groups of many Christian sects flourish who, transplanted from Turkey, were not there a generation ago. And the
emigration of Lebanese and some Syrian and Egyptian Christians to
(and, though less, re-immigration from) the New World, West
Africa, and indeed most parts of the world, is a constant feature of
these minorities. Economically, the remittances of these exiles are
an important source of livelihood for their stay-at-home friends. Few
great cities of North and South America are without a valuable and
nationally self-conscious community of Lebanese. Culturally, the
bond thus created with richer and more developed lands has been
interesting and valuable; Americanized Lebanese poets, essayists
and scholars have written acceptably in English, as have, in French,
Catholic ex-Lebanese or Syrians in France. The world-wide dispersal of active, intelligent Armenians, varying from millionaires to

cobblers, and holding every variety of passport, is a familiar phenomenon.

This often tragic mobility of the minorities is again exemplified by the recent history of the oriental Jewish communities found, for many centuries past, all over the Middle East, in which they had, under the Ottoman *millet* system and headed by their own Chief Rabbi in Istanbul, a recognized and protected place in society, and preserved their own privileges and characteristic occupations. Not as cultivators nor (save rarely) as landowners but, in almost every town in every country except Najd and the Hijaz, as bankers, traders, shopkeepers, promoters of enterprise, accountants or clerks, the Jews —politically unambitious, culturally remote, not often popular though but rarely maltreated—lived with self-respect and not unhappily, speaking the local language, represented on the local councils. But they have been ruined now by the militant Zionism of their American and European co-religionists, to whose success in founding their neo-Jewish state in Arab territory is due the new, hostile attitude of Middle Eastern governments and publics, and the catastrophe of a *millet* so long established and hitherto so safe. In Turkey and Persia the sizable Jewish communities (perhaps 75,000 and 100,000, respectively) decreased considerably in the 1950's by emigration to Israel, but in the 1960's have stabilized at roughly 50,000 in Turkey and 80,000 in Persia. The Arab lands, of course, have witnessed the mass exodus of their Jews since 1948. The ancient and large Jewish communities of 'Iraq and Yemen (over 100,000 in the former, some 50,000 in the latter) have diminished to but a few thousand each, and the Jews of Syria, Lebanon and Egypt (at least 100,000 in all) have been reduced by more than four-fifths.

Of the Jewish citizens of Israel itself something will be said later, in the course of our account of that country (p. 188 ff).

The Europeans to be found in the Middle East at any one moment cannot be said to form a minority in our present sense, enormous as has been, is and will be the effect of their presence. They are subjects of Great Britain, France, the U.S.A., Italy, Greece, the two Germanies, Japan, and the U.S.S.R. and its satellites. We may exclude, as needing no comment, the few remaining military bases (those of Britain on Cyprus and in the Persian Gulf, of the United States in Turkey); the foreign personnel of embassies and consulates; those employed by local governments in missions to their armed forces, or in specialized duties in their departments and institutions; those working on behalf of the government, or with its blessing, on indus-

trial projects or enquiries, or busy on constructional contracts
awarded by the state: in the ubiquitous oil industry, employed by
the government-authorized concessionary companies; or in other
state-approved industrial or research operations. None of the personnel thus far suggested, however important his contribution, is
likely to settle permanently in the country; and the same is true of
another category whose influence on Middle Eastern society over the
last full century has been of the highest significance in all fields of
culture and service—that is, the foreign teachers and missions, religious and secular; the staffs of institutions and establishments
whether educational, charitable, medical; and archaeologists and
students, and travellers and sportsmen. European permanent residents, less important than the above whether economically or culturally, are to be found nowadays in Turkey, confined almost entirely
to Istanbul and, doubtfully, Izmir but still a substantial community;
and to a lesser extent in Egypt, the Sudan and Persia. In Egypt and
the Sudan thousands of Greeks, with lesser numbers of Italians,
French and Maltese, have for many years been engaged (apart from
the few dozen rich and socially established) in retail trade, clerical
work, minor craftsmanship and other humble occupations; they are
to be found, in numbers much reduced by the policies of the post-
1952 Egyptian Government, not only in the cities but in scores of
villages throughout the Nile Valley. These exiled Europeans, with
often a lowly but never an abject standard of life, and with a brave
blend of nostalgia and acceptance, have mixed little with the local
population while forming a valuable element of it. But in an age of
powerful, dominant nationalism, they have an uncertain future.

The Greeks of Cyprus will be further considered when we speak
separately of Cypriot affairs (p. 185 ff).

## 5. The Turkish-speakers

Speakers of some dialect of the Turkish language-group are scattered widely throughout much of the Middle East, and form one of
its three most important elements; the other two being the Iranian-
speakers and, numerically the greatest, the Arabs. The Turks—to
use a convenient abbreviation which must not mislead—are found
as a fairly solid block in Anatolia and a small adjacent area in European Turkey; in communities of considerable but a far smaller scale,
in Persia and 'Iraq; and in scattered households or tiny groups
throughout the area.

The Turkish language-group, a member of the so-called Altaic family with its wide extension from central and northern Asia to south Russia and the Balkans, has a highly characteristic structure and a firm basis of similarity wherever found. It has at different places and periods been written in Syriac, Tibetan, Armenian, Greek and Hebrew characters, as well as in the Arabic script almost exclusively used for it in western Asia until 1928; and in Latin characters, in the Turkish Republic since that year. The language in its modern and western forms (which alone concern us here) has much attractiveness by virtue of its euphonious vowel-sounds, of which eight are distinguishable, its unusual regularity of structure, and its expressive and convenient system of prefixes and suffixes in both nouns and verbs, whereby the meaning is modified in a dozen ways from a single and simple root. The interminable and involved sentences of older-fashioned written Turkish—with the sole finite verb arriving, perhaps, after three pages!—are no longer in fashion; the Turkish of today is expressive, practicable and well equipped. Both in the Anatolian form (Osmanli Turkish, as perfected in Konya and Istanbul) and to a somewhat lesser extent in that of the Persian and 'Iraqi communities (whose dialects are often known, for contrast, as Turki) a wholesale adoption of Arabic and Persian words, carried out in medieval times, greatly altered the mass and expressiveness of the language. Most of this remains, but in Turkey itself officially sponsored efforts have been made since 1928, for reasons of national pride, to diminish the Arabic and Persian vocabulary and substitute true Turkish words. This process has been carried to great, sometimes inordinate, lengths, and it has been surprisingly accompanied by the needless adoption of French or English words to replace those available and familiar in Arabic or even in Turkish itself. A minor result of these processes is the widening difference between the current Turkish of the republic and that of Turkish-speaking communities elsewhere; these had been hitherto more closely united, linguistically, than is the case with other widespread language-groups. The gap increased farther by the adoption, under Atatürk's orders, of the Latin in place of the (fundamentally unsuited) Arabic script hitherto used in the Ottoman Empire; the details of the new transliteration were evolved by Italian scholars, on lines considered by them to be phonetic. A great gulf inevitably appeared between the old Turkish literature and the new—no unwelcome feature, perhaps, to a reforming dictator. The Turkish or Turki used in the Middle East outside the republic is still written in Arabic characters, and uses the old composite vocabulary. The Turkish language, however, whatever and wherever its evolution, must still be reckoned as relatively difficult for a European to acquire; its phonetics are subtle, its syntax unfamiliar to him, its vocabulary unaided by anything he will have known before.

The present subjects of the republic do not all speak Turkish, nor is their Turkish, notably as between educated city-dweller and uneducated countryman, dialectically uniform. Apart from resident Europeans and certain other small communities, there are appreciable groups of Arabs inside the southern border, of Kurds in the eastern provinces, of Lazes (a Muslim people of Transcaucasian, probably Georgian, origin) on the north-eastern coast towards the Russian frontier; and there are, as we have seen, Christian groups, Greeks and Armenians, whose Turkish is in most cases not their mother-tongue. To all these some Caucasians and the surviving Jews may be added. But the main community of Turks in European and Asiatic Turkey forms obviously not only by far the greatest group of Turkish-speakers in the Middle East, but 90 per cent of all subjects of the Turkish State.

This mass of population, fairly uniform in physique in spite of minor local varieties, is a mixture of aboriginal Anatolian with Phrygian, Hittite, Lydian, Kimmerian, Thracian, Persian and Greek, with medieval additions from Russia and central Asia, from Arabia and the Levant, and in later days from the Balkans. These Turks, welded first into a single group, then a nation, then a conquering Empire, yield to none in their conscious solidarity; and they now fill, with credit, all the occupations and careers usual in the modern world, including those previously reserved, until the revolutionary period 1922–1928, to members of the minority communities or to foreigners. Among the public as a whole stand, at the two extremes of social evolution, the fully educated, modern-minded, substantially Europeanized city-dweller, and on the other hand, the remote, backward cultivator or semi-nomad of the country districts. The former class has, in public and private life, most of the accomplishments, outlook and reactions of our own continent and age, with their full share of courtesy, social charm and humour; the latter has those of a tough peasantry everywhere, with its hard work, suspicion, ignorance, and naïvety. Typical Turkish qualities other than these are best shown in the middle and lower-middle orders of the towns and villages; they are those of endurance rather than speed, patience (which however must not be overstrained), discipline, personal

21. Kadhimiyah Mosque, Baghdad

22. South Gate, Baghdad

23. Date-gardener of Southern 'Iraq

24. Northern
'Iraq: the
city of Arbil

25. Government afforestation scheme, Northern 'Iraq

26. Ruwanduz: 'Iraqi Kurdistan

honesty, shrewdness rather than brilliance, acceptance of self-criticism but not that of outsiders, loyalty to established and valued figures and institutions, hospitality and kindness, outstanding military qualities, as history proves, and a singular unawareness of class distinctions. Are there, it may be asked, survivals of the callous brutality of the old Turk of the Armenian massacres, or the treatment of British prisoners in 1917? Such lapses were due, no doubt, largely to the psychological desperation caused by centuries of defeat; but they also evidenced cruelty and chauvinism of a more basic nature, and it is improbable that the strain of brutality has vanished even today. There is recent evidence that it has not.

As to religion, even though Islam has been disestablished in Turkey, the Turks are almost without exception at least nominal Muslims; indeed there has been in the period 1952–1960 something of a religious revival, fostered in part by politicians willing to use the more conservative popular elements for electoral support. Islam, therefore, whether in the form of the Sunni orthodoxy of the Sultanate and the old governing class, or that of the Sufi or heterodox sects which are widespread in Asia Minor, is still a force and a part of life in Turkey, city and countryside alike.

To the general Turcification of Asia Minor, substantially accomplished by the end of the Middle Ages, there have been latter-day additions, which indeed continue. In the nineteenth century there was a repatriation of Turks displaced by hostile occupations of Greece and Transcaucasia, and in the 'twenties of this century more Turks, probably three-quarters of a million, immigrated from Greece as part of the great population exchange following 1923. In the 'thirties and later between one and two hundred thousand Turkish immigrants arrived in Anatolia from the Balkan countries, especially Bulgaria; and the latter added to these in 1950–1951 by driving scores of thousands more, deprived of their possessions, across the border into European Turkey. A few hundred central Asian Turks have also made their way to Turkey in recent years from Soviet territory.

The Turks of Cyprus, numbering some 120,000 or nearly one-fifth of the island's population, are in part descendants of early, perhaps sixteenth-century, Turkish garrisons and colonists, and in smaller part later arrivals due to the disorders and population exchanges in Anatolia after the First World War. Their appearance, language, religion, manners and occupations and, it would seem, most of their features of character and attitude, equate them closely to their Anatolian cousins, with whom they were for so long (three centuries) fellow subjects of the Sultan. A fair proportion in the cities speak Greek, and fewer English. The Turkish villagers live in some cases distinct from, in others blended with, the Greek populations; in the towns the mixture is complete, with Turks usually a 10 to 50 per cent minority, but in places a majority. The resulting bi-nationality has produced constant communal tension, and periodic communal violence, which are far from resolved today.

The Turkish-speakers of modern Persia, loosely known as Turkomans, are various and important. Those of the Azarbaijan province, with its capital at Tabriz, represent a Turkish immigration from the east subsequent, by many years, to the Seljuq or Ottoman. Many are today an industrious, reliable, progressive people, self-conscious as one of the main minorities of Persia, but differing from the main population of the country in language, orientation and cultural background. They extend, diluted, outside Azarbaijan into the provinces of Gurgan and eastern Mazandaran, the districts of Qasvin and Hamadan and other lesser localities. Many attempts have been made to seduce them from their adherence to the Persian State, and will doubtless be made again; but they have meanwhile a tradition of good recruitment into the Persian forces, and a high military reputation. Speaking the Azarbaijani dialect of Turki (easily intelligible to an Ottoman-Turkish-speaker, but written in Persian script), they are in political sentiment clearly distinguished from the main body of Persia, far also from the modern Turkish Republic, and nearer, it may be, to their cousins in the Soviet Socialist Republic of Azarbaijan, across the border. The proximity of the U.S.S.R. has inevitably affected both their social and political outlook, as well as the direction of their trade and travel. The Azarbaijanis are Sunni Muslims by religion, predominantly agricultural in habit, but good industrial workers also. There is, in all their region of settlement, a greater or less admixture of true Persians, of Kurds, of Georgians, Circassians, and Armenians. On the assumption that Persia as a nation will survive, it may be foreseen that this Turkish minority, and the others next to be mentioned, will tend more and more to be absorbed and assimilated, with the gradual disappearance of their dialects and separate identity.

These are not the only Turkish-speaking communities in Persia. In the north-eastern province of Khurasan there are Turkoman tribes both settled and (though now diminished in numbers) also migratory, whose territory is continuous with that of the Turkmen

Republic of the U.S.S.R. They claim descent from early Turkish colonists left by Chinghiz Khan; and certainly their community sentiment or attachment seems directed more towards the lands of their origin than to those of their Ottoman third cousins. Far to the south, two Turki-speaking tribe-groups, both seasonably nomadic within fixed routes and areas, have achieved fame, not least for their own internecine rivalries: the Qashqa'i of the Fars province, who show more than traces of Mongoloid physique, and a part though not all of the Five Tribes of the same province, the non-Turkish sections being Arab. In Kirman survives the Turkish-speaking tribe of the Afshars, which gave a dynasty to Persia. In central Persia not far south of Teheran, in the areas of Qum and Saveh, is the tribal area of the Turki-speaking Shahsevan, a group highly renowned in earlier days. Thus the Turkish- or Turki-speaking element in Persia is varied and conspicuous.

In 'Iraq, as throughout urban areas of (geographical) Syria, the long Turko-Arab connection, and in particular the Ottoman administration of Arab provinces for four centuries, has left a legacy of much Turkish, and later Ottoman-Turkish, blood and culture in hundreds, or thousands, of the town-dwelling educated class. In the old days Turkish fief-holders would settle and found families (some of which survive) in 'Iraq or Syria, and in later times—into the twentieth century itself—the same would be true of a few high officials of Turkish race. The age-long use of that language throughout the administration, from 1534 to 1918, by Arab, Kurd and Turk alike, and the Turkish education, civil and military, of hundreds of young 'Iraqis in that period (more notably in the nineteenth and twentieth centuries) gave a pronounced Ottoman colouring to much of the urban society of the three *vilayets*, not all of which has disappeared. But there were, and are, other 'Iraqi Turks than these; there are the Turkomans, strung out in townships along the old Baghdad–Mosul trunk road from Qara Tepe to Arbil. Turkish-speaking in a dialect intermediate between Turki and Ottoman, hardworking and generally law-abiding cultivators and townsmen, self-contained and politically unambitious, and providers (above all from Kirkuk) of far more than their proportion of government officials both in Ottoman and in present times, they have preserved their identity against Kurdish and Arab neighbours, disliking both. Feelings of attachment to Istanbul or Ankara are not unknown, but have never been more than half-hearted; they revered the Caliph but were horrified at Atatürk's reforms. Their origin *in situ* may date back to Seljuq or post-Seljuq days; the leading families stood high with the Ottoman authorities, from whom many held fiefs which became nineteenth-century estates.

In the Levant States there are no grouped early-Turkish survivals, and the remnants of the Ottoman administration and its accompanying social influences are less obvious that in 'Iraq. Nevertheless, a number of the outstanding families of Syria are even today, among the older generation, Turkish-speaking in their domestic intimacy.

A Turkish cultural rather than physical heritage is still easily perceptible in Egypt, though remote enough from all modern features and tendencies of that country. Centuries of Turkish-Mamluk rule, followed by that of an Albanian-Turkish dynasty, and close social connections with the still suzerain Empire through the nineteenth century, left the legacy of a considerable remnant of Turkish speaking and Turkish manners in royal circles, and among the *deux cent familles*, under the now departed Egyptian monarchy. Since 1952 this Turkish veneer has been rapidly disappearing.

## 6. *The Aryan-speakers*

The Aryan or Indo-European language-group—the correct use of the two terms is disputed by philologists—is extremely widespread in the world, and contains varieties within it far exceeding those of other groups, for example the Semitic. The languages of western Europe are but second cousins of the Slavonic group or of Armenian, and third or fourth cousins of the major group called Indo-Iranian. This group divides into two branches; the Indic, which contains many of the major languages of modern India (all derived from Sanskrit), and the Iranian, which is the dominant language group in the eastern Middle East. Iranian consists of modern Persian, the official language of the Persian Kingdom; other modern-Persian varieties as spoken, often side by side with official Persian, in the provinces of Mazandaran (Mazandarani) and the Caspian area (Gilaki), and Luristan (Luri); countryside dialects spoken in Fars, Kirman and Khurasan differing less than those from standard Persian; and finally Kurdish, which differs more. Kurdish in its various and mutually unintelligible dialects is spread over a very wide area of Persia, 'Iraq and Turkey, and its era of separation from Persian dates from some centuries ago. The same may be true of the Baluchi language. All these languages, including Persian itself, use the Arabic script if and when they are written, with additional letters and a characteristically differing caligraphy. All have borrowed very widely from the Arabic vocabulary, are structurally unusually simple, and have no serious phonetic difficulties. Persian, with its very extensive literature, may be reckoned a language of much charm and resource; it greatly influenced the development of Ottoman Turkish, which borrowed copiously from it.

The Persian-speaking citizen of that ancient monarchy possesses qualities of which the origins are nowhere clearly traceable in his mixed ancestry of aboriginal Iranian, incoming Indo-European, central Asian, Mongol, Arab and the rest. His qualities are those of a quick, responsive rather than a profound intelligence, a leaning to mysticism and the unreal, with high accomplishment in words and the arts, easy acquisition of foreign cultures but always with a deep Persian superiority complex, and both broad and refined types of humour. Martial qualities, as those of patience and altruism, are generally regarded as poorly developed; tolerance is rare, unless in the form of cynicism. Manners are highly refined, impatience a sign of ill-breeding, the telling of bad news a *bêtise*. Personal honesty is assumed, integrity in public affairs notably less so. But a true appreciation of the Persian 'national character' would need to be based on a lifetime of close experience—and could then be widely erroneous; only a Persian, at his wittiest, should be entrusted with the task.

By great majority agriculturists (the pastoral tribes of the country being largely Kurds or Turks) the Persians occupy, otherwise than in a thin admixture, little of the north-west or the most westerly belt of their country, and only part of the south. The Persians, as distinct from the other Iranian and non-Iranian elements—Kurds, Lurs, Baluchis, Turks and Arabs—are concentrated in the north, west-centre, north-east and east of Persia, throughout which village life is as yet little changed from that of medieval times, while urban life has been advancing by strides.

Persians are found outside their own country principally in 'Iraq, where many households of such exiles are resident in Baghdad and Basra, and far more (though fewer than half a century ago) in the Shi'i holy places of Karbala, Najf, Kadhimiya and Samarra. No appreciable number, but at most some isolated Persian households, generally of religious complexion, are to be found elsewhere in the Middle East.

The reverse is true of other Iranian constituents in the country's population—the Baluchis, Kurds, and Lurs. The first-named, Sunni clansmen and peasants with typical tribal organization, part sedentary and part pastoral, live in the coastal area (that of the Makran province) of the extreme south, and are but a fragment of the main Baluchi group whose territory forms a major part of western Pakistan. Their interest, in the general picture of modern Persia, is strictly local; politically they are disunited and unformidable. The language is, like the Pushtu of Afganistan, derived from an Iranian group parallel to, rather than derived from, that of modern official Persian. There is a considerable Baluchi population across the sea on the north-east-facing Batina coast of Oman, and notably in the twin towns of Muskat-Matra.

In the Kurdish language, known as Kurdi or Kirmanji or both, it is not possible to trace the stages whereby, with the passage of centuries and the admixture of other local populations and their dialects, the present varieties of Kurdish were evolved, or the now clear difference between its main northern and southern branches established. The language has today, as compared to Persian, marked syntactical differences as well as many of vocabulary and phonetics, and speakers of the two languages cannot, or can barely and most imperfectly, understand each other. The Kurds as a people form an important group in western Asia; they have never at any time coalesced into a single united community, even though prolific, till the eighteen-sixties, in vigorous, short-lived local principalities. Kurdish nationalism is today a persistent, hopeless, largely expatriate growth, without a realistic programme or valid leaders. Their territory, shared on its fringes by other elements, stretches in a wide arc from Kirmanshah in western Persia across an extensive area of north-eastern 'Iraq to north-eastern Turkey nearby, as far as Erzurum and Kars, and westward almost to the great southward-flowing loop of the Euphrates. There are Kurds, perhaps some 200,000 in all, in Syria—in the Taurus foothills north of Aleppo, and in the city of Damascus, with settlements elsewhere; others, probably not exceeding 75,000 but with a full share of community consciousness, are found in Soviet Transcaucasia. The main body, however, lying athwart Persia, 'Iraq and eastern Turkey, has populations of perhaps 900,000, 1,250,000, and two million respectively in those countries. Such figures would give an estimate of some four million for the Kurds as a whole—conjectural as is this figure, and blurred as are the fringes of the community itself in terms of locality, purity and self-consciousness. The western Persian provinces occupied by a majority of Kurds are those dependent on the towns of Kirmanshah, Qasr-i-Shirin, Baneh, Sanandaj (Senna), Saqqiz, Mahabad (Sauj

Bulaq), Riza'iyeh (Urmia), Shahpur, Qutur and Maku, all in the wide strip of mountain country nearest to the 'Iraq frontier; to the eastward lie the Azarbaijani Turkomans. There are Kurdish villages, settled there by official action in the seventeenth century, far to the east in the Khurasan province.

The Persian Kurds, Sunni with rare exceptions, are in governmental eyes an unassimilated element of no great apparent loyalty to the Shah or to the Shi'i establishment. They have a background of age-long lawlessness, brigandage, local autonomy, and treasonable connections across the border with the Ottoman (Sunni) neighbours. Tribally organized, by habit agricultural with some pastoral tribes, feudally obedient to their Aghas, tough and warlike at need, the Kurds in their own countryside and deep valleys are peasants, in places nomadic herdsmen: a picturesque, attractive, far from uncivilized, virile type who have asked little, and received little, from the modern world. In the cities, which are nowhere entirely Kurdish-populated, the educated and outwardly westernized Kurd can well hold his own as writer, politician, doctor or mere conversationalist with any Persian or European, all provincial backwardness left behind.

The 'Iraqi Kurds, a 20 per cent minority in that republic are, with more Turkish and less Persian elements in their culture, similar in most respects to the Persian Kurds just described, with tribes of equal or greater fame, scenes at least equally majestic, and a broken history of valley autonomy sometimes rising to the scale of considerable principalities. For centuries the Ottoman Government, as nominal overlord, was disliked and distrusted; today that of Arab 'Iraq, for all the presence of a Kurd or two regularly in the Cabinet, is no better regarded. The many concessions made for years past in 'Iraqi Kurdistan to local feeling—Kurdish as an official language, Kurdish officials and regiments—have not availed to secure their loyalty, which indeed ceaseless Soviet efforts by broadcasts, agents and money are concerned to prevent. The 'Iraqi Kurds, with some few representatives in most towns of northern and central 'Iraq, live in the provinces of Mosul (that is, its northern and eastern districts), Arbil (but with Turkoman and Arab minorities), Kirkuk (the same), and Sulaimaniya (entire). The Yazidis, in two isolated communities in the non-Kurdish areas of Mosul province, are a puzzling fragment probably of mainly Kurdish stock though adhering notoriously to a separate religion. The latter is secret, but is known to contain non-Muslim elements including the propitiation (not the worship) of that

eminent though temporarily fallen angel, the Devil, and reverence
for Christian and Jewish, as well as Islamic, scriptures; indeed, their
religious services are in Arabic. No longer a danger to their neighbours and to travellers, the Yazidis are still dour, suspicious and
communally introvert. There are perhaps 50,000 Yazidis in 'Iraq,
a few thousand more in Syria.

   In Turkey there have been, since the great Kurdish revolt of 1925
and lesser risings in 1930 and 1936, so many transplantations, restor-
ations and renamings (such as 'mountain Turks' for 'Kurds') that
the present strength or location and condition of the Turkish Kurds
is difficult to establish. It appears true that the Kurdish areas are
now (1969) reasonably peaceful, and administered with little difference from the rest. Their separate race and language are studiously
ignored, their traditional dress is forbidden near official headquarters,
their insubordinate airs, if any survive, are chastened by repeated
blows. The whole region traditionally Kurdish, or predominantly so,
includes the *ils* (*vilayets*) of Hakari, Van, Bitlis, Mush, Ağri, Siirt,
Diyarbakir, Mardin, Elâziğ, Tunceli, Bingöl, Urfa, Gaziantep,
Adiyaman, Malatya; that is, fifteen provinces out of sixty-seven.
And there are certain minor Kurdish communities—linguistically
varied, as with the Zaza-speakers south of Erzincan—outside these.
The essential character of the Turkish Kurds and their social organization were for centuries more or less identical with those of their
cousins in the Sultan's 'Iraqi provinces and in Persia; but processes
of assimilation have now been operating, with inspiration and assistance from government quarters at every level, for fifty years, and
this cannot be without effect both on the Kurds' separate national
consciousness and on their tribal organization. These processes and
this government attitude are in some degree, and will probably be
increasingly, those of the 'Iraqi and Persian Governments also; and
Kurdish resistance to them, for all their toughness, their topographical isolation, and their separatist tradition, cannot be expected to
last for ever. Meanwhile, the Kurds are a considerable element in
the three countries, and a major embarrassment to their alien rulers.

   Speaking a dialect less remote from modern written Persian than
is Kurdish, but more deeply distinct than a mere bucolic variation,
the Lurish and Bakhtiari tribesmen of the middle stretch of western
and south-western Persia range from Dizful and Shushtar in the
south, the 'Iraqi frontier to the west, and a line north of Mandali-
Burujird to the north; in fact, a wide and beautiful mountain region,
its capital Khurramabad. The Lurs, with an interesting medieval

history of local statehood and dynasty, are today a major relic in Persia of the old days of regional separatism, aided in this case by a strong tradition and their own dialect. Along, and east of, the 'Iraq frontier region they are villagers and graziers, no longer formidable; they sometimes stray across into 'Iraq, form an element in the population of Badra, and supply, by long tradition, the famous corps of weight-lifting porters (mistakingly known as Kurds by the Baghdadis) in the streets and customs-wharfs of the 'Iraqi capital. Farther south and east the Bakhtiari, of the old-time Amirate of Greater Luristan, form a distinguishable part of the Lurish complex, speak a closely similar dialect, and are best so classified. Falling into two tribe-groups, they are among the most famous tribal folk in all Persia. With a number of fixed settlements—centres of a high culture among the sophisticated élite, which has on occasion played a decisive part in Persian politics—the majority are still seasonally nomadic, moving northward and eastward from the confines of the Khuzistan flatlands to the vicinity of Isfahan.

The important Armenian community, spread thinly but ubiquitously throughout the Middle East including Persia, is also Aryan-speaking in its own mother-tongue; these have already been mentioned among the Christian minorities (p. 106).

# CHAPTER SIX

# THE ARAB COUNTRIES

HAVING established something of the historical background, the present identity, and the constitutional forms of the Middle Eastern states of today, we pass next to a rather closer account of the facts of their geography as nature and man's delimitations have fashioned them. A few lines will be given for each separately on their topography, conditions, and climate, the composition of their populations, their natural resources and their communications. The reader who has glanced at the titles of subsequent chapters will realize that more information on the states from various aspects, but grouped by subjects rather than thus particularized country by country, is to be given later in the book. The countries' agriculture, their nascent industries, and their oil-resources will thus be described in Chapters Ten and Eleven.

In the present chapter and the next, the Arab territories and the non-Arab are for convenience grouped separately.

## 1. *'Iraq*

The Republic of 'Iraq—a kingdom until July 1958, and a republic, under military régimes, since then—is the most easterly of the major Arab states, abutting, eastward and northward, on non-Arab·territory. It has occupied nevertheless, as earlier pages of this book have shown, a leading (and for long the leading) place in Arab and Islamic history in past ages, and has claims today to be in the forefront of progressive Arab achievement—in spheres other than (at present) the political. The 'Iraqi *vilayets* were disliked by the Turks, who made them the theme of many pejorative jokes, and Syrians and Egyptians have habitually thought poorly of 'Iraqi culture and amenities. But times have changed, in 'Iraq's favour; such judgments, if ever true, are so no longer. And to the charm of 'Iraqi society, in tribe or city, such long-term residents as the present writer can testify.

'Iraqi territory amounts to about 175,000 square miles (though reputable authorities give strangely varying measurements); its extreme length is 620 miles, breadth 450. Its neighbours are, on the south, the principality of Kuwait, and Sa'udi Arabia: on the west, Sa'udi Arabia, a relatively narrow corridor of Jordan, and Syria: on the north, Turkey: on the east, Persia. The frontiers on the south and west are located in desert country, on the north and north-east in rugged mountains, in the east and south-east in the plain-country west of the Zagros ranges.

The country's sole outlet to the sea is on the mud-flats of Fao, with a frontage of some twenty miles on the Gulf, squeezed in at the Shatt al-'Arab mouth between Kuwaiti and Persian territory. Inland, though much of 'Iraq is dull and desolate country, it contains none the less great variation of terrain, including areas of wild and romantic landscape. Central and southern 'Iraq, the true delta of the twin rivers Tigris and Euphrates (whence its earlier name of Mesopotamia), is flat, stoneless, alluvial country, highly fertile, irrigable and indeed floodable, and extensively cultivated with crops and date-gardens. Its areas of broad marsh, as well as its stretches of unrelieved aridity, show that a completed drainage and irrigation system has yet to be achieved. In this region, the heart of 'Iraq, the population (exclusively Arab) is by great majority tribal outside the towns. The villages take many aspects according to the local types of cultivation and terrain, and the building materials available. The country west of Euphrates varies, except on the watered river-banks, from light steppe to true desert, the home of the great camel-grazing tribes of 'Iraq and neighbouring Syria. In the north, but short of the mountain zone, are broad plains (the ancient Assyria) cultivable, save in the driest years, on the rainfall. North and north-east of these, beyond an intermediate foothill belt, lies the Kurd-inhabited wild mountain system shared with Turkey and Persia. This is, for the most part, drained ultimately into the Tigris by the upper reaches and the tributaries of the Greater and Lesser Zab, the 'Udhaim and the Diyala. These mountain districts, which belong essentially to the Zagros system, form a region of grazing at seasonally varying levels, terraced or deep-valley cultivation, a mountain vegetation, rapid streams, hard winters and a radiant spring. The higher mountains reach more than 8,000 (and one 10,000) feet in height, and are snow-covered for much of the year. No conditions and no scenes could less resemble the average foreigner's ideas of 'Iraqi flatness.

Climatically, the country is known for its severity. In the mountains, summer heat is relatively moderate, often agreeable, especially in the 'hill stations' now available; winter cold can be intense. The foothill and undulating plain districts of the north are tropically hot in summer, with maximum shade temperatures of 110° to 115°, but they enjoy cool nights. In central and southern 'Iraq the summer heat is by 10° (sometimes by 15°) greater than this, but health and spirits are preserved by the dryness of the air and the refreshing coolness of the nights, which fails only in the southernmost parts of the delta. Rainfall varies from 4 inches a year, or less, in the uncultivable desert west of Euphrates, to 7 or 10 inches in central 'Iraq where all crops depend on irrigation, and to 12 or 16 inches on the northern plains where, in all years but the worst, rain-cultivation is successful. In the mountains, 30 to 40 inches of rain can fall, with, or in the form of, snow in the winter months. It is a country of high winds; in Baghdad summers the south-east wind is dreaded for its dust-content, the north welcomed for its comparative freshness. Fog is a rarity. On the whole, 'Iraq as a country of residence is neither unhealthy nor unpleasant—and yearly less so, thanks to the modern amenities, communications, and health services now available through the wealth due to its fabulous oil-development.

The population of the republic is perhaps 8,500,000, a figure which represents almost a threefold increase in numbers since the census of 1930. Of these, perhaps 1,250,000 are Kurds and Kurdish-speaking (p. 119), all of strong Sunni faith except minor (and not numerous) heretical communities. The Kurds, except a handful of town-dwelling households, are all to be found in the mountain and foothill zones. The Yazidis of Jabal Sinjar and the Mosul plain (p. 119) may number 50,000. The Turkomans (p. 115) of the north-east (the districts of Kifri-Kirkuk-Arbil) may number between 125,000 and 175,000. Other minorities are those of the Persians, a few thousand in all with their main concentration in the Shi'i holy cities: the Lurs (p. 120), a few hundred in the villages near the east and south-east frontiers, and in Baghdad: and the tiny Mandaean or Sabaean community (p. 107) on the south-'Iraqi river-banks. The once wealthy and numerous Jewish community, with its massive concentration in Baghdad, is there no more (p. 109); perhaps 7,000 or less remain. The Christian sects (p. 105 ff) are still a considerable element in the larger 'Iraqi cities, notably Baghdad, Basra, Mosul and Kirkuk, and provide admirable men of business, cultivators and craftsmen. There is no reliable guide to the numbers of each separate Christian community; in aggregate they may number 300,000. They include the different varieties of Uniate Catholics, and, among non-Catholics, the Greek Orthodox, Armenian, Assyrian (Nestorian) and Jacobite communities. The main body of 'Iraqi Muslim Arabs, some 6,000,000 in number between town and tribe, upland and delta, desert and date-garden, are probably about 55 to 60 per cent of the Shi'i faith, the remainder Sunni. The post-revolutionary Constitution of the republic proclaims Islam to be its official religion.

The country is for administrative purposes divided into fourteen provinces (*liwas*), each named from its headquarter town. The provinces, which are mainly but not strictly those of the Turkish régime, are subdivided on normal lines. The fourteen do not include three further units into which the western desert area is divided, for police and tribal control purposes. Baghdad, the capital, with a population of some 1,500,000, is by far the greatest city. Basra and Mosul come next, with some 350,000 and 225,000 respectively; Kirkuk and Najf are well over 100,000, Hilla nearly that, Karbala, 'Amara, Arbil and Sulaimaniya in the 50,000–75,000 range, followed by a score of lesser but largely modernized and flourishing towns. The standard of life, high or moderate among the *élite* and the upper-middle class, and self-respecting, with fair comfort, in artisan and the lower clerical circles, is low to the point of bare existence among the shanty-town or slum city-dwellers, and the less favoured of the rural villagers.

Possessor of extensive and potentially fertile lands and the water of its two great rivers, 'Iraq has an obvious—and historically verified—agricultural potential, at present in the way of increasing realization. Apart from this, has it fair material assets? Of its oil-resources, by far the greatest economic blessing and revenue-giver, more will be said (p. 254). Other mineral resources are on the whole scanty and as yet largely untapped; deposits of quartz, dolomite, and sulphur are reported (with the last-named now in the process of development), salt and gypsum have been found, indications of iron ore, copper, lead, zinc and chromite in the north are now under investigation but seem to be minor, and recent finds of large deposits of phosphates in the western desert arouse hopes of development. Forests of a scrubby, little-productive type exist in the mountains of the north, to an alleged total area of some 8,000 square miles, and scientific planting, both for timber and for soil-preservation, is proceeding. The timber now produced, mainly from the Kurdish valleys, is of walnut, plane and poplar; the oaks are stunted and of low value. Certain natural products afford interesting items of export—gum tragacanth, liquorice-root, gallnuts, and reeds for mat-making. Fishing is practised in all the rivers, with a useful but moderate rate of catch, all locally consumed without satisfying the demand; sea fishing is almost negligible. Stock-raising, traditional in its different forms, whether in the delta, the steppe, or the Kurdish mountains, has a major place in 'Iraq's economy both domestic and governmental. The animals concerned are, as elsewhere in the Middle East, sheep, goats and donkeys everywhere, cattle by the rivers and wherever pasture is adequate, buffaloes if water is plentiful, camels in the desert, mules mainly in the mountains. The export of live animals and animal products (wool, hair, casings, hides and skins) is on a considerable scale, and could be increased by improvement of breeds, processing and marketing. Existing types are of relatively low value except for meat and for draught purposes; the standard of husbandry is primitive, and diseases are widespread. Measures are in hand, however, to remedy these defects. The Arab horse, for which Basra was for centuries the trading outlet, is now in little commercial demand.

Though much remains to be done, 'Iraq has already developed an adequate system of communications. The railways are all state-owned. The major line from Basra to Baghdad, originally metre-gauge, was recently converted to standard-gauge. From Baghdad a standard-gauge line runs on the Tigris west bank to Mosul and beyond to the Syrian frontier. A metre-gauge line crosses the Tigris at Baghdad and runs north-east to Ba'quba, Kifri, Kirkuk and Arbil, with a branch extending to Khanaqin and the Iranian frontier. Another line from Kirkuk to Sulaimaniya is said to be projected. Oil pipelines run in and between oil-fields and refineries both in northern and southern 'Iraq, and on an imposing scale to the Mediterranean from Kirkuk. The road system of the country has always been embarrassed by the lack of stone in the centre and south, a deficiency now in part redressed by abundant bitumen for surfacing. Reliable roads now link all main centres, and passable fair-weather tracks run everywhere. Jordan, Syria and Turkey are all connected by road, and the two latter by rail also. There is road communication with Teheran, and with Medina by way of the central Sa'udi oases. Important road works and many new bridges have been incorporated in the development plans elaborated since oil revenues became plentiful, as they now are; further main routes of high standard are under construction. The sole seaport, Basra, is subject to the limitations imposed by its single approach (the Shatt al-'Arab) on the possible density of vessels using it, and on the draught of these by the maximum river-depth; but, within its limits, it is a well-equipped modern port. Its facilities are used by regular cargo and passenger lines of many nations. Oil export is now predominantly from Khor al-Amaya, a new mid-sea loading base in the Gulf, 20 miles off-shore. Aviation needs are served by the airports of Baghdad and Basra, which are in constant use by 'Iraqi and foreign lines of all nationalities. Lesser but reliable landing-grounds are maintained elsewhere.

The 'Iraqi currency is based on the Dinar, equivalent to £1 3s. 3d. ($2.80 US), and is controlled by its own Central Bank. The use of local and ex-Turkish weights and measures is still widespread within the country, for weight, length, and area; but these are gradually yielding to the metric system.

## 2. *The Lebanon*

Lebanese territory consists of a block of land approximating to 4,000 square miles in extent, roughly quadrilateral in shape but tapering in breadth from north to south. It is bounded on the west by the Mediterranean Sea with some 145 miles of coastline, on the north and east by Syria, on the south and south-east by Israel. The country contains a narrow coastal strip, flat or sloping; the high mountain range of the Lebanon, decreasing southward in height and wildness: the inter-montane plain of the Beka'a (Biqa') in which the al-'Asi river (Orontes), flowing northwards into Syria, has its rise, and the Litani (Leontes) flowing southwards and finally westwards into the Mediterranean: and the foothills and westward face of the Anti-Lebanon range, continued southward as that of Hermon. The highest peaks in Lebanon exceed 9,000 feet; the average altitude for the whole country is above 3,000 feet.

The territory, small as it is, is of great and varied beauty, with its Mediterranean aspect and string of picturesque (and extremely ancient) seaports, the wild mountain and valley scenery in its parallel ranges, and the fertile farmlands and gardens of the Biqa'. There is a relatively high rainfall and, in consequence, plentiful though capriciously located springs, often at high altitudes. The climate varies according to elevation and distance from the sea, from hot or temperate, humid, frostless conditions near the sea, to snow-clad mountain scenes a few miles inland, and hot summers with cold winters in the elevated but enclosed Biqa'. Rainfall diminishes fast as one proceeds inland, from 40 to 50 inches a year by the sea to 15 inches immediately west of the Anti-Lebanon. All rain falls between October and April.

The Lebanese population is of the order of 2,250,000, of whom approximately half are Christian, the body of the remainder Muslim (in the vicinity of 1,100,000), with an important Druze minority of over 100,000, and some thousands of Jews. Within the Christian population, virtually every group discussed in Chapter Five (p. 104f.) is represented in fair-sized, well-organized communities. In race the Lebanese reveal an immensely complicated mixture of many original, immigrant, and neighboring peoples. This applies equally to the Palestinian refugees, some 170,000, living in the country. Almost all Lebanese are Arabic-speaking (the official language), though the Armenians often retain, *inter se*, their own language. Some of the Christian liturgies are Syriac or Greek, and French and English are generally understood in the towns; these, especially French, are habitually spoken by the educated of all sects.

The Lebanese, to whom in spite of their diversity a 'national character' can with caution be attributed, seem paradoxically to combine toughness with gentleness, astuteness with naïvety, hard work with a Mediterranean reposefulness. They are able, progressive, emotional, articulate. With little surviving tribalism, of which confessional groupings here take the place, they exhibit strong local and community loyalties, which lead to anything between sporting competition and civil war. Outside the towns the Lebanese are village-dwellers and agriculturists, and attain a standard of life superior to that of much of southern Europe, aided not a little by remittances from tens of thousands of *émigrés* in the U.S.A. and elsewhere, who contribute a characteristic and materially advantageous feature to their society. The same phenomenon, combined with relatively advanced educational standards, many tourists, much foreign business, and the status of the Middle East's leading entrepôt and transit-station, gives the Lebanese cities their unusually cosmopolitan air.

The natural resources of the territory are scanty, yet the mixed ingredients upon which it lives produce, in effect, a greater economic stability than could be expected. Of its agriculture and industry, something will be said elsewhere (p. 241 f). Stock-raising, a feature of which is the seasonal migration between higher and lower pastures, is necessarily on an exiguous scale, though it produces dairy produce of high quality. Fishing makes a modest contribution to commerce and food supply. The area of forested land is small, but now carefully administered—in contrast to centuries of neglect; a sadly humble remnant of the famous cedars of Lebanon is to be seen. Minerals are of little importance; some lignite exists, traces of iron, a negligible

27. Damascus: the street called Strait

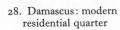

28. Damascus: modern residential quarter

29. Damascus: Barudi square

30. Village of Central Syria, near Homs

31. Ruins at Palmyra, Syria

32. A schooner captain, Rawad Island

33. Beirut, Lebanon

34. A street in Tripoli, Lebanon

35. View of Jounie (Juniya), Lebanon coast

36. Beirut, Lebanon: cliffs and flats

37. Sidon, Lebanon: harbour and Crusader Castle

38. Lebanon: the cedars

deposit of bitumen, salt derived from sea-water—and no oil. Important crude-oil pipelines, from 'Iraq and Sa'udi Arabia, enter and cross Lebanese territory to the oil-loading ports of Tripoli and Sidon respectively. More important than these is the country's tourist traffic, persuasively induced and aided by the charm and interest of the cities, mountains and ancient sites; and, transcending this, Lebanon relies above all on its profits from the many commercial, financial and social services which its geographical position, as a main gateway to Western Asia, enables it to render, and which it handles with great efficiency.

The country is divided into five provinces. The principal city is Beirut, which now contains about one-third of the population. Tarablus (Tripoli) is the only other city over 100,000 (barely), with Saida (Sidon) and Sur (Tyre) but shadows of former greatness. Beirut, beautifully situated between sea and mountain, is a city of striking contrasts, between ancient East and modern West, with all the phenomena of both. Its cultural and political life is as flourishing as its commercial, and its politics, rooted in confessionalism and the urge towards, or away from, Arab nationalism, are perpetually *mouvementés*.

The communications of the territory are adequate. The main roads are well engineered and maintained; one follows the coast throughout its length, two more run inland from Beirut and Tripoli across the mountains and into Syria, another forms an inland or inter-montane trunk-road. Secondary and local roads give access to all villages, with a multitude of 'buses and long-range hired cars. The railways are (since 1959) both state-owned: the narrow-gauge line, very slow and used for goods only, runs from Beirut across the Biqa' to Damascus to connect there with the Hijaz Railway, and nearly 100 miles of narrow-gauge track is also in use around the capital. The broad-gauge line runs by the coast from the Israel frontier to Tripoli and thence inland to Homs in Syria and beyond to 'Iraq and Turkey; another broad-gauge line also connects Rayak in the Biqa' with Homs. All the railways lose money; most goods and passengers travel by road. Air services are highly developed. Based on the Beirut airport are four Lebanese airlines (the largest, however, under partial foreign control), and most foreign airlines call regularly; the city vies, therefore, with Cairo as a major international air junction. As a seaport, it is well equipped, extremely busy, and visited by steamers of a dozen countries, for whom a score of agencies, nearly all Lebanese, maintain offices. Tripoli and Saida have a limited

traffic, though both are, as we have seen, important oil-export outlets; the other seaside towns—Tyre, Jubail, Batrun—do little business. There are no communications between the Lebanon and Israel.

The currency of the republic is the Lebanese pound, officially
£Leb. 8·62 to the £ sterling, but on the free market usually in the
vicinity of £Leb. 7·55 (or £Leb. 3·15 to the dollar). The metric
system of weights and measures is in use, not without survivals of
Turkish or earlier traditional measures.

## 3. *Syria*

The Syrian Arab Republic is a state of some 72,000 square miles,
with a population of close to 6,000,000 souls. Its borders are as
follows: to the west the Mediterranean, with a coastline of slightly
over 100 miles, and, beyond Anti-Lebanon, the Lebanese Republic;
to the north Turkey, over a great length of open frontier; to the east
'Iraq, separated by a purely arbitrary, but diplomatically agreed, line
across the Syrian Desert; to the south Jordan, across the Yarmuk
River; and to the extreme south-east Israel, which at the time of
writing (1969) occupies most of the Syrian province of Qunaitra as a
result of the war of June 1967.

By far the greatest part of Syrian territory consists of open, flat or
undulating steppe-country, with considerable stretches of true desert
on both sides of the Euphrates and its left-bank tributaries, the
Balikh and the Khabur; the triangle between the great river and the
Turkish and 'Iraqi frontiers is known as the Jazira. Westward of the
steppe, which is the home of one-fifth of the Syrian population, lie
the more populous and geographically broken parts of the country.
These, from west to east, include the narrow, fertile coastal strip,
varying from 20 miles to a few yards in width: the mountainous
areas, oriented north–south and consisting of the Ansariya range along
the coast, and south of this and farther inland the Anti-Lebanon or
Hermon ranges, with the Jabal Druze massif in the extreme south.
Between and flanking these mountains are valleys and inter-montane
plains, traversed by the al-'Asi (Orontes) river and its marshes. The
eastern area of the mountain and hilly zone is of high—or, towards the
north, lower—plateaux, dipping farther eastward into the steppe.
Here are situated the fertile and thickly inhabited regions of the
Hauran, the great Damascus oasis with its rivers 'Abana and Pharpar'
and its wonderful gardens, the ancient but less welcoming cities of
Homs and Hama, and the most populous, perhaps the most ancient,

city of them all, Aleppo with its citadel. Syrian territory is therefore extremely varied, much of it invigorating and scenically attractive, and, except for the truly desertic areas and the lava-strewn border-lands of the Kingdom of Jordan, it is for the most part capable of development by irrigation—and some of it currently in process thereof. The country is rich in archaeological remains of all periods.

The climate varies from region to region. The eastern and southern zones are almost rainless, the north has a deposit normally sufficient to support light vegetation and crops, the west enjoys up to 40 inches of rain in the mountains, with less but adequate amounts in the plains, valleys and coast. The highest peaks, notably Hermon, are snow-covered for most of the year. Temperatures and humidity vary, as would be expected, as between the coast, the mountain zone and the plains. In the latter, summer and winter temperatures are both extreme, but humidity is slight.

The religious groups within the population (with approximations of their numbers) are the Sunni Muslims (3,400,000), Isma'ili and other Shi'is (70,000), and the heretical sects of the Druzes (150,000) and the Nusairis or 'Alawis (500,000). Syria contains perhaps three-quarters of a million Christians, the largest denominations being those of the Greek Orthodox (200,000), Uniate Catholics (160,000), Armenian Gregorians (130,000), Syrian Orthodox (65,000), Assyrians (15,000) and Protestants (18,000). A few thousand Jews remain, and a few thousand Yazidis. The language of Syria is officially, and for 90 per cent of the population actually, Arabic; the ethnic or religious minorities of the Kurds, Armenians, Circassians, Assyrians and Yazidis use (amongst themselves) their own languages or dialects. French is familiar to the urban upper and middle classes, English less but increasingly. Syria also harbours a Palestinian refugee population which numbered 150,000 in 1968; to these must be added some 100,000 Syrians made 'refugees' (within their own country) by the events of 1967.

The territory is divided for administrative purposes into thirteen provinces. The largest cities are in the interior, along a north-south line from Aleppo (600,000) through Hama (210,000) and Homs (150,000) to the capital at Damascus (700,000). The port of Lataqiya (close to 100,000) is the leading city along the coast. Among the population outside the towns the characteristic forms of present-day Arab society are all represented: by the true nomads (badu) of the mid-desert camel-breeding tribes, who include some of the most famous; by the sheep-owning, partly cultivating tribes of

central-western Syria; by the wholly agricultural communities of
the open country and the river-banks, living in widely-spaced villages,
exposed to all the hazards and burdens of local tenant agriculture,
and tribal only in a diminished sense; and by the non-tribal villagers,
some in the mountain zone, some in newly-settled lands in the north-
eastern steppe-country of the Jazira. The rural standard of life is
generally low or very low, but here too there are hopeful signs. The
agricultural peasantry, who form by far the largest element in the
population, and contribute fully half of the national income, are, for
all their intelligence, so deeply conservative that the improvement of
their lot is likely to be a slow process. Until recently, private enterprise had played the leading role in developing the country's meagre
natural resources, particularly by the extension of agriculture into
the semi-arid Syrian steppe. But in the 1960's, with the introduction
of Arab socialism, the prime mover in development has become the
state. The largest and most important of its current plans is for a dam
on the Euphrates which will open to agriculture some 1,600,000
acres in the eastern portion of the country (with Soviet assistance,
work on the dam was commenced in 1968). But, as coup and counter-
coup hindered undertaking this project for several years, so the
general instability of Syrian politics seems likely to impede similar
planned economic growth in the future.

The natural resources of Syria, other than the land and water which
make extensive agriculture possible, are in fact jejune. The wide
steppe-country lends itself to camel-breeding, and the less arid
inlying areas to the animal husbandry of sheep, goats and cattle.
These, in the aggregate, produce a number of the necessities of life
and of the economy; wool and hair, and live animals, are regular
exports. The improvement of breeds and products is a constant
care of the government. Forests in Syria are limited in modern times
to the Lataqiya hinterland and the Jabal Druze, and are here rather
picturesque than productive; proper maintenance and protection present problems not yet solved. Fishing, in fresh- or sea-water, is
practised on a minimal scale. The mineral wealth of the country, as so
far discovered, is of the humblest. Syria's oil resources are slight by
Middle Eastern standards, but enough to make her a minor exporter.
A little lignite has been located, one asphalt deposit behind Lataqiya
is being exploited while more exists in mid-desert, phosphate
deposits (to be developed with east European aid) have been found,
and there are indications of chromite, iron ore, and lead. Parts of
Syria are traversed by oil pipelines from Sa'udi and 'Iraqi sources;

these pass on into Lebanon, except for one which terminates at Banyas. A smaller oil loading-point, for the export of domestic production, is being constructed at Tartus.

A fairly adequate road-system, only in part all-weather, links the inhabited areas of the country, and extends into all neighbouring territories except Israel. The (British) Nairn Transport Co. has since 1923 operated a trans-desert motor-coach service between Damascus and Baghdad. The railways, designed long ago for quite different conditions, do not satisfactorily serve the present economy. One section of the old Baghdad Railway emerges from, later to re-enter, Turkey in the extreme north: the other is a stretch of the same Baghdad Railway, as extended in the 1930's, running from Qamishliya to the 'Iraqi frontier at Tell Kochek. Neither this nor indeed the rest of the system is a commercial asset to Syria. The Damascus–Homs–Aleppo line (or D.H.P.), which in its course enters and later again leaves Lebanese territory, and affords a further connection from Homs to the Lebanese frontier at Tell Kalakh, carries a useful goods traffic but few passengers. These lines together form the Syrian State Railways. The narrow-gauge railway running south from Damascus—the old Hijaz Railway of 1908—links the capital with the Jabal Druze area, and beyond Dar'a with Jordan, but is of little economic value. In 1963 agreement was reached for the reconstruction of that portion of the line (in Jordan and Sa'udi Arabia) destroyed during World War One, but progress has been slow. The other current railway construction project, which should prove of great value to the economy when and if completed, is a line from Lataqiya to the Euphrates region via Aleppo. Until this is finished, the hinterland communications of Lataqiya—the sole important general-purpose Syrian port since the loss of Alexandretta to Turkey in 1939 (p. 77)—are poor. Syria's other ports of note, Banyas and Tartus (the latter only now being developed) serve almost exclusively for shipment of oil. There are a number of reasonably equipped airfields in the territory, with Damascus offering the best facilities and enjoying by far the most traffic. It is used by the state-owned Syrian Arab Airlines as well as numerous international carriers.

The metric system of weights and measures is officially in force in all areas, though in fact other and older standards are still in common use. The currency is that of the Syrian pound (£Syr), quoted officially at 9·09 to the £ (or £Syr 3·82 to the dollar), unofficially at rates between 9·6 and 10·1.

## 4. *Jordan*

The Hashimite Jordanian Kingdom (or Kingdom of Jordan), as distinct from the (mandated) Amirate of Transjordan, came into existence, with its changed name and status, in 1948. Its initial area was some 34,500 square miles. In 1950 a further 2,200 square miles were added by the incorporation of the central-eastern portion of ex-mandated Palestine. This same territory was occupied by Israel in June 1967, and its eventual disposition is today (1969) an open question. Jordan's present dimension is therefore legally some 36,700 square miles, realistically 34,500. The country is bounded on the west by Israel, on the south and south-west by Sa'udi Arabia (but with a small strip of sea frontage on the Gulf of 'Aqaba), on the east by 'Iraq, and on the north by Syria. It has no common frontier with Egypt.

The territory west of Jordan (today occupied by Israel) is that part of Palestine whose Arab character had not been (until recently) threatened by Zionist colonization. Roughly quadrilateral in shape, but with a deep wedge driven into its western flank to secure Israeli access to Jerusalem, the territory runs, north to south, from the neighbourhood of Janin to (and beyond) that of Hebron. It contains the Arab towns of Nablus, Tulkaram, Ramallah, Jericho (Ariha), and Hebron (al-Khalil). Part of Jerusalem and its eastern environs were the centre of this area until 1967, when they were occupied by Israel—without the world's recognition. The West Bank is a temperate region of hills, with olive groves, fruit gardens and terraced as well as open-field cultivation. The Jordan Valley, deeply sunk between its lines of hills rising on either side, lies within Jordan territory to the extent of some 50 miles as the crow flies, far more as the river winds. The riverain plain, extremely fertile, is in places 12 miles wide and is all irrigable; it ends, on the south, where the river pours its waters into the bitter saltness of the Dead Sea, 1,290 feet below sea level—the lowest place in the world. South of the Dead Sea, the Jordanian-Israeli border is the median line of the broad, barren Wadi 'Araba, running south-west to the head of the Gulf of 'Aqaba.

East of the valley lies a broad upland, rainfed belt of which the favourable, cultivable section lies to the west of the Hijaz Railway. The belt is some 30 miles wide on its northern face at the Syrian border, which is formed by the Yarmuk river, and is narrower and less fertile, to the point of almost total aridity, as it falls southward to the latitude of Ma'an and beyond. South again of this, and everywhere east of the railway, Jordan is a desert country, too dry for cultivation, largely lava-strewn, and humanly valueless except for the scanty, almost invisible camel-pastures of the desert tribesmen. The cultivable area contains the towns or major villages of Irbid, Mafraq, Jarash (with the famous ruins), Zarqa, 'Amman the capital, and al-Salt.

The Palestinian population west of Jordan is typical of the Arabized amalgam of peoples familiar in every country of the Levant—'Arabs' in every valid test as well as in their own opinion, and the world's acceptance, for fourteen centuries. East of Jordan the mixed relics of earlier peoples are probably scantier, the purer stocks of Arabia a majority; but the difference may in fact be slight. Tribalism, widespread in the old Transjordan, is little represented west of the river; there, and in the uplands from Irbid to 'Amman, the population are village-dwelling cultivators, devoted to the soil and to their homes. The total population of Jordan in mid-1968 was perhaps 2,200,000: some 1,600,000 of those were to be found east of the river, including 500,000 'old' refugees (those who were displaced from Palestine in 1948) and 250,000 'new' homeless persons (who fled the West Bank in 1967); the remaining 600,000 were in the territory under Israeli occupation. The Jordanians (excluding the refugees) are believed to consist of some 75,000 nomads or semi-nomads, nearly 800,000 townsmen, and over 500,000 cultivating villagers. The dominant city in Jordan is the capital 'Amman (which tripled in population between 1952 and 1967), with some 350,000 inhabitants. Zarqa is the next largest (125,000), while some of the towns of the West Bank are in the 50,000–75,000 range. Among a great majority of Sunni Muslims are found perhaps 200,000 Christians, with the Greek Orthodox the largest community, followed by Catholic Uniates and Armenians. The Cherkes and Chechen settlements are mentioned elsewhere (p. 102); they are not numerically important.

Jordan has no mountains other than those, reaching a maximum height of 5,000 feet, which form the eastern escarpment overlooking the river. There are no considerable rivers other than Jordan, and no lakes except its share of the Dead Sea. The climate of the territory is one of great heat, whether in the Jordan Valley or on the plateau to the east; in the latter, the winter can be severe, with hard frosts and snowfalls. Rainfall is in most years adequate to cultivation without irrigation on the high land both sides of

Jordan, ranging from 15 to 25 inches a year; but east of the Hijaz Railway it falls to 8 inches or less, and crop-growing cannot be attempted.

Jordan is a poor country, viable only on the humblest standard of life, and quite unable (except with generous aid from the outside) to afford the military, diplomatic and social-service *train de vie* which Middle Eastern states now consider essential to their self-respect. It has existed largely on subsidies from foreign friends, first Great Britain, later the United States, since 1967 its oil-rich friends. Its own resources are scanty. The greatest part of the country, being arid steppe-desert, is devoted to a sparse and penurious animal husbandry maintained, as their sole means of existence, by the nomad tribes; this keeps them alive, supplies some local needs of the sedentary folk, but leads to the export of only humble quantities of wool, hides and skins, and animal fats. Of agriculture in Jordan, something will be said elsewhere (p. 241 f), and the same is true of its industries (p. 249 f). No oil has been discovered. There are limited areas of forest, of some potential importance, in the north ('Ajlun district) and in the south (near Ma'an). These are now officially maintained, but irreparable damage was done to them in the period 1908–1918 by the Turks, seeking fuel for their Hijaz Railway. For a fishing industry, the Gulf of 'Aqaba offers the only possible location, and fish abound. The country's mineral resources, other than oil, may possibly exceed those in the other states of the Fertile Crescent, thanks to the Dead Sea and the Wadi 'Araba. In these two natural declivities, important deposits of phosphates, potash and bromine, and a lesser but still useful presence of gypsum and manganese ore, have been discovered in recent years, and a liberal economic policy has successfully encouraged considerable foreign investment in their exploitation.

Great improvements have been made in late years, through funds allotted by United Nations, the U.S.A., and Great Britain, to the road system of the country. Excellent metalled roads now connect the capital to all main centres, including the port of 'Aqaba, the towns of central and northern Jordan, and Jerusalem. Passable un-metalled roads serve outlying areas in the agricultural districts, on both banks of Jordan. Bus, lorry and car traffic is light but adequate to needs. The Hijaz Railway runs from the Syrian frontier near Dar'a in the north to a point south of Ma'an, and in 1963 a contract was let by the governments of Jordan, Syria, and Sa'udi Arabia for the line's reconstruction in Jordan and Sa'udi Arabia. The port of

'Aqaba has been improved beyond recognition and, although reliant on road traffic to the rest of the country, has recently been handling over 1,000,000 tons of goods annually, thus reducing Jordan's dependence on Syria for transit. Air traffic, including that of Royal Jordanian Airlines, uses primarily the airport of 'Amman, where a number of European, American, and Middle Eastern lines call regularly. The territory is crossed by two oil pipeline systems: that of the 'Iraq Petroleum Company which up to 1948 carried oil from northern 'Iraq to Haifa (and has been unused and derelict since that date), and that, still operating, of the Trans-Arabian Pipeline Co. (Tapline) taking Sa'udi crude to Sidon in the Lebanon.

The currency of Jordan is the Jordanian dinar, equivalent to £1 3s. 3d., or $2·80 US. Where local or Turkish weights and measures have been outgrown, and for all international purposes, the metric system is used.

Before leaving Jordan, a fuller account must be given of the Palestinian refugees, that tragic population whose greatest concentration is in Jordan and whose existence over the last twenty years represents so notorious a problem of Middle Eastern society. The term 'Palestinian refugees' applies properly to that internationally designated and succoured body of people who left their homes in Palestine during the turmoil of threats, invasion and violence that accompanied the creation of the state of Israel in 1948. Their flight was due partly to the preceding 'temporary' exodus of the middle-class, which left a void in the Arab community; then to simple terror of the destruction of home and family; finally to acts of outrageous brutality by Jewish militant elements (the massacre at Dair Yasin is the most famous) and the panic resulting from these. When the shooting gradually halted, there were some 500,000 refugees in Jordan, about 200,000 in the Egyptian-administered 'Gaza Strip', 80,000 in Syria, and over 100,000 in the Lebanon. Once out of their homes, they were not (with a small number of exceptions) allowed to return, in spite of a specific resolution of the UN General Assembly in that sense. Their houses, gardens and lands were Israeli-occupied from that day, separated from their owners by a *de facto* frontier-line which represented the limits of the land held, on a given day of 1948, by the Israeli forces—a line, therefore, not defensible on any reasonable or humane basis, and one which cut villages in half or separated them from their own lands. Amendment of this line in Arab favour was always rejected by the Israelis; and meanwhile the refugees were to only a limited extent absorbed in adjacent Arab countries. Many of those who had money or a profession, or a craftsman's skill or civil service experience, were able to establish themselves in one country or another (including the oil-fields of the Persian Gulf) and to make new lives. Thousands (perhaps up to 100,000) of these categories found permanent-seeming homes in Jordan itself—whence, in large part, the rapid expansion of its urban life, and a valuable contribution to the kingdom on many levels. Since all refugees in Jordan became, by King 'Abdullah's decree, Jordanian citizens, thus in a day doubling and greatly diversifying the population of the kingdom, the scale of the resulting social revolution in the territory is evident, with political effects at least equal; the incomers included dozens of *ministrables* and their educated followers, and the acquired territory in West Jordan contained such important political centres of Arab nationalism as Nablus and Jerusalem. A very few of the refugees were helped by work on agricultural projects within Jordan, notably in the Valley. But the majority were, in the nineteen years from 1948 to 1967, without permanent homes, a burden to themselves, to local society, and to the world at large which, through United Nations (UNRWA) funds, played the main part in keeping them alive. UNRWA itself, the 'United Nations Relief and Works Agency for Palestinian Refugees in the Near East', was established by the UN General Assembly in December 1949, and is supported by governmental and private subscriptions; its local headquarters is in Beirut.

The rest of the refugees—practically all of those in the Gaza Strip and many of those in Lebanon and Syria—lived permanently in camps. The authorities of the host countries, while far from indifferent to their plight, tended on the human plane to regard them with a certain weary distaste and on the political to dismiss major projects for resettling them as a politically and emotionally inadmissible confession that Israel was here to stay and that their homes were lost forever. The refugees themselves lived in a state of frustration and bitterness which eventually proved gravely dangerous to the peace of both the Middle East and the world. For long politically quiescent, in the 1960's their youth increasingly found political hope and emotional release in military activities against Israel—with results which compounded the refugee problem.

The war of June 1967, which perhaps only the Palestinian liberation groups desired, had results far different from their dreams. Instead of a return to Palestine, a new exodus was set in motion: about 525,000 Arabs, both Palestinian, including 175,000 1948 refugees fleeing for the second time in their lives, and non-Palestinian (Syrians from the Jaulan heights, Egyptians from the Sinai and Canal regions) left the territories occupied by Israel either during or shortly after the hostilities. Their story has been drearily parallel to that of the 1948 refugees, the chaos of flight, gradually replaced by the 'order' of a miserable existence in ramshackle camps, barely supported by international charity. Up to spring, 1969, no progress was made towards the rectification of the plight of either group of refugees, those of 1948 or 1967. They remain in their dismal camps, a perpetual seed-bed for bitterness, hatred, and violence which show no signs of abating. They are indeed both the most tragic by-product of war and the greatest barrier to the achievement of peace in the Middle East.

## 5. *Egypt* (*United Arab Republic*)

Egypt, which even after September 1961 has continued at its own wish to be known as the United Arab Republic, occupies a territory in many ways remarkable. Its geography is admittedly unique; its recorded history, as we have already seen, is the most extended of any, with but one possible rival; its surviving ancient remains in tombs, pyramids and monuments are the wonder of the world. Its strategic situation as a junction and through-way for world traffic is of unequalled significance. Its political and social position today among the Middle Eastern countries is one, not indeed of admitted primacy, but at least of claimed and partly accepted predominance in size of population, scale of commercial and industrial operations, social and cultural evolution, progress in education and the professions. These considerations, together with the social charm of so many rural and urban Egyptians at every level from *fallah* to Minister, make all the more regrettable both the undoubtedly grave economic and political crises in which the country finds itself in the late 1960's— the former a result as much of nature (in the guise of population growth) as of events controllable by the state, the latter more purely the outcome of the errors of policy-makers.

As a habitable area the country is (as Herodotus remembered) 'the gift of the river Nile', claimed as greatest of all rivers by those sensible to its spell, and richest in history and legend; without the Nile the whole of Egypt would be a mere uninhabited Saharan waste.

Lower Egypt consists of all the country from Cairo (inclusive) north-wards to and with the Delta; the latter, 8,500 square miles in area, contains the various branches of the Nile-Damietta (Damyat), Rosetta (Rashid) and the rest: the flattened mass of fertile silt brought down by the river over many thousands of years: a dozen populous cities, hundreds of villages, and a teeming rural population. Between them and the open Mediterranean lie four shallow, partly silt-filled lakes, and east and west of the whole river and delta system stretch broad uninhabitable deserts of utter aridity. Upper Egypt is the river-side plain, from 2 to 15 miles broad, reaching from the Sudan frontier at Lake Nasser to near Cairo. This is all cultivated to the limits of its waterable acreage, and is flanked on either side by rainless desert from the Red Sea to the Libyan border. The area of the whole country is some 385,000 square miles, of which 96 per cent is total desert, leaving but 15,000 square miles at most of cultivable land. The extreme length of Egypt is 675 miles, its greatest breadth 770. Its frontiers, drawn across sheer desert, are on the west with Libya, on the south the Sudan, on the north-east Israel; northern and eastern boundaries are provided by the Mediterranean and the Red Sea. No geography could be less complicated. The Sinai peninsula, separated from the rest of Egypt by the Suez Canal (and in 1969 under Israeli occupation), may be regarded as either Asian or African.

Otherwise than on Nile-side and in the Delta, the country is every-where uninhabited except by the scanty population of five oases (Faiyum, the most important, and Kharga, Dakhla, Farafra and Siwa), all in desert west of the river: by the towns and settlements along the course of the Suez Canal, and on the Mediterranean coast. The whole of these together contain less than 5 per cent of the Egyptian population.

The First Cataract (first as we proceed up-stream), due to a partial blockage of the river-bed by hard rock, occurs near 'Aswan (Assouan) in upper Egypt and is the site of the famous (and earliest) Dam. (The other four Nile cataracts lie in the Sudan.) Between the Nile and the Red Sea is a belt of hilly or mountainous country, running parallel to the coast and in places reaching 7,000 feet. Elsewhere the Egyptian deserts are undulating rather than flat, and are varied locally by deep depressions of which the best known is that of Qattara in the northern-most quarter of the Western Desert. Sinai has a few coastal villages and a famous monastery, with most of its area the domain of the camel-breeding Bedouin. The largest cities of Lower Egypt, accord-

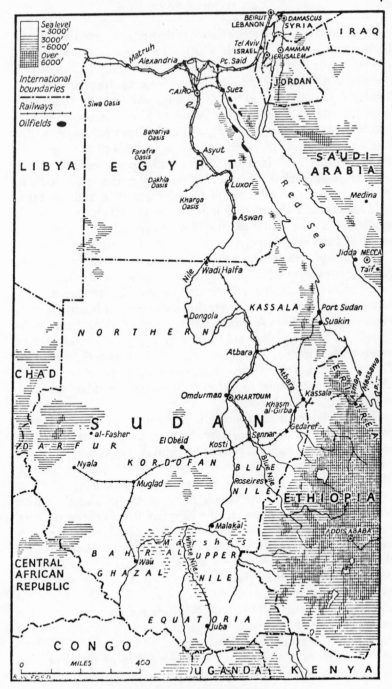

EGYPT AND THE SUDAN

ing to the census of 1966, were Cairo (with over 4,000,000 inhabitants, the largest city in the Middle East), Alexandria (1,800,000), Giza (570,000), Port Said (Sa'id, 280,000), Suez (260,000), Tanta (230,000), Mahallat al-Kubra (225,000), Mansura (190,000), Imbaba (170,000), Zagazig (150,000), Damanhur (145,000), and Ismailia (Isma'iliya, 140,000); and in Upper Egypt Asyut (Assiout, 150,000), Faiyum (130,000), Aswan (Assouan, 125,000) and Minya (110,000), with a number of towns, of both regions, in the 50,000–75,000 range.

The territory is divided for administrative purposes into sixteen provinces, eight each in Upper and Lower Egypt; in addition to these are five special governorates (of Cairo, Alexandria, and the three Canal cities), and the four 'frontier districts', relatively scanty in population, of the Red Sea, the New Valley (the western oases, excluding Faiyum), Matruh (the Mediterranean coast) and Sinai.

The climate of the territory varies between narrow limits. Rainfall, almost non-existent in Upper Egypt, can amount to a maximum of 6 to 8 inches a year in the Delta and on the Mediterranean coast. Summer heat is everywhere severe, but least so on the Mediterranean, where the Alexandrian summers are reckoned tolerable. Sandstorms brought up by the south wind (the Khamsin) of early summer are a severe trial. Winter is everywhere delightful in its cool brightness. The annual rise of the Nile, without which Egypt could not survive, takes place from August to October; by December it has subsided, and in April is at its lowest.

The population of the country is well above the Middle Eastern average in respect of homogeneity. Not less than nine-tenths of the people are of traditional modern-Egyptian type, whose blood-mixture, except for minor upper-class nineteenth century Turkish additions, has long settled down to produce a prevailing physique: a type representing a thickened, more muscular, slightly darker Mediterranean. As a character, the Egyptian has on the whole been a popular figure in the world; an upper class of charm, high culture and wealth (though often with too restricted a social conscience) has pleased its foreign acquaintances; the professional and middle class, far more extensive than elsewhere in the Middle East, commends itself by its intelligence, courtesy, and capacity for progress; and the mass of the *fallahin* in Delta and Nile-side are known as laborious and patient, yet responsive and humorous. Only the lowest stratum of the urban proletariat shows itself at times to contain its full pro-portion, or more, of violence or delinquency. Among such European long-term residents in the country as were also sensitive observers, life among Egyptians has had little that was unpleasant, much that was delightful, to offer.

Of a total population of nearly 32,000,000, over 90 per cent are Sunni Muslims of the Hanafi and Shafi'i sects, and these, in the towns, include many adherents of one or other of the still vigorous Sufi fraternities (p. 92). Islam is, under the post-revolutionary constitution, the official religion of Egypt. Foreign communities, from among whom many individuals—Greeks, Italians, and other Europeans, and also Syrians and Lebanese—have in the past obtained Egyptian passports, have played a part in the country's affairs more than proportionate to their size, and have contributed largely in culture, finance, and commerce. This, since the modern upsurge of xenophobic nationalism, is much less clearly the case today; indeed, the numbers of such communities have of late been notably reduced by emigration or expulsion. The same is true not only of British (including Maltese and Cypriot) and French subjects, whose numbers in the Egyptian cities have fallen rapidly since 1956, but also of the long-resident Egyptian-Jewish community, now greatly diminished by movement to Israel. The position of the Armenians (including both Gregorians and Uniate Catholics) is, in the current political atmosphere, fairly but not wholly secure; of the other Middle Eastern Christian communities (Greek Orthodox and Greek Catholic, Syrian Orthodox and Syrian Catholic and Maronite) who are mainly of Syrian and Lebanese origin, substantially the same may be said. These are cultured, progressive, valuable members of society—but are imperfectly at their ease in post-1952 Cairo. The Copts (p. 106) are an Egyptian minority on a different footing; numbering perhaps 2,000,000, mainly peasants but also landowners and town-dwellers, these are authentic Egyptians with no other home or allegiance, and are differentiated from the Muslim majority only by their refusal, 1,000 years ago, to change their monophysite Christianity for Islam— and differentiated also, in some measure, by the special and valuable gifts in commerce, the professions and administration peculiar to their community. The majority of Copts have kept their ancient faith, minorities have accepted Protestantism, others Catholicism, while conversions to Islam were, and perhaps are, not infrequent. The Copts have, as loyal Egyptians, played an active part in politics, usually on the side of nationalism, never in any non-Egyptian interest. Yet in the atmosphere today prevailing their Christianity and distinctness seem to militate against their acceptance by Muslim feeling as completely reliable compatriots. Coptic, as a language, is no longer spoken or written, but survives in their mixed Arabic-Coptic liturgy.

To the outside world it may appear that the main Egyptian effort since 1952 has been made in the field of foreign affairs, with the pressing of campaigns of threat or seduction, invective or persuasion, directed intermittently to Arab neighbours and the western powers; and indeed a restless, sometimes intemperate, yet usually intelligible foreign policy has been and is in process of development. Its objects have been those of Egyptian aggrandisement and prestige (in part, at least, with the purpose of increasing Egypt's own popular self-respect and dignity), pre-eminence in the Arab world if this prove possible, and the acquisition meanwhile, by a proclaimed neutrality, of maximum material aid in every form from both western and eastern sources. But in fact the thoughts and efforts of Egypt's ruling military clique and her more intelligent citizens are, and ought to be, still more anxiously concerned with her internal problems. The greatest of these is the assurance of her food supply, standard of living and economic stability in the face of a seemingly uncontrollable population increase which has more than trebled the body of the nation since this numbered 9,000,000 souls in 1897. The true object of policy would be to achieve the uplift everywhere of currently (and traditionally) low, or deplorable, living-standards among both rural and urban poor; and with it should go a massive increase of education, enlightenment and health, and the diminution of social inequality and injustice. These objectives are in fact being sought with much sincerity, though not always with patience nor the wisest of planning. The means by which, in the restless uneasy atmosphere of Cairo and its officer-ministers, these ends are being pursued include a major or indeed ruthless revision of the land-tenure system with strict limitation of privately-owned acreage, and of rents chargeable; they include trade agreements with all and sundry, a drive towards industrialization (with provision for profit-sharing and a ban on exaggerated salaries); they include a widening and tightening of state control and ownership, and a complex of social, technical and administrative steps taken to increase rural prosperity. Part of this is the planned completion, at the earliest date, of the giant High Dam at Aswan (p. 84), a project nearing completion: and the establishment, for all to see, and using the confiscated wealth of the exiled Royal family, of exemplary planned rural communities devoted to showing what can be done, in Egypt now, with sufficient energy, capital and modern methods, to create a new type of rural life.

Together with these objectives and methods, the administration of the revolutionary government has in hand a rapid overhaul of, and much innovation in, the public services of education, medical establishments and village improvement. These and many other measures taken governmentally in the Egypt of today, amounting as they do to the adoption of a thorough-going socialist régime, do not and will not commend themselves to all—least of all to democrats (since personal liberty is largely sacrificed), or to the formerly privileged classes; some of the steps taken may well be misconceived, others ill-financed, others already a partial failure. But all show a genuine, almost a frantic, effort by the best leadership now available to deal with the appalling, yet visible and assessable, problems of this deceptively simple-looking territory. (The simple and effective expedient of birth-control, advocated by government authorities, is repugnant to the Egyptian masses.) Meanwhile, in all that pertains to social and economic organization a spirit of revolution, dating from 1952, still prevails in Cairo, activity throbs (sometimes painfully) in every field, aspiration towards social and material advance is limitless, and the voice of those (no negligible fraction) who detest the present methods and objectives is faint or drowned. On the subjects of Egyptian agriculture (including its all-important irrigation, and its famous cotton) and her industry, more will be said elsewhere (p. 243, 248 f); but it must be emphasized here how predominantly Egypt is still today (as it has been from all antiquity) an agricultural country in respect of its needs, its traditions and the livelihood of 75 per cent or more of its people, even while it is resolved more and more rapidly and widely to adopt modern industry as the prayed-for, perhaps the sole, solution of its problems.

Egypt is endowed, far less than its broad surface might indicate, with natural resources. Forests are unknown, fisheries make only a minor contribution to wealth or food, stock-breeding—in spite of current researches and pilot-schemes—must be impracticable on any important scale, mineral wealth is limited to very modest deposits of phosphate rock, manganese, gypsum, talc, iron ore and lesser items. These are being exploited, with the first two already being exported, and will be developed to the maximum. The oil finds of the 1960's (p. 253) are more than promising, with the prospect of Egypt becoming a small-scale exporter in the 1970's. Tourism and Suez Canal tolls are sources of income which political misfortune—or folly—can temporarily disrupt but not destroy, and a human resource of value is the export of teachers and technicians to other Arab countries—a resource of even greater political and social importance than financial. But, with all that Egypt's agriculture, its industries, and its every resource and ability can do for it, and with even the best of management and good fortune, it is still not clear how, short of miracles, this country—a paradise, perhaps, for a small or moderate population—is to support, and still less to elevate to living-standards far higher (as is desired) than the present, a population growing even now by 750,000 souls a year.

Flatness and aridity render the achievement of a communications system in Egypt perhaps less arduous than elsewhere. Roads, passable if often inferior, run everywhere. Railroads, intensively developed since the mid-1800's, serve adequately the Nile Valley (including Kharga oasis) northward from 'Aswan, and the Delta, the Mediterranean coast, and the Canal Zone; some 2,900 miles of line, and a further 860 miles of light (agricultural) track are in use. Aviation is highly developed, Cairo competing with Beirut as the main Middle Eastern staging-post for inter-continental flight. All main (western) airlines regularly use Cairo; other airports in the country in daily use are those of Alexandria, Port Said, Matruh, 'Asyut, Luxor and 'Aswan. The state-owned United Arab Airlines covers the country as well as most of Europe and the Middle East. River navigation, of which about 1,000 miles is on the Nile, the rest on its major branches and canals, is of great service. And the Suez Canal stands out as a highway of truly international status.

This unique waterway, which was authorized in 1854 by grant to de Lesseps from the Khedive Sa'id, begun in 1859 and opened in 1869, cost a mere £16,000,000; it would, *ceteris paribus*, cost ten times that sum today. It was for nearly a century administered by and for the Universal Suez Canal Company (an Egyptian-registered Corporation, with headquarters in Paris), until its abrupt nationalization by President Gamal Abdul Nasir in 1956, by an act whose legality some lawyers (and all Egyptians) have defended, others have attacked. Under Egyptian control, the Administration (including pilotage) of the Canal in the post-1956 years was efficient; plans for its deepening, widening and improvement were progressively carried out. The increase in revenue to Egypt since nationalization was tremendous; in 1966, over £80,000,000 sterling (all the more useful because in scarce hard currency) accrued to the Egyptian government: a dividend of which the true value was much increased by Egyptian gratification at her successful defiant take-over and subsequent administration of the Canal, and the status of owning and controlling so famous and remarkable a work of man. The Canal, 101 miles long (excluding approach channels each end) has a minimum width of 200 feet and a depth sufficient for the passage of vessels of 37-foot draught. A railway and a freshwater canal run beside it throughout its length.

Since the war of June 1967, the Canal has been closed to traffic, and acts as a frontier between two hostile armies rather than as the useful servant of world trade and progress which its builders intended. The loss to Egypt of the revenues of this waterway have been grievous, and only a subsidy from the oil-rich Arab states has enabled Egypt to forgo them. In the meanwhile, the survival of world trade without grave strain and the increasing use of giant tankers for the transport of Middle Eastern oil to Europe—a trend well begun before the closure of the Canal—have caused speculation that the days of the Canal, when political conditions allow its reopening, may be numbered. This trend of thought is perhaps pessimistic; the Canal can be modernized and improved to accommodate most traffic demands upon it, and its use indisputably means an immense saving of mileage for the user (a voyage, for example, from London to Bombay saves 4,500 miles by taking the Canal, and one to the head of the Persian Gulf 5,000): only politics, it may be, prevent the Canal from resuming its old place in world trade.

The Egyptian pound, £E, is officially worth 19s. 2d., or $2·30 US, but about half this in free money markets. It divides into 100 piastres, or *qurush*. The metric system is in general, always in official, use; but as a measure of area the Egyptian *fiddan* (4,200 square metres, or 1·038 acres) still prevails. The *rotl* of 0·99 lb is widely met. Many other local weights and measures are found in agriculture and trade; the *ardab*, a measure of capacity (43½ gallons), is much used for the sale of grain and cotton seed.

## 6. *The Sudan*

The Anglo-Egyptian Sudan of 1899–1955 enjoyed always the interested goodwill of the outside world, and not least that of Great Britain who, with her purely formal Egyptian partner, bore the entire responsibility for the country's nurture and progress. Critics of colonialism, indeed, would do well to study the condition of this territory before the first date mentioned above, and at the second; a greater transformation for good, in terms of human happiness, can rarely have been witnessed in any country in so few years. Here, it seems, was the colonial system—never viewed by Britain in the Sudan otherwise than as a temporary expedient for rehabilitation—at its very best; and in fact the administration, in this the solitary case where Great Britain enjoyed continuous years of power in an Arab country with no 'local authorities' to collaborate with or conciliate, was the work of able and devoted men. The superior type of a great majority of Sudanis, the picturesque vastness of their country, the magic of the Nile, perhaps also the unforgotten drama of Gordon and Kitchener, have added to the attractive popular image of the country abroad.

The Sudan Republic, as it became in 1956, has an area of 970,000 square miles (more than sixteen times that of England and Wales), an extreme length of 1,400 miles, a breadth of 1,200. Its boundaries were indicated on an earlier page (p. 14). Its frontage on the Red Sea is of over 400 miles in length, a strikingly desolate coastline with but two ports, Port Sudan and the now largely derelict Suakin. The country can be viewed as consisting of five main natural provinces, linked by their overlapping contiguity and by the all-dominating Nile. The northern area extends from Lake Nasser (on the Egyptian frontier) to Khartum; here the river is flanked by rocky plains varied by isolated groups of hills, among which occasional but very rare rainfall can produce a few thorn-bushes, with, towards the south, acacias in the *wadi* beds. The whole region is denuded, almost soilless, and irrigable only by raising water from wells or from the river; it is the home of camel-grazing nomads, and of the sedentary owners of the narrow strip of cultivation and date-gardens along the Nile.

The Red Sea Hills region (the western flank of the great Afro-Asian rift-valley) contains a belt of impressive mountains, some over 7,000 feet in height, amid which are valleys where rough thorn grows on the lowest ground and increases, towards the Eritrean border, to a more copious vegetation. The higher hills, with greater moisture, can support small trees which include the wild olive. The maritime plain east of this hill-system is featureless and desolate, largely fringed with coral reefs; it can however after rain afford some grazing, and the deltas of the Gash and Baraka rivers, near Kassala and Tokar, are annually flooded and grow valuable crops, including cotton.

From south of Khartum, and stretching far west through Kordofan to Darfur, lies a predominantly sandy region, with light rains which are all locally absorbed without visible drainage. Towards the south, the undulations in the sand-plain die out. The vegetation comprises short grass and trees which include the gum-arabic acacia; grazing is good, and the crops grown in favoured districts are considerable. This, the central Sudan, is the most populous and developed area of the country, with the greatest present activity and the most hopeful projects in cultivation and stock-breeding. It includes, in contrast to predominant flatness, the steep Nuba Mountains of Kordofan province, and, far to the west, the Jabal Marra ranges of Darfur, which rise to 10,000 feet and look westward over the Republic of Chad and its westward-flowing rivers.

South of this central area lies the wide belt where red sand gives way to the dark soil which covers all but the most southerly part of the lower half of the Sudan. With little drainage within its own limits, the area is crossed by stream-beds carrying impermanent water from catchment areas at a distance. The surface is for the most part covered by vast treeless plains of grass or, to the south, by savannah forest. Grazing is plentiful, wide areas are cultivated. Scattered hill-systems break the monotony, and amidst these sufficient water accumulates, in wells, to provide for sedentary village life. South of the twelfth parallel of latitude heavy rain falls, and over many thousands of square miles the Nile disappears in the featureless, trackless swampy wastes of the *sudd*, through the dense growths of which a passage for river-transport is barely maintained.

South of this wide zone lies the typically African forest area, which, with its equally non-Middle Eastern population, covers three provinces of the Sudan Republic (Upper Nile, Equatoria and Bahr al-Ghazal), but, for reasons given (pp. 11, 103), will not detain us here.

It emerges from this too-brief glance at the country that it is characterized by vast spaces and intractable deserts which occupy the greatest part of its surface: by a rainfall varying, from north to south, from almost nothing to tropical plenty: and by an extreme summer heat. It provides in fact, even if we ignore (as here we do) the all-African conditions of the deep south, most varied environments; and to these, as elsewhere, the response is that of camel-nomadism, sheep and cattle semi-nomadism, and cultivation by villagers in river-side settlements, in irrigated estates, and on favoured rain-fed slopes and depressions in open country. Cultivation follows diverse, and in cases unusual, methods (p. 245); and its serious increase, in extent and productivity, can only follow the development of irrigation, for which the single source is the river.

The Nile—its 4,160-mile overall length compares with the Mississippi's 4,520—is the dominant feature of the country, as it is of Egypt. The river is the supplier of drinking and irrigation water, and of

fish; it is also the unique central highway. Its waters, contributed by
Uganda, Kenya, Ethiopia and Eritrea, have been the subject of many
diplomatic exchanges. The most important of all these rests (at
present) with the Nile Waters Agreement made between the Sudan
and Egypt in November 1959: an agreement which, superseding a
British-sponsored arrangement of 1929, seems to secure the reasonable interests of both countries, makes possible the Egyptian High
Dam (with payment of £15,000,000 compensation for 40,000 evicted
Sudanese), and enables the construction of two major dams in the
Sudan, one on the Blue Nile at Roseires (the first phase of which
has been completed), the other on the 'Atbara at Khashm al-Girba,
recently finished, with a resulting 500,000 acres opened to irrigation.
Similar arrangements for water control with Ethiopia must one day
be made. In the Sudan, the extent to which irrigation from the Nile
is practicable (otherwise than by hand or animal-lift, or by the now
numerous mechanical pumps) is limited by the relative smallness
of the area accessible to flow canals; none is thus accessible from
the White Nile, and little from the Blue Nile other than the extremely
important Gezira area, between the White and Blue Niles just above
their confluence. The Gezira Scheme is described elsewhere (p. 245).
The annual rise of the Nile, unique among rivers for its regularity,
begins in June, and its high level continues till October. The flood-
season water is derived mainly from the Blue Nile, with its enormous
seasonal variation, and the 'Atbara, the seasonal discharge of the
White Nile, below Khartum, varying comparatively little. When all
is considered, it does not appear that the Sudan (especially with its
vast but ill-manageable reservoir of the *sudd*) will foreseeably suffer
from water shortage; but full and fruitful utilization is another
matter.

The human occupants of the Sudan, about whom something was
said on earlier pages (pp. 103ff.), are within limits diverse, even if we
omit the pagan Africans in the three provinces of the south. Apart
from a much greater variation between environments in this country
than in Egypt, the basic Arabization of earlier population elements
(themselves of differing stocks) has been less uniformly effected than
in the northern neighbour, and no single prevailing Sudanese type
can be matched to the relatively uniform Egyptian. For example the
Nubians of the riverain area of northern Sudan, originally non-
negroid, have in historical times been heavily mixed with negro
blood, and later received a lesser addition of Arab; these are mostly
bilingual between Arabic and their own dialect, and rarely inter-

marry with 'Arabs'. The Donagla, of Dongola (Dangala) province, are less negroid, more Arabized, but keep their own tongue. The Fung, on the other hand, though descendants of the old seventeenth-century Fung conquerors and imperialists, speak both Arabic and a Berberine (Nubian) language, but not their own. These varieties are matched by those found among the Beja tribes (who include Kipling's Fuzzy-wuzzies) of the Red Sea Hills; these are folk who speak their own Baidawi or Khasa tongues as well as Arabic, and had lived already for long centuries in their present countryside before the first Arab incursion—in spite of claims, among leading headmen, to descent from the Prophet's own Arabian tribe! Yet their social organization and way of life is strictly that of Arabia. The Baggara tribes, cattle-breeders (as their name implies) in central-western Sudan, use an Arabic of their own, but combine a large mixture of Negro blood with an outspoken pride of race and status; and even more do the camel-breeding nomads stress their pure Arab origins, which an unfriendly critic might dispute. The Nuba of south and east Kordofan must be pronounced non-Arab by most criteria, and so also the backward Fur people of the high mountains of Darfur.

The population, including nearly 4,000,000 in the south, was estimated in 1968 as roughly 14,800,000. Of the non-southern 11,000,000, about 3,000,000 live in the three provinces of the north (Northern, Kassala, and Khartum), and nearly 8,000,000 in the centre and west (Blue Nile, Kordofan, Darfur). The vast majority of all these are Sunni Muslims, divided, however, to an extent politically important, between variant sects and fraternities with differences based more on personal loyalties (not least as between Mahdist and Mirghani leadership) than upon niceties of doctrine. Among the whole body of residents in the country, perhaps 80,000 are Europeans, Egyptians, West Asians or Mediterraneans, some 25,000 varied African non-Sudani races, and more than 80,000 West Africans from ex-French or ex-British territories. The Christian elements are not numerically imposing; they include about 175,000 Catholics of the Latin or the various oriental rites, a few thousand each of Greek Orthodox, Armenians, and Copts, perhaps 90,000 Protestants, and a few hundred Jews. The resident Lebanese and European (notably Greek and Italian) element has made, over the last half century, an important contribution in retail trade, commerce, and officialdom; but this is diminishing in the post-independence period.

The country's natural resources, apart from its agriculture (p. 245), are not impressive. The search for exploitable minerals has been pursued for many years, and lately with intensity; the list of 'traces' or alleged prospects is formidable; but thus far only iron ore and copper are being developed. No oil has been discovered, and the territory is of low promise. Hydro-electric sources, not having been provided by nature, can be secured only in connection with river-barrage works. Among wild products, gum-arabic is important and, after cotton, affords the most valuable item of export; the Sudan provides the world with some 90 per cent of its requirements. Timber found in the south, and along the Blue Nile, is valuable, but insufficient for export; yet 'forest' areas are estimated at 400,000 square miles. Dum-nuts ('vegetable ivory'), mother of pearl, ivory and salt, are occasional exports. The inexhaustible papyrus of the *sudd* has little apparent value. Bee-keeping provides only for a local market. Stock-breeding is practised in nearly all inhabited areas of the country and, in whatever form, is a major source of livelihood; but exports from this source, amounting in value to an average of 5 per cent of the country's total, are confined to limited quantities of live cattle and sheep, and of hides and skins. Fishing is a widespread occupation, and the Nile is bountifully stocked; some salted fish is exported. The relative paucity of the gifts of nature bestowed on this vast territory suggest, indeed, that its economic and in consequence probably its social progress must needs be laborious and slow; yet the Sudani scene appears at once more pleasant and hopeful, and less constricted or threatened, than that of its northern neighbour.

The nine provinces into which the Republic is divided have all been mentioned. That of Khartum is in population the smallest, but contains the 'metropolitan area' of the capital itself with Khartum North and Omdurman (Umm Durman), giving a joint urban population of some 450,000. The other provincial capitals are on a smaller scale; the Sudan is the least urbanized of all Middle Eastern countries. According to 1965 estimates, Wadi Madani (capital of Blue Nile province) has 65,000, al-Fashir (Darfur) 30,000, Kassala 50,000, El Obeid (al-'Ubaid, Kordofan) 62,000, Juba (Equatoria) 15,000, Malakal (Upper Nile) 11,000. Even smaller capitals are Wau (Bahr al-Ghazal) and al-Damir (Northern). Major towns other than provincial capitals are Port Sudan, 80,000; 'Atbara, 48,000, with its railway junction and workshops; and Mongalla in the far south. Wadi Halfa in the north is no more, submerged under the waters of Lake Nasser.

The roads of the country, except within towns, are mostly no more than formed earth or gravel tracks, passable except after rain; when the latter is heavy or persistent, road communication ceases. The length of such motorable track in the Sudan is roughly 30,000 miles. Radical improvement of the road system by extending modern road construction is now in hand; the first modern, all-weather-surface road between major cities (Khartum and Wadi Madani in the Gezira) is nearing completion, and plans for the construction of a similar road between Khartum and Port Sudan (a distance of some 575 miles) are being studied. The railway system is extensive: a line runs northwards from Khartum to Egypt by way of the river through al-Damir, 'Atbara, and abu-Hamad, with a branch from abu-Hamad to Kareima (Kuraima). From 'Atbara a line runs to Port Sudan and Suakin *via* Haiya, with another from Haiya southward to Kassala and on by way of Gadarif to Sannar (Sennar), site of the Blue Nile dam. A line from Sannar goes to Roseires. The former is joined also to Khartum by a river-side line *via* Wadi Madani, and westward from it a line crosses the White Nile at Kosti, and proceeds to al-Rahad and el-Obeid. Al Rahad has lately been connected with Nyala in Darfur province, *via* abu-Zabad. The most recent construction is that of a line which takes off from the last mentioned at Mujlad in Kordofan province, crosses the Bahr al-Ghazal, and reaches Wau in the province of the same name. This line was built entirely by Sudani engineers and labour. The present Ten-Year Plan calls for the extension of this last-named from Wau to Juba in the south and for the building of a line from Nyala to El-Geneina (near the Chad border). The total of completed track in the country, all of 3 foot 6 inch gauge, is about 3,375 miles. It is all state-owned. River steamers, owned by Sudan Railways, provide communication where there is no other, or to supplement land-transport; services, with a total mileage of 2,300 miles, run to and from Juba, and up the Bahr al-Ghazal to Wau, and on the Dongola loop of the middle Nile to connect with the Egyptian services.

Sea-transport facilities are necessarily confined to Port Sudan, a fully-equipped modern port used by many inter-continental shipping lines. The Ten-Year Plan provides for a survey for another port, which will probably be Suakin. Air travel is locally in the hands of Sudan Airways, which operates both internal and international routes, the latter notably to Aden, Asmara, Entebbe, Jidda, Cairo, Beirut and London. Foreign airlines call regularly at Khartum.

The Sudani pound, £S, which since independence has superseded the Egyptian, has a value of £1 4s. 0d. (or $2·87).

## 7. Sa'udi Arabia

This enormously spacious, desertic kingdom, homeland of the Wahhabi sect of Sunni Islam (pp. 85, 95), covers some four-fifths of the Arabian peninsula. The north-Arabian extension into Jordan, Syria and 'Iraq is non-Sa'udi, as are the south-western (Yemeni) highlands, the south coast and its hinterland, the south-eastern mountains, and more than half of the Persian Gulf littoral. The rest, belonging all to 'the Kingdom' (as its neighbours call it), leaves it an area of 950,000 square miles, exceeded among our range of countries only by the Sudan, and more than ten times the size of England, Wales and Scotland. Its neighbours on the north are Jordan and 'Iraq: on the west it is bounded by the Gulf of 'Aqaba and the Red Sea, on the south by the Yemen, Southern Yemen and the Sultanate of Oman, on the east by the Trucial shaikhdoms, and the territories of Qatar and Kuwait. It enjoys, therefore, more than 1,000 miles of sea frontage on the Red Sea, and 300 on the Gulf. Its land frontiers are without exception drawn across desert country, officially defined to the north and south with respect to Jordan, Kuwait, and (in part) the Yemen, and largely disputed towards the Persian Gulf.

Viewed from west to east, the narrow plain along the Red Sea coast is barren, without natural harbours, obstructed by reefs and coral, and carrying in its few miserable villages the scantiest of populations. The largest of these settlements, from north to south, are Wajh, Yanbu' (the port for Medina), Jidda (by far the most important, being one of the chief cities of the territory and the port for Mecca), Rabigh, Lith and Qunfidha. Behind and parallel to this desolate coast-strip, a line or belt of not less barren volcanic mountains stretches from the Jordanian to the Yemeni border, with its ridges and peaks higher in the north and south, lower in the latitude of Yanbu' and Jidda in the central sections. The terrain athwart, and east of, this mountain zone is of appalling desolation, relieved only by the scanty pastures used by a few fragmented camel-tribes, and by the oases created by the rare fortune of a water-source at Tabuk, Taima, al-'Ula, Khaibar, Medina (the famous refuge and burial place of the Prophet), Mecca itself, Ta'if (with 5,000 feet of elevation, and the summer resort of the Hijazis), Khurma, Turaba and Abha the capital of 'Asir. None of these, except the Holy Cities and Ta'if, would deserve mention except for their rarity as urban settlements. The population of Jidda is now in the vicinity of 250,000, Mecca 230,000, Medina nearly 75,000, and Ta'if 40,000.

The whole Arabian peninsula is a plain of ancient rock severed from
Africa (which is the same) by the deep fissure of the Red Sea, and
disturbed locally by volcanic action, whence the Hijaz mountain
ranges and the flat lava-strewn uplands which flank them. All Arabia
is elevated on its west side and tilted gently downwards towards the
east. The country east of the Hijaz mountains, therefore, is still high,
covered by light layers, here and there, of younger rocks and varied by
local ridges and depressions which have created the conditions for
oases. The central area of the Kingdom is composed not of a single
featureless plain, but a variety of desert surfaces (p. 16 f.), scattered
ranges of low hills and broken ridges, hundreds of dry water-courses,
and rare wells or water-holes which make life possible for the nomadic
camel-breeding tribesmen. To the north of the central area lie the
sheer deserts of the Nafud, to the east those of the Dahna, to the
south that of the totally waterless, Sahara-like Ruba' al-Khali, or
Empty Quarter, proverbial for its forbidding lifelessness. The oases
of the centre, however—the true heart of the Sa'udi Kingdom—are
considerable; and they permit, in changeless, inner-Arabian fashion,
a not uncultured and not uncomfortable urban life, to which the
recent and fantastic oil-wealth of the kingdom has contributed, for
the fortunate few, a measure of modern luxury. The main oases are
those of Jauf in the far north, Ha'il in the Jabal Shammar, Buraida
and 'Anaiza in the Qasim district (with populations of perhaps 30,000
each), Shaqra and Riyadh (the capital, with a rapidly-swollen population of perhaps 300,000 and a galaxy of royal palaces) in that of
'Aridh, with Laila and Sulaiyil towards the south-west. These and a
score of lesser oasis-centres, with their scanty but sufficient water,
their gardens and exiguous crops and herds, their permanent mud-
brick dwellings, mosques and mosque-schools, support the settled
life of modern Arabia. In and around the palaces of the Sa'udi
princes—and no royal house was ever more philoprogenitive—where
the oil-revenues are spent or squandered, luxury and ostentation
abound, and the old austerities are forgotten.

In Eastern Arabia, towards and along the Gulf coast, the flatness
of the terrain is broken only by minor ridges and sand dunes, and
these, in coastal areas, give place to flat gravelly plains and wide
areas of salt-marsh. Inshore water is shallow and full of sandbanks,
giving difficult approach to the land for shipping. The most populous
oases—prior, that is, to the oil-age which has covered eastern Arabia
with ultra-modern settlements of western industrial type—in the
al-Hasa (al-Ahsa) province of the Kingdom, are those of Hofuf

Qatif and 'Ujair. North of the province lies a Sa'udi-'Iraqi Neutral Zone, delimited in 1922 under British sponsorship because no boundary line between the two parties could otherwise be agreed; a similar Neutral Zone between Sa'udi Arabia and Kuwait was divided in 1965, although oil exploitation continues to be shared.

The Kingdom is divided for administrative purposes into five provinces. These are the Hijaz on the west, a broad strip astride the coastal mountains: 'Asir in the south-west, which is permitted something of a privileged status: the Najran area, inland of 'Asir towards the Yemen border: the main subdivisions of Najd, the wide central area, which we have already named: and the al-Hasa province on the Gulf, with its capital at Dammam. Administrative methods are everywhere capricious and unformulated, but the current tendency is on the whole towards more semi-representative bodies in the towns and districts, powerless though these may be. There is no law save that of the Qur'an and the Shari'a.

The climate of the Kingdom is one of extreme severity. Rainfall over all of it, except the better-watered south-west area adjoining the Yemen, ranges from nothing to 8 inches a year; this can, exceptionally, be increased by sudden and violent falls which for a few hours turn the *wadi*-beds into torrents. Some of the rain, it appears, is carried below ground by aquiferous strata down the west-to-east slope to, or nearly to, the Gulf shores, where it furnishes wells and springs otherwise inexplicable. (Such water comes out in fresh springs in the sea off Bahrain.) The aridity of 99 per cent of Sa'udi Arabia is not improved by its high desert winds, its frequent dust storms, and its heavy coastal humidity; but days in winter can be sharply cold, in contrast to the very high summer temperatures of up to 120°.

Population estimates for this inhospitable land vary wildly, from over 7,000,000 (the officially-sanctioned figure) to less than 4,000,000 (by outside demographers). Apart from a few hundreds of miscellaneous (but always Muslim) foreigners in the Red Sea and Persian Gulf coastal towns—Somalis, Baluchis, Negroes, Persians, Indians—the people are all Arabian Sunni Muslims, perhaps half of whom (including, of course, the royal family and court) profess Wahhabism, and half other doctrines. No Jews are permitted in the territory. The movements of the rare Christians who visit it, including diplomats, are strictly controlled; none are allowed in Mecca or Medina. Outside the towns, and in some measure within them, tribal ways prevail, in forms less modified or modernized than in any other country: a feature to be expected in view of the strength and antiquity of the Arabian tribal tradition, and the possession of a terrain in most of which no life other than the nomadic could be supported. Among these Arabia tribes still so organized, and still leading patriarchal lives in conditions literally unendurable to others, are found some of the most famous and historic of communities in the tribal world. Yet even here modern ways are intruding; the rapid creation of a population in the eastern region modern at least in its livelihood is producing pressures for non-economic change which not even the ubiquitous monarchy has been able (or found it wise) totally to resist, and the state's own desire for the further exploitation of its natural resources pushes it in the same direction—that of partial modernization. Thus a structurally-modern educational system (with its emphasis admittedly on technology rather than the more speculative arts) is rapidly expanding, slavery was abolished in 1962—the implementation of which measure amongst the tribes will of course be a long process—and hesitant steps towards governmental modernization are under way, with the recent institution of electorally-nominated (but royally-appointed) local councils.

Mineral wealth other than petroleum had long been negligible, gold itself, worked since the 1940's, being abandoned; but recent surveys have been optimistic, reporting major finds of uranium, copper (already being mined), phosphates, pyrite, and iron ore for whose processing a rolling mill opened at Jidda in 1967. Fishing and charcoal-burning occupy a few hundreds, at the lowest subsistence level. A little pearl-fishing is carried on from the al-Hasa coasts. Agriculture is possible on a small scale around the oases, where crops, dates and fruit are grown to the limits of the water supply, and the bedouin find it possible, in years of relatively good rains, to grow small patches of wheat in desert depressions. The rearing of sheep is similarly desired, but similarly limited, pastures capable of supplying herds being widely variable from year to year, and always inadequate to large numbers. Camel-breeding is the livelihood of the great tribes, and its produce enables them to buy their grain and other essentials from the oasis shopmen. An interesting experiment, begun fifty years ago by the great King 'Abdul 'Aziz ibn Sa'ud, was that of settling the *badu*, formed into fraternities and therefore called Ikhwan, or Brothers, in subsidized settlements intended to be static and agricultural, for which purpose they were sited where water could be made available. But the loss of their camels seemed to increase rather than lessen the Islamic zeal of the ex-nomads, and this turned often to open indiscipline; nevertheless many of the colonies persist, and may point a way to ultimate detribalization. The largest of them is Artawiya, in eastern Qasim.

In the days before the economic revolution produced by the oil industry, reliance of the State finances (then scarcely worthy of the name) was on the Mecca pilgrimage and the money which it was possible to extract in fees from the pilgrims, and by supplying necessaries to them. This, the greatest of all Islamic pilgrimages and a statutory duty for every Muslim, is now well organized; it is no longer used as a money-extracting occasion, though indeed the very large travel-organization to deal with the Hajjis' land, sea and air travel is not unprofitable, nor are Sa'udis excluded from its benefits. Careful precautions against epidemic disease are taken. Licensed guides escort the pilgrims who come in the sacred month in their tens of thousands (up to 200,000 in a year) from every Islamic land, to perform the ritual ceremonies at Mecca and to keep the Feast of the Sacrifice. Most, not quite all, visit Medina also. Religion apart, the Hajj has all the social importance of a universal meeting-place of the Faith, and politically that of providing opportunity, at the very heart of Dar al-Islam, for mutual information and debate, for reaffirming (one may hope) the part of Allah in wordly politics—and perhaps for admiring the wealth and achievements of the House of Sa'ud. All sects take part equally; it is a yearly return to Islamic essentials.

The communications system of the country has seen dramatic improvement in recent years, a process still continuing. The main ports are Jidda on the west coast, now undergoing large-scale modernization with the construction of eight new piers, and Dammam on the Persian Gulf, a deep-water facility connected to the mainland by an eight-mile causeway. In addition Yenbo, the port of Medina, has recently been improved to accommodate modern shipping. Modern-type roads have been widely extended, and now connect Jidda with Mecca, Mecca with Medina and Ta'if, Riyadh with Hofuf and al-Kharj, while in 1967 the 950-mile 'Trans-Arabian Highway' from Jidda to Dammam via Riyadh was finished. Current plans call for 5,000 miles of surfaced road by 1970. Other roads, except those company-built in the oil territory, are merely tracks, usually passable, making all the major oases at least relatively accessible. The old Hijaz Railway is being repaired to link again the Holy Cities with the Fertile Crescent (p. 136), and should mean more and easier pilgrimages. Telephone and wireless services, especially for official use, are well developed. Sa'udi Arabian Airways, owned by the state but American-operated, maintains air services with

Beirut and Cairo as well as internally. The main airfields are at Jidda, Riyadh, and Dhahran (the ex-American base).

The standard currency is the Sa'udi Riyal, successor (in the eyes of the state but not those of the nomad) to the Maria Theresa dollar; its official value is 1s. 10d. (or SR 4·50 to $1·00). The Sa'udi Arabian Monetary Agency acts as a Central Bank.

## 8. *The Yemen*

The Republic (the successor, since 1962, to the Imamate) of the Yemen, scenically and climatically perhaps the most favoured region of all Arabia—it is the original Arabia Felix—has been also the most isolated inhabited area in the Middle East, and the least penetrated (if we except, perhaps, the highlands of Oman) by European influences. This has resulted, in part, from its geography, and its difficult routes of access which discourage all but the most persistent visitors: and in part from the policy of its rulers who, themselves medieval, remained for centuries highly suspicious of the outside world. Enjoying, at least in its upland districts, the best of climates and a generous rainfall, and threatened by none, the territory has yet contrived to be strikingly backward, insecure, and unhappy.

The area of the territory is some 75,000 square miles, with a sea frontage on the Red Sea (which forms its western boundary) of just under 300 miles. Its territorial neighbours are Sa'udi Arabia on the north and east, the new People's Republic of Southern Yemen on the south. The frontiers have in each case been the subject of much diplomatic review, without ever achieving final delimitation; nor may the Yemen-Southern Yemen boundary long endure, given the instability of both states. The Red Sea islands near the Yemen coasts (the Farsan group, Kamaran (Qumran), and Perim) do not form part of Yemen territory; the two latter are claimed as part of Southern Yemen, while the Farsan archipelago is Sa'udi.

The country falls into easily distinguishable zones, of which the first is the flat, barren and almost uninhabited maritime plain. The main part of this is separated from the sea by swamps and lagoons, inland of which a sandy and rocky wilderness, traversed by arid river-beds, occupies the width of the plain, some 30 to 50 miles in depth. Next, inland of this, lies the western foothill area, trackless, deeply intersected by ravines, and rising to an elevation of some 3,000 to 4,000 feet; here more vegetation appears, and though largely of desertic type supports life for some villages and a scanty population of graziers. The highly elevated but deeply intersected region most characteristic of the Yemen, the high central upland, is heavily vegetated, fertile, and able to support a considerable population, reckoned as not less than 5,000,000 souls. The plateau maintains an height of from 6,000 to 9,000 feet, but many peaks and ridges are higher, and one, claimed as the highest mountain in Arabia, reaches nearly 14,000 feet. The highlands are, thanks to the rainfall, widely cultivable, whether in open areas or by an age-long system of terracing in which irrigation, from impounded rain, is practised with rare skill and profit. Inland from the plateau, where it slowly loses height and merges in the true deserts of southern Arabia, the population thins to vanishing point and Sa'udi Arabia is entered. The country contains no rivers; the westward- or eastward-flowing rain-torrents lose themselves in the sands of the Tihama (coastal plain) without reaching the sea, or in those of the central deserts. Rainfall is assessed as some 15 to 20 inches a year in the northern and central highlands, 30 inches or more in the south-west where the monsoon reaches in from the Indian Ocean, and an almost negligible deposit on the coastal plain. The winter season on the highlands can be cold, down to and below freezing point, with frequent snow-falls; but in summer the region is temperate, its near-equatorial heat tempered by altitude and cloud-cover.

The population of the lower, seaward slopes, that of the coastal towns and villages and of the terrain along the Aden Protectorate frontier, consists of Shafi'i Sunni Muslims, among whom on the coast is a small proportion of domiciled Africans—Somalis, Dankilis, and Ethiopians. The people of the highland area are Zaidi (p. 93) in religion, as is or was the family of the Imam; these may constitute in all rather less than half the Yemen population. In the deep hinterland a fair-sized community of Isma'ilis (p. 94) survives. There are no Christians, and the Yemeni Jews have, except for a tiny minority, left their homes for Israel, after the many centuries in which they formed an abiding element in the south-Arabian population.

The leading cities of the Yemen are San'a, the capital, and Ta'iz, with populations estimated, before the civil war and its effects, at figures of roughly 100,000 and 80,000. Both cities are at high altitudes, respectively 7,250 and 4,600 feet. Other major towns of the highlands are Ibb, Yarim, Dhamar, Manakha, 'Amra and Sa'da. The cities of the Tihama are Hudaida, the country's principal port, with a population now nearing 50,000, and Mokha, once famous, long in decline, and now being rebuilt.

Pre-republican government—and, as far as can be ascertained, Royalist rule in the areas currently under their control—was largely a régime of the static but pervasive tribal system, with all its means of control and its loyalties. Central government was irregular and arbitrary in the extreme: all real power, even over the smallest details, was in the hands of the Imam—as long as he could avoid assassination, or trust any of his sons. In the cities, a refined Islamic civilization of ancient pattern, and some scholarly culture, persisted. The Republican régime, as befits a 'modern' state, has introduced a constitution, an assembly, and other trappings of progress, but the long-drawn civil war (and the bitterness with which it has been waged) makes speculation difficult as to how much Yemeni society has indeed yet changed.

The rural standard of life, at least in the highlands, is in general less depressed than that of many Middle Eastern countries. Yemen's natural resources have already been suggested—good soil and climate, agriculture and fruit growing, with its famous coffee and newer, but now increasingly important, cotton. There is opportunity and space for livestock breeding, that of sheep, goats, mules and camels; hides and skins are exported. Honey is produced on a scale unique in the Middle East. The narcotic drug *qatt* is widely grown and universally used, with little regard paid to its debilitating effects on physique. There is little sea-fishing. As yet, no mineral resources of any value (including oil) have been located.

Foreign assistance has played an indispensable part in the development of the Yemen's communications system and the beginnings of a modern economy. Facilities at the port of Hudaida, an open roadstead, have been improved considerably with the help of the USSR, which has also constructed another port, with deep-water access, at Ras Kadhib near-by. The old port of Mokha has been partly rehabilitated. A Chinese mission has completed a sorely-needed all-weather highway from Hudaida to San'a, and the United States has built a similar road from Mokha to Ta'iz and San'a. Other than these routes, thus constructed with foreign help, internal communications are dependent on unsurfaced and precarious tracks. In recent months Yemen's first modern factory, for textiles, was built at Bajil, and another, constructed with Chinese aid, now operates in San'a. The comprehensive Egyptian aid, in all departments of life, which so greatly helped (or, many would say, created) the Republic, has much diminished since 1967, but the Soviet Union has stepped to take its place. The country has as yet no railways.

There is a roughly organized internal aviation service, under local control but with foreign pilots and staff.

The Yemen's currency was, until 1964, the Maria Theresa dollar. In that year a new monetary unit, the Yemeni Riyal, was introduced. It has an official value of 8s. 11d. (YR 1·071 equals $1·00 US).

## 9. *Southern Arabia*

The composite territory next to be described consists of a belt of country, narrow at its south-western and deep at its north-eastern (Oman) end, in all some 1,700 miles in length and bordered, on the whole of its southern face, by the Arabian Sea. The western half is the Republic of Southern Yemen, the eastern half the Sultanate of Muscat and Oman. The inland frontier of the former is with the Yemen and Sa'udi Arabia, of the latter with Sa'udi Arabia and, at its northern end, the territories of the Trucial shaikhs. The inland frontiers pass everywhere through utter desert—that of the fearsome Empty Quarter—and are therefore undemarcated.

The main geographical features of the Southern Yemen, which is divided administratively into six provinces, are a dull, harbourless, unfertile coastal plain of varying width, with the Aden area and Makalla the only considerable urban centres: a wide inland area of barren broken hills and valleys: a district of higher mountains, 5,000 to 8,000 feet in height, as Yemen territory is approached: and a high table-land region in the two eastern governorates, cut through by the great rift of the Wadi Hadhramaut and its associated depressions. Inland of it all, to north and east, lie impassable deserts. The islands of Socotra (Saqatra) with the 'Abdul Kuri and the Brothers groups across the Gulf of Aden, as well as Perim, Karaman, and the Kuria Muria islands are also part of Southern Yemen. The total area of the state, whose boundaries on its landward sides are largely undefined, is some 112,000 square miles. The country with its coastal humidity, its extreme summer heat, its dust storms and aridity, has climatically little to recommend it, though a wild and desolate beauty awaits visitors to its remoter districts. Rainfall varies from some 3 to 5 inches a year at Aden to five times that amount, or more, in the mountains. The surface, when not wholly barren, is covered with a light thorny scrub and in places by incense-giving dwarf trees; cultivation exists along torrent-beds, in the Hadhramaut basin, in districts near Makalla, and elsewhere where well- or cistern-water can be spared.

The country's population has been variously estimated at figures from 900,000 to 1,500,000; a total of somewhat over 1,000,000 seems most likely. The state's leading urban area is that of Aden, until 1967 directly-administered British territory; this, with its suburbs of Shaikh 'Uthman and Little Aden, contains some 250,000 souls. Aden's population, attracted by the opportunities available in the busy port, naval-base and oil-refinery town, is varied; a majority of Arabs (a large proportion of whom are immigrants from the Yemen proper), several thousands each of Somalis, Indians and Pakistanis, and, until the withdrawal of the British, perhaps 5,000 Europeans. The political turbulence of the 1960's and the nationalism of the new Republic have, as usual, generated continuing pressures on the non-Arab groups, and their role in Aden's future will certainly be less than what was theirs in its past; the British administrators are already gone. Until recently, the city was a prosperous and growing complex; the refinery at Little Aden, the British garrison which was spending £12,000,000 a year locally, the city's general entrepôt activities for the area of the Horn of Africa, and above all its bunkering services for vessels heading north through the Suez Canal combined to make Aden the leading, and certainly the most modern, city of the Arabian Peninsula. In addition to sea traffic, it served a dozen regularly visiting airlines at its airfield at Khor Maksar. But its fate since South Yemeni independence is dubious; years of political strikes and demonstrations and latterly a 'war of liberation' within the city, the 'revolutionary' policies of its new rulers—who have managed to alienate exactly those countries which contributed most to the city's birth and development—and the closure of the Canal, so disastrous for Aden's trade and bunkering, have resulted in an economic crisis of the late 1960s which only some combination of internal stability, foreign aid, and political fortune can solve. The only other city of economic importance within the country is Makalla, with a population of the order of 25,000. The new state's capital is Medina al-Sha'b.

Until independence in 1967, the remainder of the territory (Aden Colony excluded) was divided into twenty-four petty, backward sultanates or shaikhdoms (see Appendix A) grouped by the British into two Protectorates, a Western and an Eastern. These, until their submergence by the revolutionary forces in 1967, were one of the most primitive areas of the Middle East, medieval in both culture and structure, and only slowly changing under British tutelage. Throughout both Protectorates, covering territory which until the 1930s was largely lawless and unorganized, a very fair degree of security had been achieved by the patient efforts of the handful of British representatives. An excellent start had been made in education by the foundation and inspection of primary, and even some secondary, schools; a beginning of other public services had been made, life and property was safeguarded, feuds and bloodshed ended, economic development encouraged by funds to aid practicable small-scale agricultural and other projects. The emigration of thousands of Hadhramis to the Netherlands East Indies (as they then were) was for a century a main source of wealth to the important cities of the Wadi—Tarim, Sayyun, Shibam—and, though this resource is now no more, Indonesian influences in the Hadhramaut are still visible, and have been a progressive agency; these imposing wilderness-surrounded cities remain, within the small circle of their social and religious élite, strikingly advanced and even luxurious. Elsewhere, penury is extreme, illiteracy until recently universal, and the world outside unimagined. The livelihood of the people derives from their scanty and precarious agriculture (which includes some tobacco and some cotton), fishing on the coasts, and limited sheep and cattle-raising. Camel-droving, once a main source of livelihood, has been superseded by motor transport. No oil has been discovered, and no exploitable minerals are known to exist. A local livelihood is often augmented (or replaced) by one gained by enlistment in British-sponsored (and British-paid) forces, or by flight to the towns or the sea. A number of Adeni and Hadhrami tribesmen have settled in Great Britain, others in Ethiopia, Sa'udi Arabia or East Africa. The prospects for any more rapid or progressive development under independent rule are far from bright, regardless of the intentions of the new government; neither the wealth nor the experience nor the man-power indispensable for meaningful change seem to exist.

The remote island of Socotra, also part of Southern Yemen, lies 150 miles from Cape Gardafui and has an area of 1,400 square miles and a population of some 10,000. It is self-supporting in dates, cattle and sheep. The Kuria Muria islands are geographically part of Oman, but when the British government attempted to return them to that state in 1967, the government of Southern Yemen refused to agree. Their population is less than 100.

The Sultanate of Oman, with 1,000 miles of coastline, occupies the rest of southern and south-eastern Arabia, stretching eastward from the Aden boundary at Ras Dharbat 'Ali to the narrow entrance to the Persian Gulf. It has some 600,000 to 700,000 inhabitants, within a territory of roughly 90,000 square miles. The country has five main areas. The first of these is the detached province of Dhufar in the extreme south-west, a district treated in all respects as the sultan's private estate. This has a pleasant and fertile coastal plain, flanked by the broad ring of the Qara hills, and is well watered by monsoon rains. There is some cultivation and good cattle-breeding. Salala is its capital, Marbat its port. The second constituent district is the totally barren, uninhabited area of both coast and hinterland between Dhufar and the southern end of the main Oman mountain range. The third is the fertile and populated Batina coast running from north-west to south-east, to Ras al-Hadd, between the Gulf of Oman and the mountains. This is an area of famous date-groves, scores of villages, a passably motorable track, and the sea-side towns of Muscat (Masqat) with its twin Matra, Sib, Khabura and Suhar. The fourth district is that of the mountains—the impressive range of the Jabal Akhdhar (p. 16), wild and desolate but with its vivid green areas of vegetation, its small urban or village centres, *wadi*-bed camel tracks, and a few easier passes practicable for wheeled vehicles, improved to that standard during the last few years. This is a region of heavier though uncertain rainfall, less severe climate. It is made habitable by the cultivation of grain, dates and fruit in far from negligible quantities, by skilful irrigation, and by the breeding of the famous Omani camels. The fifth and last zone of the Sultanate is the sandy or gravelly plateau west of the mountains, sinking and merging westward into the Ruba' al-Khali, and containing rare oases, such as those of the Buraimi group, but otherwise only the scantiest of bedouin life.

The Omani population is, outside the towns, uniformly Arab, mostly Ibadi (p. 92), and devoted to its feud-ridden tribal organization. The latter is a complex of ancient devotions and antipathies, exacerbated by the theocratic claims of ambitious divines or their champions. The whole territory has known little political or social tranquillity, while prevailing poverty has precluded any but the slowest development. It is further weakened by an active tribal and sectarian separatism in the mountain zone (a struggle which the radical pan-Arabists encourage from abroad and in United Nations), and by border quarrels with Sa'udi Arabia. The capital, Muscat-

Matra, is a city of mainly non-Arabs—Baluchis, Indians and Pakistanis, negroes, elements numerous also in the Batina coastal towns.

The Omanis live on their dates, fruit, fish, grain, and the produce of their camels. There are no industries other than domestic. No significant minerals other than oil have been found, though some coal may exist; oil has only recently been discovered in commercial quantities, with important production and export dating from 1967 (p. 256). The British contribution to a Development Fund to assist progress in the areas of agriculture, roads, schools, health and defence, became needless as massive oil-revenues now accruing will inevitably change all aspects of life in Oman.

Airfields exist at Salala in Dhufar, on the barren Masira Island off the south-east coast, and at Bait al-Falaj near Muscat. A weekly air-service links Muscat with Bahrain. Steamers from and to India call at Muscat weekly, others occasionally. The small ports of Suhar, Khabura and Sur offer no protection from the weather.

The media of exchange are the Maria Theresa dollar and the Indian rupee.

### 10. *The Persian Gulf States*

The sole area now outstanding, from this cursory tour of the Arab countries, is the southern shore of the Persian Gulf, excepting that part thereof, the al-Hasa coast, already mentioned (p. 156) as a province of Sa'udi Arabia. This leaves us the Trucial Coast, the Qatar peninsula, the islands of the Bahrain group, and the amirate of Kuwait. The whole of this region is one of extreme desolation, almost totally without natural resources (save one!), devoid of natural harbours, without the possibility of any but the most exiguous agriculture, unendowed with adequate grazing, and lacking, indeed—except on a part of Bahrain Island—even a modicum of vegetation. The coastline is encumbered with shoals, deep water channels are hard to find, winds are sudden and unpredictable. Rainfall is scanty, though not quite unknown, and even minimum potable water-supplies can be a grave problem; they exist almost solely at Bahrain and in or close to the foothill area of the Oman mountains. The coast is humid and malarial.

The TRUCIAL COAST, the stretch of country extending some 400 miles from Ras Masandam (the northernmost tip of Oman) to the base of the Qatar peninsula, affords, with its featureless, sandy and

salt-marshy hinterland, space for the domains of the seven independent Trucial shaikhdoms: an area amounting to some 50,000 to
100,000 square miles according as one may guess or claim an approximate, because never defined, inland boundary. A 1968 census reported a greater than anticipated population of 180,000, of whom
over four-fifths live in the coastal towns which are the shaikhs'
capitals, less than one-fifth in inland oases, notably the Buraimi
group. All are Sunni Muslims, and all sedentary except a few camps
of camel-herdsmen. The social organization is tribal. The occupations
are date-tending, pearl-diving, camel breeding, fishing, rarely and
scantily crop-raising, and, far more important, working in one or
other of the great oil-fields of the region. An important source of
revenue since 1937 has been the 'interim payments' made to the
rulers by the operating oil company for oil concessions granted, and
the employment given locally by oil exploration parties; of recent oil
developments in the Abu Dhabi Shaikhdom and in the offshore area
of Dubai more will be said later (p. 256). Until recently, the British
government had taken the lead in development planning, including
agricultural experiments and technical training, and in 1965 this was
institutionalized in a Development Office; but now Abu Dhabi,
thanks to oil, can assume the major role.

The independent shaikhdoms are seven in number (see Appendix
A); four are insignificant (though Ras al-Khaima is among the more
populated); Sharja has good pretensions to stability and progressiveness; Dubai is the best potential port and the largest town (some
55,000 inhabitants in 1968); but Abu Dhabi has the most territory,
sudden fantastic wealth, and every likelihood of becoming dominant.
Peace between the shaikhs has been secured by the good offices of the
British, who have also protected the territories externally. The future
of these services, as well as that of the shaikhdoms themselves, is
much in doubt since the British decision (1968) to withdraw its
military forces from the Gulf region in 1971. There has been,
hitherto, no administration in the states other than that, strictly
patriarchical, of the rulers themselves, in which the British have
played no part.

Steamers call weekly at Dubai, where construction of a deep-water
port is currently under way. Daily air services link Dubai and Abu
Dhabi with the rest of the Gulf, and a few Middle Eastern airlines
call at Dubai or Sharja.

The QATAR shaikhdom, with an area of about 4,000 square miles
and possibly 70,000 inhabitants (50,000 in Doha (Dauha) town, the

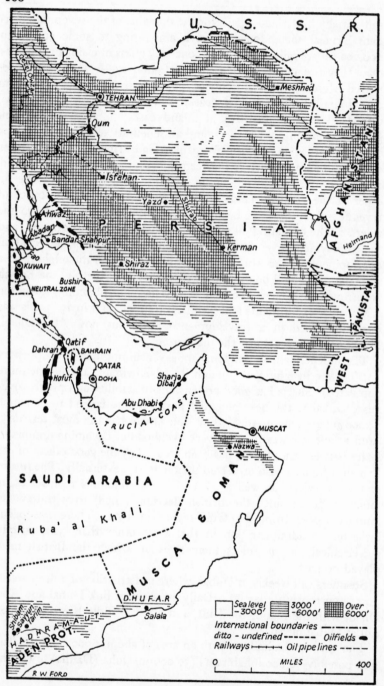

THE PERSIAN GULF

capital) mainly of the Wahhabi faith, is in amenities for human residence no improvement on the Trucial Coast, with which it is geographically continuous. Its boundary with the Sa'udi Kingdom has never been agreed. Since the large-scale discovery of oil (p. 256) which since 1950 has totally transformed the economics of the peninsula, the old and miserable livelihood of the Qataris from fishing, pearling and camel-breeding is forgotten; the oil company is now the dominant employer and benefactor, and the *per capita* income of Qatar's fortunate citizens was estimated for a time as the highest in the world—instead of, as but a half-generation ago, among the lowest. As in Abu Dhabi, the population is appreciably leavened by the presence, in oil-company employment, of hundreds of non-Qatari Arab technicians, office workers and labourers.

Besides Doha, now under transformation from a sprawling, squalid village to an opulent ultra-modern city and nucleus of a welfare state, there are three or four other villages, as well as the settlements, ports and multifarious activities of the oil company. Umm Sa'id is the deep-water port created by the latter, 20 miles south of Doha; Zakrit, equally a company creation, on the west side, has only shallow access. The Shaikh of Qatar, although no enemy to physical modernization, continues to maintain absolute control over the internal affairs of his state, with an Advisory Council his only nod to liberalism. The prevailing level of enlightenment among his own subjects could, until very recently, scarcely have been lower, but education for the young and for many adults (including that provided by the oil company) has made and is making rapid strides.

BAHRAIN is the largest island (30 miles by 10) of a group of eight, the others being Muharraq, Sitra, Umm al-Nisan, Hawar (close to the Qatar coast) and four more, all smaller except the last-named. They lie between the Sa'udi coast and the north-west tip of Qatar. The total area is some 215 square miles; the population is over 200,000, of whom the capital city, Manama, has rather less than half, and Muharraq about 40,000. Apart from resident or visiting foreigners (Indians, Pakistanis, non-Bahraini Arabs, Persians and British and American oil-men) the subjects of the Shaikh are about half (Shi'i) Baharina, who are alleged aboriginal islanders, and half Sunni Arabs, to whom the shaikhly house and most of *les gens bien* belong. The never-relinquished Persian claim to the island need not here concern us, though the large Shi'i element is not unconnected with it. The climate is of typical Persian Gulf type, but the many amenities of the island make it easily tolerable.

Plentiful water and cultivation exist in the northern half of Bahrain island, less or scarcely any in the southern part or on the other islands. Manama and its villages, deep in date-gardens and admirably tended horticulture, are the Gulf's most attractive centre. A causeway, with a central breaching-section for shipping, links Bahrain with Muharraq, where a busy, well-equipped airport was finished in 1961. New port installations were completed in 1962 at Mina Salman, which is now the centre of a growing shrimping industry. Much new building has occurred in recent years, and a new planned city, Isa City, which will provide spacious and spaced accommodation for an estimated 35,000 inhabitants, is now under construction. Urban services—those of public health, light and power, road transport, town-planning, education, broadcasting, and security—have now, after many years of enlightened if patriarchal rule and more than 35 years of oil-wealth, reached a high standard. Excellent artesian wells exist, and the main settlements enjoy piped supplies. The Anglo-American oil-field and refinery operatives, some hundreds strong, live in their own township, in the barren centre of the island; this does not include the Bahraini labour-force. Bahrain is host also to a British diplomatic mission, and a small naval base, which may be 'phased out' by 1971.

The occupations of the Bahrainis in oil-less days, pearling and ship building and maintaining the services of a main entrepôt for Arabia, are of lesser importance than oil and oil-refining—Bahrain's refinery being the second-largest in the Middle East. But the educational level of the people and the state's abundant natural gas promise much for light industrial development. A few British advisers and experts aid the Shaikh, at his request.

The amirate of KUWAIT, north of the (Sa'udi) coastal province of ál-Hasa and of the Kuwaiti-Sa'udi Neutral Zone, is unique among the .sovereign states of the world for its combination of small and desolate territory, fewness of inhabitants, and enormous wealth. Its territory at the head of the Gulf, measuring some 6,000 square miles of almost totally waterless desert, contains, apart from a few camps of indigenous or visiting nomads, a single city, Kuwait. This, a mid-eighteenth-century tribal foundation, has grown from about 70,000 inhabitants in 1930 to 450,000 in 1969. About half of these are native-born Kuwaitis, the rest are 'Iraqi, Egyptian, Syrian, Palestinian, Lebanese, Sudani, Omani and other Arabs, Indians and Pakistanis, most of these being employed either in the oil-fields or in the many enterprises, public and private, which oil-wealth has made possible. About three thousand Americans and Europeans are temporarily resident in the amirate. The official currency, the Kuwaiti Dinar, has a value of £1 3s. 4d. or $2·80.

The state's accession to multi-millionaire status, amazing in its suddenness and scale even by Middle Eastern standards, has transformed Kuwait in half a generation from a small, isolated, impoverished community of medieval type, living hungrily on pearling, boat-building and smuggling, into an extreme form of welfare state equipped with every facility, benefit and adornment that money can buy, and confronted only by a problem unknown to its forebears— that of how best to dispose of its income. Nine-tenths of the old walled town has been destroyed, a modern city of planned boulevards, modern architecture and materials, fullest urban services, shops and banks, consulates, clubs and factories, hotels, offices and palaces have arisen. The new schools, colleges, technical institutes, clinics and hospitals, housing estates: the power stations, water distillation plants (since the principality is waterless), and sewage system: the airport and deep-water harbour: all these and much more are the pride and amazement of modern Kuwait, and the outcome of its successive Development Plans, initiated in 1949. All services are given free, all are immensely costly; and the contribution of it all to 'the Good and the Beautiful' and to human happiness in the person of the Kuwaiti townsman may perhaps remain, after all, a debatable quantity.

# CHAPTER SEVEN

# THE NON-ARAB COUNTRIES

## 1. *Persia (Iran)*

PERSIA, if a country of the Middle East, is not less one of Central Asia. Geographically it forms the western half of the Iranian plateau, of which the eastern half contains Afghanistan—an almost equally Iranian country, in population and language—and the Baluchistan province of West Pakistan; but its religious and cultural contacts have been predominantly, though by no means exclusively, with the Arab world, and its modern outlook and interests lie towards the West. The long continuity of the Persian record, the achievements of its early imperial conquerors, its artists, scholars and poets, its place in world-accepted romance and legend, and the high intelligence of its present *élite*, gives Persia a singular status among the nations of western Asia, or indeed of the world. This is little diminished by the evident weaknesses of Persian public life, and the seemingly insuperable difficulties encountered there in establishing a secure, liberal régime. Indeed, the talents of this gifted people seem to lie even less than might be expected in the direction of political wisdom, or sound administration.

The territory, of which Iran is the time-honoured and widely used designation—as it is of the 'Aryan' peoples and language group—was by official order so known during the reign of Riza Shah; since then the name Persia (taken from the province of Fars in the south) is again permitted.

It extends over some 630,000 square miles, having thus more than double the area of Turkey, two-thirds that of the Sudan, and almost half the extent of India. Its boundaries on the north-west run with those of the U.S.S.R., across the Aras (Araxes) river, and with those of Turkey across a wilderness of wild mountains. From deep in Kurdistan to the head of the Persian (now known, however, throughout the Arab world as the Arabian) Gulf runs the Perso-'Iraqi frontier. Persia's southern boundary is the Gulf itself, and, outside the Strait of Hormuz, the Gulf of Oman and Arabian Sea. The eastern frontier divides the country from Pakistan in the south, from Afghanistan in the centre, and from the Turkmen Republic of the U.S.S.R.

in the north, where the southern shores of the Caspian complete its delimitation.

Loosely described as a high plateau, Persia falls in fact into a number of diverse areas, each with a special character but close and overlapping intercommunication. The north-west, substantially the great province of Azarbaijan, contains a tangle of high mountains (up to 14,000 feet) continuous with those of eastern Turkey. They are in places stony or lava-covered, with deeply-cut intersecting valleys, the broad river-valley of the Aras, and a number of narrower raised or inter-montane plains. Lake Urmia, only less salty than the Dead Sea, and the marshes surrounding it lie in the heart of an extensive, flattish agricultural plain. The capital of Azarbaijan is Tabriz (population, according to the census of 1966, some 400,000); other main towns are Riza'iya (110,000, formerly Urmia) on the Lake, Ardabil (80,000), Maragha (44,000), and Khuy (45,000).

Western Persia, from south of Azarbaijan to the Strait of Hormuz, is dominated by a broad mountainous tract up to 150 miles in width, and containing peaks exceeding 12,000 feet in height. This is known, loosely and generally, as the Zagros range, the middle and southern sectors of which contain the famous Persian oil-fields. The mountain-ridges are of fairly regular north-west to south-east tendency, but with varying directions of river-drainage. The whole tract, in at least the northern part of which earthquakes are a looming terror, is diversified by hill-cultivation, in places terraced, by fairly abundant pasture-land which supports cattle-owning transhumant tribes, by some stretches of forest, by much barren rock and soil-less hillside, and, towards the east, by depressions enclosing sometimes salt-marshes, sometimes the low-lying, cultivated and garden-bearing plains which contain historic cities. Of the latter, the best known in western Persia (including the eastern fringes of its mountain-system) are Hamadan (125,000), Kirmanshah (188,000), Yazd (77,000), Kirman (80,000), Kashan (62,000), Burujird (59,000), Isfahan (425,000), and Shiraz (270,000). In, or on the hilly fringes of, the extensive flat alluvial plain (so untypical of Persia) formed by the delta of the Karun and Karkhan rivers, lying west of the southern Zagros and extending eastward to the 'Iraqi frontier, lie the cities of Dizful, Shushtar, Ahwaz (207,000), Khorramshahr (formerly Muhammara), and Abadan (270,000), the oil-city. On the barren and humid Gulf coast are Bandar Shahpur, Bushire (abu Shahr), Linga, Bandar 'Abbas, and Jask.

Eastern Persia, a broad belt of territory reaching some 800 miles

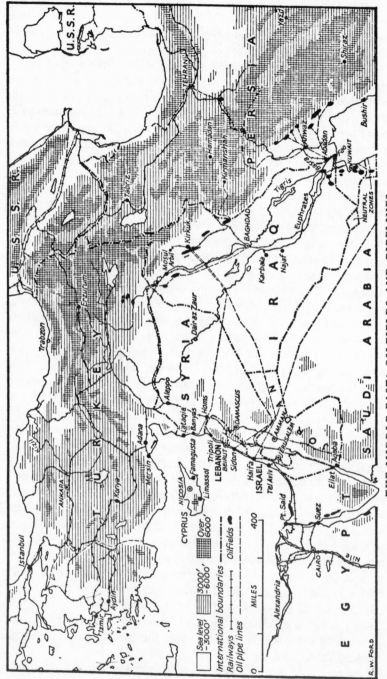

THE MIDDLE EAST: OILFIELDS AND PIPELINES

R. W. FORD

from north to south, contains the great and famous city and shrine of Meshhed (410,000) and the lesser towns of Quchan, Sabsawar, Sultanabad (Arak), Birjand, Zabul, and Zahidan (Duzdab). This region, intermediate between the central deserts and the Afghan and Pakistani frontiers, has no unified character or dominant features; the mountain ranges, in places high and imposing, follow no obvious system. Cultivation, except in the Meshhed area to the north, is limited to a few areas of higher ground, much of the land is sandy desert, and salt-depressions abound. The rivers, except for short streams running south into the Gulf, have no permanency or outlet. In the wide Sistan depression, athwart the Afghan frontier, salt-marshes and a lake are formed by the waters of the Helmand and other rivers which enter the country from Afghanistan; before ceasing to flow they afford water for considerable cultivation—and, in bad years, can produce dangerous floods. But most of the area is otherwise arid, windy, sandblown and desolate, though it would seem surprisingly to have supported a denser population in past ages. The south (Gulf) coast is separated from the central deserts by a stretch of desert barred, from west to east, by high barren ridges; these enclose the Jaz Murian basin, fed by enclosed rivers which produce an extensive salt-marsh area and lake; pasture is poor, cultivation scanty, and the date-gardens, where these can exist, are of low quality.

The heart of Persia consists, at an altitude varying from 1,000 to 5,000 feet, of a vast area of undrained, almost rainless desert, partly sandy and stony, partly of glutinous mud covered by crusts of salt, partly of marsh into which men, animals and vehicles can sink and disappear. The area is one of sheer desert, scarcely traversable unless at the fringes, and uninhabited; only on the higher edges that rise towards the enveloping ring of mountains is there human life and cultivation, the foothill areas themselves being fertile and favourable. The great deserts of the centre themselves cover more than a third of the whole area of Persia, with the result that the geographical centre of the country is its least populated area.

They are separated from the Caspian Sea by the last region of Persia to be here mentioned, the broad foothill belt and the massive range of the Elburz, with its westward and eastward extensions. These merge into the systemless massifs of Azarbaijan and of Khurasan respectively, with Elburz itself, surmounted by the superb Demavend (18,500 feet, the highest mountain in the Middle East) barring the central approaches to the sea. Elburz and its flanking ridges provide a rich variety of scenes, conditions and climates; they afford fertile soil for cultivation, good or poor grazing, forest, ravines and bare hillsides, precipitous as well as gentle slopes. Rainfall on the northern face of the mountains can amount to one hundred inches a year, the highest known in the Middle East except that of a small area of north-eastern Turkey. The coastal plain is fertile and thickly populated; a line of sand-dunes and salt-marshes lies between it and the sea. The Caspian itself lies 90 feet below sea level; it is sinking further annually, and thus renders life more and more difficult in the ports along its coasts. (It contains about a quarter of the proportion of salt found in normal sea-water.) Persian cities on this coast are Resht (142,000), Pahlevi (35,000), Babul and Bandar Shah. Just south of the Elburz range (indeed within sight of it) lies Persia's largest metropolitan area, its capital Teheran (2,500,000) with its northern and southern suburbs of Tajrish (155,000) and Rayh (100,000); nearby are Qazvin (78,000) and Qum (135,000).

Though the modern capital has, thanks to its extraordinarily rapid growth since the Second War, more than three times the population of any other Persian city, in terms of prestige the situation is far otherwise; a dozen of the major Persian cities have an outstanding local and often imperial history, from which survive not only a world of history and romantic legend, but also buildings of great dignity and beauty or, elsewhere, of the highest claims—as at Meshhed or Qum—to religious appeal. Impressive Achaemenid and Sassanian, as well as early Muslim, ruins attract scholars and tourists.

The climate of the country contains, naturally, a score of varieties, from the extreme heat and high humidity of the Karun plain and the Gulf shores, with a rainfall of 4 to 10 inches a year, to the still greater heat and still scantier rainfall of the central deserts, and to lower but still severe temperatures on higher ground inland, alternating with harsh winters. Rainfall varies from the very high deposits of Elburz to almost none at all. In temperature and moisture, and therefore not less in vegetation and livability, the north and north-west of the country excel the south, centre, and east. The season of maximum rainfall varies; in the north, apart from the Caspian provinces, it is rainiest in early spring, in the south in midwinter. Deposits vary capriciously, between wide limits, from year to year. Humidity is high on the Gulf shore in summer, on the Caspian it is almost perpetual. The sun is everywhere powerful; the air, inland, is usually dry and clear except when dust storms occur.

Of the racial composition of the country—Persians, Kurds, Lurs

39. A view of Limassol, Cyprus

40. Kyrenia: castle and harbour

41. Cyprus: Nicosia–Limassol road

42. Jerusalem, Jordanian sector: the Via Dolorosa

43. Jordan: ruins at Jarash

44. Jerusalem: Jordanian pottery-maker

45. Cairo, from the
Ibn Tulun mosque

46. Cairo: Liberation Square

and Turks—something was said on previous pages (pp. 116 ff.). The total population claimed (in 1966) was over 26,000,000; that this census was accurate is highly dubious. As against an overwhelming Shi'i majority, a Sunni minority of about 1,500,000 is estimated, including the Kurds. Lesser religious minorities are those of the Zoroastrians or Parsees, known locally as Gabrs (18,000), the Jews (80,000), the Armenians (150,000), and the Nestorians or Assyrians (50,000). Some thousands each of Roman and Protestant Christians (here including the European and American residents) may be found at any one time, mainly in the cosmopolitan capital or the oil regions. Persia is divided into thirteen provinces, with Teheran having a unique status under its own Governor-General. These are subdivided into counties, districts and groups of villages. The Baluchistan region is classified as 'special', but lies within the province of Sistan for administrative purposes.

The country's population, small in relation to its wide area, and influenced by its varied and largely desertic surface, lives rather in a multitude of smallish habitable areas than in a few major stretches of fertile country. The chief exceptions to this tendency are in the flat-lands of the Khuzistan province at the head of the Gulf, the regions of Lake Urmia and Tabriz, and the Caspian shore. In the rest of Azarbaijan, in an area of the central north-west (Hamadan-Kashan), and around Meshhed, population is relatively dense; but everywhere else it is sporadic and sparse and indeed, as we shall see elsewhere, in part nomadic. The great majority of Persians are, however, village-dwelling agriculturists, primitive and conservative in method, poor and lowly in living standards. Animals—sheep, goats and cattle—producing meat, hides, wool and hair, cheese and butter, and manure for gardens are the wealth of the transhumant grazing-tribes and of many villagers, and contribute something to exports. Cottage industry is still extensive; it includes silk-weaving, embroidery, metal-working and wood-carving, as well as carpet-making. Both industry (of which more will be said later, p. 247ff.) and mining, although still relatively small contributors to national income and occupation, have expanded rapidly in the 1960's, together growing at a rate of 10 per cent annually. This is partially due to the state's promising mineral wealth, only now being fully uncovered: both iron and coal exist and are being worked, lead, chromite and red oxide are being exported, and other deposits now under exploitation are bauxite, copper, manganese, zinc, silica, and barite. Persia's vast petroleum resources are mentioned elsewhere (p. 254f.).

The forests of the territory—40,000,000 acres are so classified, though much of this is of low quality—have some importance, and produce useful quantities of walnut, maple, beech, box and oak. The usual pests of oriental (perhaps of any) forests have been operative for centuries in the form of goats, fire and wood-cutters; but with American aid good work has been done in recent years towards rehabilitation and a competent Forest Service. Forest lands were nationalized in 1963 to insure conservation and planned exploitation. Fisheries in the Persian Gulf add considerably to the local diet but fish are not a significant Persian export, other than the famous caviar of the Caspian, no longer under concession to the USSR but now controlled by a state-sponsored monopoly.

The construction and maintenance of an adequate communication system, in a territory on this scale and with all its land-surface problems, is a task far exceeding the capacity of the Persian treasury. Roads, of which limited stretches are admirable, are more generally indifferent or poor and, being used by very limited motor-traffic, are disproportionately costly to maintain. Although current plans call for one-quarter of the development budget to be devoted to communications, the creation of a first-class system in the near future is scarcely imaginable, however indispensable to the development of the country. In 1965, Persia had only 3,100 miles of surfaced road; in rural areas, animal pack-transport is still the norm. Railway lines, dating only from the 1930's or later, now run from the head of the Gulf at Bandar Shahpur (and also from Khorramshahr, the lines joining at Ahwaz) to Teheran, *via* Dizful and Qum; from Teheran to Qazvin, Zanjan and Tabriz—with a branch line to Lake Urmia—and the U.S.S.R. frontier at Julfa; from Teheran to the Caspian at Bandar Shah and on to Gurgan, and also eastwards to Shahrud and Meshhed; and a line from Qum to Kashan. Railway construction in the 1960s has concentrated rather on grandiose intercontinental projects aimed at linking Persia with Turkey to the west (a line to Tatvan on Lake Van was opened in 1964) and Pakistan on the east; a monumental track from Kashan via Yezd to Zahidan in the extreme south-east is now under construction. But the whole of this system leaves, it is obvious, a great part of Persia with no railway communications, and little prospect of any.

The territory can boast no single reliable deep-water harbour, and its shipping is thereby greatly embarrassed. On the Caspian the small ports are in constant danger, or in actual process, of silting or sanding up, and only Bandar Shah has any considerable (nearly all Russian) traffic; on the Gulf, Abadan and Kharg Island are solely, and the fresh-waterless Bandar Mashhur mainly, devoted to oil export; Bushire and Bandar 'Abbas, open roadsteads, have difficult interior communications; Khorramshahr, far up the Shatt al 'Arab (a waterway wholly 'Iraqi-controlled), is small and ill-equipped. Apart from the Shatt, the middle and lower reaches of the Karun offer the only river-navigation in Persian territory, and have been so used (under originally British initiative) for a century; transhipment at Ahwaz is necessary. Tug and barge traffic plies across Lake Urmia.

Persia is linked to Europe and the middle and further East by a number of foreign airlines using Teheran airport, which was completed in 1958. The other largest cities each have its own adequate landing-ground, for military and civil use. All internal civilian flights are the monopoly of the government-controlled Iran National Airlines.

The Persian unit of currency is the rial, with parity of 75·75 rials to one dollar, or 182 to the £ sterling: these rates are subject to modification in market transactions. The metric system is employed throughout the country, though older and indigenous measures are widely used in country districts. The Persian official year is solar, New Year's Day being 21st March.

## 2. *Turkey*

The Turkish Republic extends to an area of almost 300,000 square miles, of which some 9,000 are in Europe, across the Bosphorus, Sea of Marmara and Dardanelles, and 290,000 in Asia. Excluding its European remnant, the country forms a rough quadrilateral; its east-west length is 950 miles, and north-south varies between 300 and 400. In Europe, its neighbours are Bulgaria and Greece; in Asia its northern, western and (in part) southern boundary is formed by the Black, Marmara, Aegean and Mediterranean seas (excluding, however, almost all the Aegean islands, which are Greek), its southeastern by the republics of Syria and 'Iraq, its eastern by the kingdom of Persia and the Armenian and Georgian republics of the U.S.S.R. None of these boundaries, except the sea, correspond with any geographical realities; those on the east and south-east are drawn across wild mountainous country.

Eastern Turkey is a tangle of high ranges, barren and sometimes lava-covered uplands, towering volcanic cones which include Ararat (16,910 feet), a great lake (Van), and deep valleys with drainage which provides the sources of the Euphrates, Tigris and Aras. The population here is scanty, vegetation limited, communications difficult. To the south and south-west of this region lies another, entirely different in type; it is the northern extension of the north-Arabian Fertile Crescent, consisting of treeless, open, flattish or undulating lands, at far lower altitudes than the mountain zone but higher than the Syrian desert across the border. In this area of fair grazing and spacious rain-cultivation lie the cities of Gaziantep ('Aintab), Urfa, Diyarbakr, Mardin; in the high mountain zone are those of Malatya, Elâziğ (Mamuret al-'Aziz), Erzurum, Erzincan, Kars, Van and Bitlis.

The central plateau of Turkey is largely barren, with a low population outside the cities and with cultivation confined to favoured, largely riverain areas. The region is ringed on the south, north and east by mountains, and has itself an average altitude of 3,000 to 5,000 feet; in some of its higher districts it is elevated to 6,000 to 8,000 feet with isolated peaks, or volcanic cones, ranging up to 12,000. The landscape is diversified by a number of salt lakes, mudflats and marshes, but elsewhere is drained by the considerable rivers which flow into the Black Sea—the Kizil Irmak, Yesil Irmak, and Sekariya. The main cities of this area are Eskişehir, Kutahya, Afyonkarahisar, Ankara, Çorum, Tokat, Sivas, Kayseri (Caesarea), Niğde, Konya, Karaman. On the north side of this region, and stretching west-east in a 20- to 40-mile strip inland of the whole Black Sea coast, is a broken mountain region barring the way to the central plateau to the south, and falling sharply to the sea on its northern face, leaving little room, except in limited areas, for a coastal plain. The mountains, which combine with the sea and the rich rain-fed vegetation to give delightful scenery, grow higher to the east, beyond Trabzon. Besides the major rivers which, having drained central Turkey, break through northward to the sea, there are a number of short, torrential streams falling in the same direction. Turkey has no navigable river. Coastal cities, on the Black Sea—containing, however, no good natural harbour—are Zonguldak, Inebolu, Sinop (Sinope), Samsun, Ordu, Giresun, Trabzon (Trebizond), Rize. Inland of the coastal ranges lie some comparatively lowland areas. The whole region is one of continuing, sometimes alarming, volcanic activity.

Turkey's southern, Mediterranean coastal region and its hinterland are divided from central Turkey by the wide, lofty and imposing mountain system of the Taurus, the irregular folding of which has determined the configuration of the coast. To the north of the ranges occur lakes and salt-marshes; in their midst, a broken desolate area of extreme isolation: and to the south, coastal districts even more isolated, but containing two considerable plains. The western of these is that of Antalya, which remains incompletely developed by reason of malaria and bad communications; the eastern is the Cilician plain, famed for its fertility and containing the major cities of Mersin, Tarsus and Adana. The plain represents the alluvial deposits brought through the Taurus by the rivers Çakit, Seyhan and Ceyhan. The last area of Turkey to be reviewed is that of the coastlands of the Aegean and Marmara. These provide the most favoured region of the republic, both in Europe and Asia; the area includes the Aegean hinterland along the course of the westward-running rivers—the Simav, Gediz, Menderes (Meander) and Daraman—as well as the broken, deeply indented coastline itself, and the broad flattish basin on both sides of the Sea of Marmara. This region contains a high proportion of the Turkish people, living in admirable climatic and other natural conditions in proximity to some of the most famous cities and beautiful and historic seascapes in the world. The role of this district in human history, from remote antiquity onwards, is well known, and not less its function as a direct gateway from the west into Asia Minor and beyond. Its famous cities are those of Istanbul, Edirne (Adrianople), Kirklareli (Kirk Kilisseh) and Tekirdaǧ (Rodosto) in Europe, and, in Asia, Adapazari, Ismit, Iznik (Nicaea), Bursa (Brusa), Balikesir, Akhisar, Izmir (Smyrna), Aydin, Denizli, Muǧla.

The climate of Anatolia is as various as its land-surface, with extraordinary variations of heat and cold between districts as well as between seasons; in parts of the central plateau the summer temperature can be over 100 degrees Faht., the winter — 15 degrees, and the rainfall can vary from 100 inches a year at the eastern end of the Black Sea coast, to 10 inches or less in some interior districts. The western and south-western coastal regions enjoy a perfect Mediterranean climate, with mild wet winters and hot summers. In the Marmara lowlands, conditions resemble those of Great Britain, especially in its rapidly changing weather. From all the above it will appear that almost any natural condition desired or dreaded by man can be found in Turkey, and almost every form of response thereto has been adopted by the varying ways in which life is lived, from Kurdish semi-nomadism to intensive fruit-growing, from extensive sheep-farming to the close area of tea or tobacco gardens.

Agriculture apart (p. 238)—and this in Turkey is extraordinarily varied—the natural resources of Asia Minor are considerable. Its mineral wealth, exploited in remote antiquity in the forms of gold, copper and iron, is the most considerable in the Middle East; if its development to some extent lags behind, this is by reason of the low grade or limited scale of most deposits, their scattered locations and difficulty of access, and the lack of available risk-capital to exploit them. The state plays the dominant role in mining activities through its Institute of Mining Research and its Etibank, whose subsidiaries control the country's major coal, copper, lead, sulphur, and chromite mines. The Zonguldak region on the Black Sea coast is Turkey's most important coal-producing area, although recent discoveries of large reserves have been made in the Elbistan region in eastern Turkey; coal is of course a major asset to industry, and up to 8,000,000 tons a year are produced. Deposits of iron ore are widely spread in the country, but exploitation is no more than partial owing to difficulties of transport and treatment. The major fields are at Divriği between Sivas and Erzurum, near Gaziantep in the south-east, and the Camdağ mines conveniently located near the coal of Zonguldak. Over 1,500,000 tons of iron ore were produced in 1967. Chrome has long been an important Turkish resource, and its exploitation of this mineral is reckoned as the second greatest in the world; it is found chiefly in western Anatolia and the Lake Van region in the distant east. Lignite occurs at many locations and on a commercial scale, the country's copper needs are met by domestic production and a useful export of that mineral is made, and lead and zinc are both found at widely scattered locations. Turkey enjoys a world monopoly of meerschaum clay (found on the plateau near Eskişehir). A variety of lesser minerals which diversify, without as yet greatly enriching, production, are known to exist in Turkey— alum, antimony, asbestos, manganese, mercury, sulphur, wolfram and emery. The last-named, found on the island of Naxos, gives an exportable surplus, as do antimony, boracite and manganese. The wolfram deposits have increasing importance. Production of minerals has, on the whole, increased encouragingly, and the search for more is being vigorously pressed. Petroleum (p. 253/4) is disappointingly scarce.

The forests of Turkey are the most extensive in the Middle East, and all, since 1937, government-controlled. They are found at different levels and in different conditions in many parts of the country, and cover an eighth of the surface of Turkey. Most are of low quality and meagre yield. A modern forestry administration has (at least on paper) been installed, and efforts, which should not be viewed with excessive optimism, are made to limit the progressive deterioration which has been continuous in the past through unauthorized cutting, charcoal-burning, fire, neglect—and goats. Some new planting is in hand. The annual value of forest output is low but not negligible.

Fishing is an activity of little economic importance, though practised in some degree in all seaside areas. Some recent development has taken place, with American aid. There is a limited export of fish, but not as great as the country's coastal waters warrant.

The plateau of Anatolia affords a home and livelihood to the millions of livestock which are among Turkey's riches, and their immediate contribution in milk, butter and meat is a main support of hundreds of villages, even though modern forms of dairy-farming are little adopted; and is the whole-time concern of (a seeming anachronism in modern Turkey) the Yuruk (nomadic) herdsmen who move seasonally between higher and lower pastures. Draught-animals have still a high place in local agriculture and village transport. The export of hides and skins, wool and mohair, is valuable. The Anatolian wool is of coarse quality, though exported on a major scale; the silky hair of the famous 'Angora' goat, on the other hand, is highly prized and indeed unique. Water buffaloes are kept, for transport and ploughing and their milk, mostly on the Black Sea coast.

Turkey is divided into sixty-seven Ils or provinces, subdivided into districts and cantons (the latter having elective councils). The largest city is Istanbul (population, according to the 1965 census, (1,750,000); next come the capital Ankara (900,000), Izmir (415,000), Adana (290,000), Bursa (210,000), Eskisehir (175,000), Gaziantep (158,000), Konya (155,000), Kayseri (125,000) and almost a score more with populations over 50,000. Yet only one-quarter of the Turks are city-dwellers, three-quarters being countrymen. The population of the Republic is now near 33,000,000; of these some 3,000,000 live in European Turkey, the remainder in Asia. Population has grown rapidly in the past generation; in 1927 it was less than 14,000,000. It has increased by an annual proportion varying between 2·3 and 3·0 per cent per year since then. Turkish resources, underdeveloped as they now are, could doubtless support a larger than present population. Thanks to the long continuous Turkish occupation of Anatolia, their tradition of conquest and government, their religion, their policy of assimilation (aided at times by the expulsion or massacre of minorities) the present population is unusually homogeneous, not indeed in racial origins but in sentiment. A large proportion of the 2,000,000 Kurds in the eastern provinces is by now largely assimilated as Turks; the same may apply to the 30,000 recently immigrant Bulgarians, and to the 25,000 Lazes and 90,000 Circassians. It is probably less true of the 350,000 Arabs (all in the Mardin-Urfa area), and untrue of the surviving Jews, roughly 50,000 in number, or the Greeks and Armenians in two or three main cities of the west. Not much more than 1 per cent of the population is non-Muslim, though a fair proportion, possibly one in six, are believed to be non-Sunni but to follow instead some semi-heretical Shi'i persuasion within Islam (p. 94). A proportion of the Arabs above-mentioned belong to the Christian sects of the Chaldaean, Syrian and Greek Uniates, and the Armenian Orthodox, but the numbers of each community are uncertain. Islam, no longer officially the State religion, is nevertheless widely revered and practised; the more old-fashioned Turk, in particular, is to all appearances a model Muslim. All races and creeds alike are treated, it is claimed, with impartiality by the government, though in practice certain discriminations (and, *vis-à-vis* the Greeks, a still powerful antipathy) continue to be observed.

The size of the country and the difficult terrain of tangled and passless mountain tracts, added to the prevailing (including governmental) poverty, render an efficient system of communications difficult to achieve, even though this is acknowledged as indispensable for social and economic reasons and to remedy the isolation in which live a high proportion of Turkish villagers, notably in the south-west, the extreme east, and the Black Sea littoral. The road system has, accordingly, been greatly extended and improved during the last generation, in part with American aid; there are now at least 20,000 miles (part macadam, part graded earth) of national highways, as much again of fair provincial roads, and an uncertain length of passable tracks. The country is now spanned by the CENTO-sponsored 'Asian Highway' which provides an all-weather route from Europe to Persia. Buses, fixed-route taxis and innumerable ox-carts are all constant road-users in addition to trucks and passenger cars. Railways, inadequate a generation ago, have been similarly developed with a view both to economics and to strategy, including internal security. They are since 1947 all state-owned, and give generally a reliable service. Much of the country is still, and will no doubt long remain, without railways by reason of the immense difficulty and cost of construction, and the unrewarding traffic; but most of the chief cities of the interior now enjoy railway communication, and this extends also to the east, to Erzurum, Tatvan on Lake Van, and beyond to Persia; eastwards also from Diyarbakr to Si'irt; and northward to the Black Sea at Zonguldak and Samsun. Other new lines have been built in central and western Anatolia. Turkey now has over 5,000 miles of railway, much of which has been, or is being, double-tracked. But it cannot be pretended that the combined road and railway system, improved as it has been at great cost, gives Turkey anything like an adequate communications system.

Partly for this reason, the country's merchant navy has, in recent years, been fostered and much increased. Total tonnage, all state-owned through the State Seaways Administration, now exceeds 1,500,000 tons, and a total of some 3,000 vessels. These have a monopoly of the coastwise trade (in many areas the sole link with the outside), and a respectable share of Mediterranean and Aegean traffic. The chief ports besides Istanbul—by far the greatest, and now under further development on the Asiatic side—are Izmir, where new installations have been added, Zonguldak, Samsun, Trabzon, Eregli, Mersin and Iskanderun. New harbours have been built at Hopa on the Black Sea, Bandirma on the Marmora, and Antalya on the Mediterranean. Turkish State Airlines (the T.H.A.O.) includes participants both domestic and foreign, and gives an excellent internal service. The main airports are those of Istanbul and Ankara, but twenty more are in use. Turkey is served, internationally, by the scheduled services of a dozen foreign (European, American and Middle Eastern) airlines, with agencies and facilities at Istanbul and Ankara.

The Turkish pound stands at £T 21·79 to the £ sterling (or 9·08 to the dollar). The money in circulation, apart from nickel and silver, consists of Central Bank notes. The metric system of weights and measures is in force, since 1934. The Gregorian Calendar, replacing both that of Islam and that of the half-westernized Ottoman compromise, was adopted in 1925.

## 3. Cyprus

Cyprus is a territory markedly differing from any other in the Middle East by its racial content, its history and its current politico-social problems, and by being an island—the third largest in the Mediterranean. It lies some 250 miles from the Egyptian, 70 from the Syrian, 40 from the Turkish coasts. The area of the island is 3,570 square miles, its greatest length 140 miles, its greatest width 60, the average width (excluding the narrow eastern extension) about 40.

The dominant physical features of the country are at once obvious:

a sharply defined ridge of hills, rising to 3,000 feet and reaching from west of Kyrenia to the north-eastern tip: a mountain massif, that of Mount Troodos (6,400 feet), in the west-centre of the island; and a flat plain, the Mesaoria, lying between these two and open to the sea on its west and east flanks. Both the coast and the mountain area, which is heavily forested, are of great beauty. The territory is full of picturesque medieval and modern buildings, and of ancient Greek and Roman remains. The climate is of normal Mediterranean type, with a hot summer in the plain and a mild winter, and liability to frost and snow above the 3,000-foot line. The rainfall can be as much as 40 inches a year on the higher ground, but as low as 10 inches in the Mesaoria plain. The drainage of rain from the slopes, and even that of melting snow, is so rapid that no rivers exist other than short-lived torrents. Conditions on the island, despite its smallness, are remarkably varied, and nowhere disagreeable.

Apart from agriculture (p. 241), which is here obviously limited by the chronic dryness of the agricultural lands and their restricted acreage, and a few light industries on a humble scale, the resources of Cyprus are not impressive. The tourist trade is valuable. Supply to, and employment by, the British forces in their detached enclave are assets; so also is the country's central position as an air-travel halt and junction. The Cypriot forest, on and all around Mount Troodos, covers nearly one-fifth of the island (or 670 square miles) and, besides its uncommon beauty, can supply nearly half the local needs in timber. The utmost care is taken to minimize the dangers and evils of fire, goats and marauders. Neither fishing nor animal-herding and breeding are of more than parochial importance. Mineral exploitation has been a main source of the island's wealth. Exports of cuprcous pyrites, cupreous concentrates and iron pyrites each amount to millions of pounds annually, and gypsum, chrome, umber and asbestos are of lesser—but some—value. But the island's mineral reserves are gradually being depleted, and the place of mining in the economy is declining in the 1960s; thus the share of minerals in total exports has decreased from over one-half in the 1950s to 37 per cent in the mid-1960s, and the number of people employed in mining has dropped from 6,000 to 5,000.

The population of Cyprus was in 1968 estimated at 625,000, as against less than 200,000 in 1878; it is increasing by about 10,000 a year. About one-third of the people are town-dwellers, the remainder live in the Greek or Turkish or mixed villages, with a humble but by no means miserable standard of life. There is a steady movement from the countryside to the towns. Among the latter, each the head-quarters of one of the six provinces, are Nicosia, the capital, with a population of 106,000, Limassol (48,000), Famagusta (40,000), Lanarca (21,000), Paphos (11,000), Kyrenia (4,000). These populations include small minorities of Maronites, Armenians and other Christian sects, and a few hundred European foreigners. They include also the considerable Turkish minority, one-fifth of the whole, of which we spoke on an earlier page (p. 113).

The bulk, approximately four-fifths, of the people claim, as is well known, to be Greek. It is true that no Greek territory lies nearer than 250 miles away, across the sea; that Cyprus has never, throughout history, been under Greek mainland rule; and that the Cypriot dialect differs appreciably from mainland Greek. Nevertheless, their own Greek culture, speech, sentiment and nostalgia combine to make unrealistic any claim that the islanders are 'not really Greeks,' and as such they must without question be considered. They are, of course, Greek Orthodox in religion, with their own auto-cephalous Church of Cyprus: their Archibishop having been, since August 1960, the first President of the Republic. Many members of both the major communities speak each other's language, and English is widely understood in the towns.

As to communications, the island's road system is greatly improved and now fairly, though not wholly, adequate to the demands made upon it by the growing motor-traffic. The number of road accidents, reported to be abnormal, is probably due to recklessness of drivers rather than to the roads, of which over 1,300 miles with hard surface exist, and some 2,700 without; these are impassable on very few days in the year. Nicosia has an equipped airport, used by one locally-based company, and a dozen more belonging to Middle Eastern states or to countries of Europe. Air transport benefits by the poorness of Cypriot harbours, of which not one is adequate to modern needs. Limassol and Larnaca are open roadsteads with no protection from the weather, and the use of lighters is a necessity; the quay at Famagusta, the island's main port, can accommodate only vessels of shallow draught and moderate length, larger ships having to anchor in the outer harbour. Greek, Italian and Israeli shipping lines provide regular passenger service, and others, including British, serve cargo requirements by at least weekly calls.

The Cyprus pound equals £1 sterling ($2·40 US) and subdivides into 1,000 mils. British weights and measures, those of the metric system, and older indigenous or Turkish units are all in use.

## 4. Israel

The area of the State of Israel—excluding the 26,000 square miles of Egyptian, Jordanian and Syrian territory occupied in 1967, whose ultimate disposal is at present an unanswered problem—is some 8,000 square miles. The territory is less extensive than the Palestine of the British Mandate, but larger by about one-quarter than the area allotted to the Jews by the United Nations proposals of 1947. The deviations from mandated Palestine are 150 square miles on the Mediterranean coast beyond Gaza—the 'Gaza Strip'—and some 2,200 square miles of Samaritan and Judaean highland in central-eastern Palestine. Israel thus defined consists, in effect, of the fertile coastal plain of the mandated territory; of the foothills west of the central range, and part of that range itself; of the flat, rich vale between Mount Carmel and the Jordan, the vale of Esdraelon (or Emek Yezreel): the historic district of Galilee, which includes the plain of Acre ('Akka), an area of broken hill-country, the descent to the Jordan, and the lakes of Hula (now drained) and Tiberias. Besides these, Israel includes a wedge-shaped corridor leading to Jerusalem, the western portion of that city—the annexation by Israel of the eastern part in 1967 being unrecognized by the world—and almost all of the southern desert of Palestine, bounded by the Sinai wilderness to the west and the Wadi 'Araba to the east; this, the Negev, gives Israel half of its total area. These two boundaries, converging on the Gulf of 'Aqaba, leave to Israel, as its priceless southern sea-outlet, a gap of some 8 miles on its shores. In terms of neighbours, the Republic is bounded on the north by Lebanon; on the north-east by Syria; on the east and south-east by Jordan, all the way to the Gulf of 'Aqaba; on the south-west by Egypt; and on the west by the Mediterranean. None of Israel's boundaries has been confirmed by international agreement; from 1949 to 1967 they were only provisionally fixed by armistice between Israel and her neighbours, while since 1967 and that year's expansion of the territory under Israeli control they have been precariously governed by cease-fire agreements.

Climatically, Israel is a typically Mediterranean country, with warm or hot summers and mild, rainy winters. The low-lying areas toward Jordan, and even more the Valley itself, can offer summer temperatures of over 100° F, and a high humidity. Snow is uncommon in the lowlands, not infrequent though rarely heavy in Jerusalem, and a regular feature of winter, to considerable depths.

in the hills of Galilee. This latter area has an annual rainfall of 40 inches or more, which decreases southward, by stages, until in the Negev and along the coast below Gaza it drops to 8 or 5 inches or less. Prevailing winds are south-westerly. On the whole, the temperate, sunny and delightful climate of Israel is among its uncontroversial assets.

The composition of the population, which was 90 per cent Arab in 1919, and between 60 and 70 per cent in 1940, underwent a total change in the year 1948 and thereafter; the great majority of the Arab population departed (for reasons elsewhere described, p. 137 f.) from the main part of Palestine which was thenceforward to be Israel, and the numbers of immigrant Jews rapidly and vastly increased: a process authorized and encouraged by the policy, or indeed the *raison d'être*, of the new state, which offered an unquestioning welcome to any Jew in the world who wished to enter. The population of the territory, in which about 200,000 Arabs and Druzes remained, rose rapidly; by early 1967 it had reached 2,650,000, of whom 2,340,000 were Jews, 223,000 Arab Muslims, 58,000 Arab Christians (mainly Catholic and Uniate), and 31,000 Druzes. The Arab minority in Israel, while sharing in the economic and social benefits afforded by this most modern of Middle Eastern states, were for long subject to various restrictions and suffered a community isolation separating them from the mainstream of either Israeli or Arab life. The conquest of densely-populated Arab areas in 1967 placed an additional million Arabs under Israeli rule, raising the spectre of an eventual Arab majority in a Jewish state should these areas be permanently kept by a new, 'greater', Israel.

The formidable immigration of Jews was the dominant feature not only of the demography but of the entire public scene in Israel in its first two decades. The immigrants, qualified or unqualified to start new lives, with every variety of capacity or helplessness, every age and background, came predominantly from Europe in the earliest years following mid-1948: from Hungary, Austria, Poland, Germany and the Balkan countires, with a few from southern, very few from western, Europe and fewer from America. From 1950 onwards began the flood of immigrants from eastern and African countries, whose situation there had deteriorated, to the point of unbearability, thanks to Muslim resentment. Scores of thousands came, accordingly, from the Yemen and Aden, from 'Iraq, Persia and Turkey, from Egypt and north-west Africa, from Ethiopia, Afghanistan, Turkistan and China. In the twelve years following 1948 the proportion between

European and eastern or African Jews entering Israel seems to have been approximately 46·5 per cent of the former, 53·5 of the latter. There is little need to emphasize the immense range of human types involved, from blond Nordics and Slavs to Berbers, Mongolians, Indians and black Africans; yet all were Jews, all became—and, with allowance for emigration, nine-tenths remained—Israeli citizens. So much, an observer might ruminate, for the ever-repeated assertion that Jewry is a 'race'! The predominance of oriental immigrants (one of numbers, not at all of wealth, skill, culture or standard of life) will doubtless in future years be emphasized by their more rapid rate of increase, and cannot but exercise a heavy influence on the future of Israel.

No task of the young State has been more arduous, nor more essential, than the assimilation and settlement of the immigrant masses whom, in a high percentage of cases, fear and poverty and misery, rather than suitability, had selected. They have been received, fed, housed, set to work, instructed, directed and redirected until somehow and in some occupation the point of 'settlement' has been reached. The techniques for this series of co-ordinated processes, always with emphasis (partly practical, partly doctrinaire) on the *land* and on manual labour, have been constantly improved, and have no doubt gone far to create, out of amazingly disparate material, a feeling of single nationhood and of willingness to face Israel's appalling problems.

The dominant language of the country is a revived and simplified Hebrew, which is taught to all immigrants and has become the *lingua franca* as well as the official language (jointly with Arabic) of the state. This decision, involving the subordination of the languages actually spoken by the multifarious incomers (Ladino, many forms of Yiddish, and almost every major language of Europe and Asia), has made assimilation and absorbtion more immediately difficult for the novice, but has also, on a larger view, made possible a measure of homogeneity and nation-wide communication as no other solution could have done. Arabic is spoken by the Arabs and Druzes, and is known to older Jewish residents. English is the most usually heard of European languages, though English-speaking immigrants have not in recent years exceeded 1 per cent.

Meanwhile, the face of the country has been changed. Not only has a new, alien population, from the four corners of the earth, replaced the former age-long dwellers in that familiar and delightful countryside, but new settlements or villages, some temporary, some permanent, have been sited and sprung up in many hundreds, existing cities have increased in size two or six or tenfold; examples are Tel Aviv with Jaffa (in 1967 390,000 strong, and almost all Jewish), Haifa (increased from 120,000 to 220,000), the portion of Jerusalem acknowledged as Israeli (196,000), Beersheba (from 2,000 to 65,000), and a number more grown to the 25,000–50,000 range. Entirely new cities have been founded in Galilee, in the Negev, and on the Gulf of 'Aqaba. In spite of the ambition, and the economic necessity, to work the land and grow food, the Israeli population in 1967 was estimated to be over three-quarters urban, less than one-quarter rural. Agriculture has, nonetheless, a high priority among the employments to which the young of both sexes are channeled during their period of national service.

Israelis settled on the land have adopted, or have conformed to, forms of social organization peculiar to the country, and representative of its strongly socialist climate. Life in the famous Kibbutzim is entirely collective, with private property forbidden and all family life restricted; in the villages of more normal type private property and personal responsibility are allowed. In 1967, out of 801 rural settlements, 232 were Kibbutzim, with 82,000 settlers; a greater number lived under one of the less exacting régimes. Arab villages numbered about 100.

More will be said on later pages of Israeli efforts in the fields of agriculture and irrigation (p. 242 f.) and of industry (p. 247 ff.). In both, the scene in recent years has been one of phenomenal activity. This has been based in equal parts on scientific direction and planning, on the devoted labour of all concerned, and on the provision of capital. The latter has come from three sources: one, the now vanished Arab population (in the form of lands, citrus-groves, gardens, wells, houses, public buildings and installations); secondly, from international and foreign national agencies: and thirdly, and most notably, from the government of the United States and the immensely wealthy and influential Jewish public in that country, upon whose abundant contributions rests, in simple fact, the viability of the State of Israel.

The natural resources of the country are scanty. Its minerals, the search for which has been vigorously pressed, include some iron ore in Galilee and the Negev and, mainly in the latter, copper (near Eilat), manganese, mica, gypsum, phosphates, salt, silica, and china clay. Excepting phosphates (now a major export), the above amount to very little at present; but the extraction of potash, bromine and

magnesium salts from the Dead Sea is a major enterprise—its installations have been resited since 1948—and it produces both valuable
raw materials for the chemical industry and useful exports. There
is no scope in Israel for extensive animal husbandry, but cattle are
raised intensively for meat and for dairy produce. Fishing on commercial lines is practised off the Mediterranean coast and in the
Gulf of 'Aqaba by a fleet of trawlers and other craft; the Sea of
Galilee is actively fished, and the breeding of carp in ponds in many
of the agricultural settlements is a developing industry. Forests, a
feature of the Palestinian landscape in antiquity, are today represented by some medium-scale but increasing modern plantations.

Israeli territory being small and unobstructed, an adequate system
of communications, mainly inherited from the mandatory government, presents serious difficulty only in the partly untrodden, sandblown Negev, and sometimes also in providing access to the remoter
new settlements. New main roads have been constructed, or old
tracks improved, in connection with the port of Eilat and the potash-
extraction installations, and to link Tel Aviv better with Jerusalem.
Road traffic is everywhere dense. The railways, maintained and improved, remain substantially as they were designed under the Mandate; that is, the coastal railway from the Egyptian to the Lebanese
frontier: the Tel Aviv–Jerusalem line: and the Esdraelon line from
Haifa through 'Afula to the Jordan Valley. More recent lines join
Lydda to Beersheba and Beersheba with Dimona to the south; the
latter line is being extended to the phosphate deposits at Oron in the
Negev, and plans call for the line's ultimate terminus to be Eilat. The
relations between Israel and her neighbours preclude any trans-
frontier communication, by rail or otherwise. Of the country's
seaports, Haifa was until recently the best equipped and the busiest;
a well-found modern harbour, it serves the country's north. The
poor and unnatural, but once necessary, port at Jaffa-Tel Aviv was
closed in 1965, its place being taken by the new deep-water harbour
at Ashdod further south, which, with all its equipment, can be
expected to handle an eventual 4,000,000 tons annually. Eilat,
Israel's invaluable outlet to the East, is being developed as rapidly
as possible; its traffic includes Israel's vital oil imports, piped from
it to Haifa for refining. In 1965 a supplementary facility on the Gulf
north of Eilat port was opened. Israel's merchant marine now
includes tankers, dry cargo vessels and passenger ships to a total of
nearly 100 vessels, with some 700,000 tons displacement. This is a
needed resource to a country whose land frontiers are blockaded and

47. Cairo: the new Corniche road

48. Archimedes' screw: primitive water-lift on the Nile banks

49. Egypt: a village market at Bardis, near Baliana

50. Railway construction: Central Sudan

51. Village agricultural show, Sudan: dancers and drums

52. Cotton growers, Gezira

53. Ferry across the Blue Nile, Khartum

whose needs of import and export are paramount. In the field of aviation, the country's main centre is at Lydda, with lesser fields at Tel Aviv, Eilat, and Jerusalem. Two local airlines exist, the largest (El Al) having major international scope. Many non-Middle Eastern carriers call at Lydda.

The metric system is used in Israel; for land-measurement the Donum, of 1,000 square metres (a quarter of an acre), is the unit. The Jewish year 5729 begins on September 13, 1969. The unit of currency is the Israeli pound (I£), for which the rate of exchange is I£8·40 to the £ sterling (or I£3·50 to the US dollar).

# CHAPTER EIGHT

# PUBLIC LIFE

## 1. *The Disunited States*

FOR the devotion of a chapter to governments and politics, in a work on 'social geography', there is more justification in the Middle East than could be pleaded in, for instance, a West-European or North-American area, since in these an interest in government and politics is for most people swamped by a score of others—business, social or sporting—and the visible effects of government action or inaction are less conspicuous. In the lands of the Middle East, on the other hand, 'the Government' is all-important, politics are the dominant concern for a large, and the most dynamic, part of the population. The State is the most pervasive of influences, the greastest and often the only repository of important capital, the initiator and controller in industry, communications and agriculture. It is the agency, far more than any form of private enterprise, responsible for creating the new conditions of life which have profoundly modified the ways of urban society. It is the sole provider of super-community and super-tribal authority, greatest direct employer of labour, possessor and bestower of the highest prestige. It is inevitably, therefore, from many angles a significant social factor. Moreover in every country, even Arabia, the servants of the government, the civil service in its every grade, form a highly important body, a numerous, characteristic, and privileged class. It is true that the transition from the low standard of nineteenth-century conditions in the Ottoman Empire, Persia and Egypt, to those of a more active, better trained, more honest official class, is as yet far from complete; there are still, almost everywhere, too many civil servants, too generally ill-paid, extremely diverse in type and merit—from over-meticulous to haphazard, from deeply entrenched veterans to the new and callow, from more than doubtfully to rigidly honest, from arrogant to democratic—and often infused with overdoses of political fervour or departmental narrowness. But the elements of scandal or comedy, or even farce, frequent enough in the Serais or police-barracks of Ottoman times, are by degrees disappearing; genuine service to the public is becoming a less unfamiliar concept, and a national is superseding a merely bureaucratic pride. Indeed, the *effendis* of today and tomorrow mark a vast advance on those of yesterday, and now form a generally creditable as well as an important social element; much goodwill and more competence are available in the civil services, and directors and ministers of excellent ability are far from uncommon. Indeed, the adverse factors which persist are generally those implicit in the backward, heterogeneous publics, in military interventions in civil government, and in the aberrations of dictators, rather than in the shortcomings of officialdom.

As to the shape of government itself, our survey of Middle Eastern populations may have suggested doubts about the applicability of the nation-state form of grouping to a region in which languages, races and minorities are spread so sporadically across the map; but could this be otherwise? To the sovereign-nation system there appears, in the modern world, no alternative; in the Near East the example of one self-conscious Balkan fragment after another breaking off from the Ottoman Empire long ago established precedents which the present Arab states—but, to their chagrin, never the Kurds, and never the Armenians—have been successful in following; and the similar record of imperial disintegration, or imperial policy, in favour of small independent states is, of course, plain to see in Africa, Asia and elsewhere in the mid-twentieth century. Moreover, in the possession of the recognized qualifications for nation-state rank, which are common territory, history, tradition, language, outlook, and sense of mutual belonging, or most of these, the modern Middle Eastern states, thanks in part to their long if often unedifying experience of politico-administrative forms and provincial delimitations under the Ottoman monarchy, do not fall short to anything like the same extent as do the new states of Africa; most of them can make a fair or strong case for national status, and all have successfully done so. That the secular nation-state conception is far removed from the original Islamic principle of a single religious-political community of all Muslims everywhere must, of course, be recognized; but this creates no practical difficulty, and is remembered only by the most conservative and pietistic elements in the states concerned.

Meanwhile among the Middle Eastern nations, as they now exist, national spirit is conspicuously developed. Those governments and publics which have enjoyed national status for centuries—Turkey, Persia and (practically, though not wholly in form) the central- and south-Arabian States—continue to be vigilant that no affront to, or

implied diminution of, their independence be sustained; and this is
even more the case among the nations 'liberated' to enjoyment of that
privilege since the First War—the ex-Ottoman Arab States, with
Egypt, the Sudan and Cyprus—in all of which their highly sensitive
nationalism places insistence on 'complete independence' as its
primary demand or pride. This, however, is not the only constituent
of this ever-quoted (and in Europe largely decried) nationalism which
is, and will for years remain, the strongest and most pervasive political
force in the region. It contains, indeed, its element of genuine, perhaps idealistic, patriotism, its nostalgia for what was best in a
glorious past, its resolve that the cherished State shall be not only free
but benevolent, an inspiration towards uplighting living-standards
and securing justice, and a visible negation of old inferiority com-
plexes implanted by centuries of subordination. Nevertheless, and
though few western nations are blameless in such regards, it must be
said that nationalism in its Middle Eastern forms, with its visible
elements of (often officially supported) xenophobia, chauvinism and
boasting, too often takes forms inimical to liberty and enlightenment
within these countries, and damaging to their prestige abroad: the
former from its narrowness, insistence on uniformity, and competitive inflammatory influence on rival politicians, the latter from its
malicious suspicion or rancour, and its easy adoption of bad international manners. It is, however, idle to expect the publics and
leaders of Middle Eastern states to progress beyond nationalism, or
even to purge it of its evident crudities, at a stage of their independent
development in which manifestations of egocentric jingoism are, it
seems, an inevitable phase of growth.

   In view of this prevalent, deeply felt territory-nationalism can
there be hopes of some form of multi-statal grouping—unity,
federation, or association—between our territories? an association
desirable, no doubt, on many grounds and perhaps made more
conceivable by the peculiarly haphazard distribution of races and
communities in the Middle East and, more positively, by the powerful
factors of much common history, of propinquity and constant intercommunication, of largely similar conditions, as between the various
states? Or can there truly be hopes, even, of the ever-proferred, ever-
elusive Arab Unity? It must be answered that, for anything wider
than the last-named possible grouping, there is no present hope whatsoever; Turkey, Israel, Cyprus, Persia—these are all far too distinct,
too self-consciously isolated by their own exclusive national feeling,
too suspicious of their neighbours, for any close link between them,

or between them and the Arab states, to be presently conceivable. The Arab states themselves, as we have seen (pp. 101–2), possess solid and lively factors of unity; and a political extension of this, they repeatedly tell us, such as to create a new world-force and reflect the single voice of the Arab people, with more power and unanimity than their disappointingly ill-knit and ineffective League of Arab States has ever done, is one of their most cherished aims. Then, why not?

The reasons, sadly convincing, are various but interconnected. The first and most basic is the existence of differing levels of social and educational evolution in the states concerned. Second is the power and narrowness of the local patriotisms which the education and policies of the past fifty years have exalted. Thirdly, one must observe the strength of vested interests—of royal houses, officialdom, the tribes, the minorities, the armies, the men of commerce and industry—which militate against any form of super-statal union which might, and in cases certainly would, adversely affect their personal and sectional interests. Fourthly, ideological cleavages in the Arab world, the absence of any consensus among 'reactionaries', 'moderates', and 'revolutionaries' on the basic form or principles of any new régime, are becoming wider with each passing year. Fifthly come the visible animosities between existing states—between 'Iraq and Syria, for instance, or Egypt and Jordan, or Sa'udi Arabia and most of her neighbours in the peninsula. When one adds to these factors the intensely individualistic strain of the Arab character, with its dislike of outside or any other authority, and the lurking doubts among many as to whether the task of managing the suggested super-national group (federal or federated or unitary) would not prove beyond the powers of any leadership at present available in the Arab world, the prospects for effective Arab unity must be regarded as dim. Certainly the record to date—the failure of the Egyptian-Syrian union of 1958–1961 and the current difficulties of the oil shaikhdoms of the Persian Gulf in agreeing on even the loosest of federations—points in the same direction, towards the unlikelihood of the achievement of Arab unity in the forseeable future.

## 2. *The Field of Government*

In peninsular Arabia, rulers are still convinced that *l'état c'est moi*, and their families—habitually numerous, often idle and extravagant— are insistent that this formula (than which they can conceive no other) includes themselves. In these principalities, therefore, except in so far as world-opinion (or the urgings of European advisers, if permitted) may have faintly penetrated, very different conceptions of the legitimate sphere of government are held from those of the modern world, including their sister Middle Eastern states to the north and west. It is the latter, and the activities of their more developed administrations, that we pass now to consider.

It is needless, unless for completeness, to mention that in every such state is found a body of Law; a body far removed from its purely Islamic predecessor (the Shari'a), even though it may still permit the use of the latter (except in Egypt and Turkey) for cases of personal status—marriage, divorce, alimony, guardianship. The modern and repeatedly revised law-codes in current use, civil and criminal, are based on French or British or Swiss or Italian originals, and on local latter-day statutes. To administer these, all the governments maintain, properly separated from their legislative or executive branches, normally adequate Courts of Law, local and central, at all levels of First Instance, Superior, Appeal and Cassation, as well as the religious or community Courts limited in their jurisdiction to affairs of personal status. These systems, supervised by a Minister of Justice, are for the most part comprehensive and respectable. They are presided over nowadays by judges and magistrates of modern education, graduates of their law-schools, who have (except in the Shari'a courts) superseded the *qadhis* of old. It may be said that, not without their frequent short-comings, sometimes humours, occasionally scandals, the codes and courts of Middle Eastern countries now present on the whole a far from discreditable picture, are conducted with dignity and integrity, and are supported by a general public opinion in these qualities. There has been, beyond question, an important rise in standard during the last half-century. Both bench and bar provide careers for many of the professionally educated members of the middle class, for whom, too often, employment is difficult to find; and it is no longer anywhere (unless in the tribunals of Arabia) a near-certainty that the rich litigant will win his case, and the well-connected criminal be acquitted.

Trained and armed forces capable under normal conditions of securing law and order, and apprehending the wrong-doer, are no less a matter of course. A more or less adequate Police and/or Gendarmerie is maintained, reasonably drilled and equipped—as were indeed, in their time, those of the Ottoman (but far less the Persian) power. In these forces, and the Prisons administrations which accompany them, there is today more goodwill and honesty, less oppression and corruption, than ever before. Behind these are supported, upon a great or small scale (and often absorbing a lamentably large share of the revenues of the state) regular military, naval and air forces, which range from the important formations of the Turkish Republic to the relatively petty units of Lebanon or the Sa'udis. Such forces have an appreciable social importance by reason not only of the part they play in the maintenance of order, but also from their contribution to visible national pomp, glory and ceremonial, and from the particular status of the officer-class—with, it must be added, its notable readiness to stray into, and then to dominate, the political field.

With the same difference in scale, and no less in effectiveness, the Middle Eastern states follow all modern practice in assuming the duties of a Public Health Service, and that of Education. Medicine as a career attracts many of the best types of citizen; good medical services are recognized as of inestimable value to the country, and incidentally catch the eye of foreign observers; and the only limit to governmental effort in this regard is that of material resources— money, buildings, equipment and, in most of the territories, trained men. Within such limits all the Governments, each in their degree, aim at measures intended to decrease the danger of epidemic disease, to stamp out those hitherto endemic (malaria, bilharzia, the eye diseases), to minimize adverse local factors (bad housing, dirt, polluted water, food infection, etc.), and to care for school children, as well as to provide specialist and general hospitals, asylums, and dispensaries in every district. There is, in this field, no lack of intelligent goodwill, and progress is continuous, to an extent extremely striking and heartening to those who have watched it for the last four decades. The recruitment of a few foreign specialists is still unavoidable, and the refusal of many local doctors to face village or provincial life is unfortunate.

In Education the effort, in all but the least advanced of the states, is equally sincere; all or almost all have would-be comprehensive systems, from kindergarten to university, and in most of them primary education is (at least in law and intention) nowadays compulsory, even though in effect it reaches only a proportion of the population, ranging from 5 per cent to 80, and may leave hundreds of villages, still, with no school at all. But, aided very substantially in some countries (Lebanon, or the Sudan, for example) both by century-long missionary educational effort and by that of the local minority communities, Christian and Jewish, the states have for some years—indeed, ever since their attainment of independence—placed the advancement of education, and war on the still prevalent illiteracy, in the fore-front of their programmes: as part of which go also technical and professional training and the despatch of young men to foreign universities (British, American, French, more recently Soviet and East European) for higher education. (Governments habitually show less interest in a question actually of acute relevance; it is, what careers, what outlets are available, or likely to be, for the new highly-educated class?) To direct scholastic programmes can be added the state Broadcasting services, the maintenance of cultural institutions (galleries, museums, libraries), and that of the ancient sites, monuments and objects in which most Middle Eastern countries are so exceptionally rich.

Nor are those of Health and Education the only public services which these governments today, in contrast to the conceptions of a century ago, feel bound to render to their publics. In most territories, legislation had been passed dealing with conditions of work in industry—hours, holidays, safety, amenities, minimum wages, compensation for injury; in some cases there is an inspectorate to enforce these, in others such regulations are largely ignored in practice, except by the foreign companies. Wages tribunals and Employment Exchanges have been set up by some of the states. Laws and regulations governing Social Security or Social Insurance have been published in most countries, and if in fact applied (which is no matter of course) do something, and will certainly do more in the future, to provide by pensions and care for the aged or distressed; the serious problems of financing and organizing such schemes have not in general, however, been fully solved. Both the law and the practice of Trade Unionism vary widely from one territory to another. In some, little has been done; in others, state-authorized Unions exist in some industries or in single factories, but are ill-organized and may or may not be permitted by law to withdraw their labour. In certain territories the Unions have been primarily politically-minded, as in the Sudan or pre-independence Aden; elsewhere, and often following European advice, Trade Unionism follows normal objectives by more or less normal methods. The grouping of individual unions into confederations is increasing, but is still limited by the specific and local nature of the demands and outlook of most, and by their untrained leadership. There is in some cases international affiliation to the W.F.T.U., in others to the W.C.F.T.U. The countrywide Histadruth in Israel combines Trade Union, Social Security, trading, contracting, co-operative and directly industrial functions on a very large scale and relieves the Israeli government of many of its functions in these respects. The Co-operative movement has taken root, with government initiative and fostering, in the industries or agriculture of a number of territories, and is capable of making an invaluable contribution. In this whole field of labour welfare and security, organization and self-help, the governments are increasingly aware of their opportunities, and progress may be expected as rapid as the evolution of the public itself permits.

The finances of the state call in the Middle East as everywhere for metriculous budgeting, accounting and auditing, processes which are lacking only in the patriarchal Governments, and are in course of introduction even there. The assessment and collection of revenue is still open, in certainly half of these countries, to well-based criticism for its low efficiency, its inequality, its favouring of some interests (such as landowning) over others, and its not infrequent scandals. Allied to financial administration goes the provision of central banking, the establishment of para-statal banks for special purposes connected with development and the provision of credit, and, through an *ad hoc* ministry or department, the control of a mass of state-owned, or endowment-owned (that is *waqf*), property in land and buildings. The government is bound to assume also the burden of overall development planning, often by Five-year or Seven-year Plans, for all types of progressive projects: projects which involve the allocation of a great part of the state revenues. Such planning (sometimes in touch, also, with outside agencies capable of providing funds) is usually entrusted, under the Cabinet, to specialized standing committees or Development Boards.

Government is equally concerned, centrally or locally, with planning of another kind—with *urbanisme*, street and park construction, slum clearance, water and electricity supply, and the provision of housing. In this field, so central to, and so revealing of, the current aspirations of the Middle Eastern states, the last forty years has important progress to show in every country, and indeed in almost every city except the poorest and most remote; many centres have been completely rebuilt, with wide streets, full public services and amenities, and an imposing range of buildings, public and domestic. The state interests itself no less in village improvement, with better road-access, modern water and electricity supply, and the telephone; it can, in 'Iraq or Syria, initiate schemes for summer hill-stations, and takes steps, almost everywhere, to provide for the important tourist industry. All main communications—roads and bridges, railways, airports and their equipment, ports with dredged channels and jetties, river navigation (in 'Iraq, Egypt, the Sudan), posts and telegraphs—are within its activities. In the field of industry, most Middle Eastern governments, as we shall see, have by now taken steps, some upon an important scale, to build or finance factories, develop mines, engage in (or, more commonly, delegate to foreign concerns) the vast petroleum industry, and in general play the dominant part in industrial development which in other regions devolves more usually upon private or joint-stock capital. In the domain of agriculture, still easily the prevailing source of national livelihood, the state guarantees, or modifies, or today sometimes essays to revolutionize, the land-tenure system and landlord-peasant relationships, initiates research into plant-types and cropping methods, teaches widely the results of such research, improves marketing facilities, gives thought to stock-breeding, forestry and fisheries, drains marshes, erects flood protection works, and carries out irrigation projects on a scale vastly beyond private capacity.

In these endeavours, fundamental to modern Middle Eastern self-realization, countries of our region have had powerful and willing friends. There have been first, the sympathetic, aid-giving governments of the United States, Britain, and the U.S.S.R., and, to a much lesser extent, others. Such aid has taken the form of direct help, in a crisis of famine or epidemic: or of a grant of funds, by gift or loan, for a development project or series of projects, as of Great Britain to Jordan, or Russia to Egypt, Syria and 'Iraq, or China to the Yemen, or America to Israel, Turkey and Persia. Other forms of aid have been missions of technical enquiry and appraisal, or the compilation of economic reports, or the despatch of a military mission, or gift of military munitions. In all these and other ways, outside nations of both the western and the eastern blocs have made, with whatever mixed motives of altruism or self-interest, the most direct of recent and continuing contacts with the Middle East: have trodden their streets, ranged their countryside, discussed business in their offices, known at first hand their citizens and homes. The greatest contributions in these fields have been those of the United States who, through one or other of its specialized agencies, has provided abundant funds, experts and goods in kind to most of our territories, under the headings of Development Assistance, Technical Co-operation, or Military Support, more particularly for development in Israel and Persia, and (largest of all items) for military aid to Turkey. The U.S.S.R. has given less; nevertheless, its aid dramatically increased in the 1960s, to the point where by 1969 it provided the bulk of outside assistance to Egypt, Syria, 'Iraq and Yemen. Great Britain has directly aided Jordan, Oman and the Trucial states and provides technical assistance to others.

A second group of similar contacts has been multiplied by and through United Nations, of which almost all the Middle Eastern states are members. The part played by U.N. in the politics of our region in the last two decades has, indeed, been both various and continuous; here however it must suffice to mention the type of beneficent activity shown locally by certain of the many U.N. agencies. Such, obviously, are those of U.N.R.W.A. (p. 138), concerned with Palestine refugees and involving the maintenance of offices at Beirut, 'Amman, Damascus, Cairo, Jerusalem and Gaza; of the Truce Supervision Organization (U.N.T.S.O.), established in 1949 to maintain the Armistice Agreements of that year, but since 1967 the tenuous U.N. presence on the cease-fire lines; and of the Peace-Keeping Force in Cyprus (U.N.F.I.C.Y.P.), set up in 1964 to separate warring Greek and Turkish Cypriots. The U.N. Children's Fund, U.N.I.C.E.F., is represented by offices in Ankara, Beirut, Cairo and Teheran. The Economic Commission for Africa, E.C.A., is concerned with Egypt and the Sudan; the similar Commission for Asia and the Far East covers Persia. The Economic and Social Council, E.C.O.S.O.C., itself has an office in Beirut; that of Food and Agriculture, F.A.O., in Cairo; that of World Health, W.H.O., at Alexandria; and the International Labour Office, I.L.O., in Ankara, Beirut and Cairo. There are U.N. Informational Centres at Baghdad, Beirut, Cairo, Khartum and Teheran. The U.N. Educational, Scientific and Cultural Organization, U.N.E.S.C.O., has held meetings in the Middle East. Finally, and of greatest practical importance, the International Bank for Reconstruction and Development (the 'World Bank') has repeatedly conducted economic surveys in the region and has made loans for specific projects on a scale sufficient to give it locally a leading place as a development agency. The International Monetary Fund, I.M.F., has aided some of the states in their currency or exchange difficulties: the U.N. Special Fund has made many grants to governments to 'create the conditions' favourable to foreign or domestic investment: and the Expanded Programme of Technical Assistance, which works through all existing U.N. machinery and, jointly with the Special Fund, maintains resident representatives at virtually all Middle Eastern capitals, has spent and is spending millions in practical forms of aid.

## 3. *The Field of Politics*

The few pages to be devoted to this subject—pages which will show (if it were doubtful) how close is the connection in the Middle East between political activity and other main aspects of society—will deal in succession with the general character of local politics, the main issues upon which its debates concentrate, and the more characteristic political methods normally employed. Our account will necessarily be generalized for most, and the most typical, Middle Eastern countries, while not entirely true for any one of them, and will for this purpose ignore the entirely different conditions in Israel on the one hand and in the Arabian states on the other.

The days when government and its visible agencies were objects of fear and hatred to most of at least the non-urban public are over, except in the wilder tribes or remotest hill-communities; but the population elements are, on the contrary, still numerous among which the rule of law and the processes of orderly government have still an uncertain hold and little favour. Public opinion in support of lawful authority is far from unanimous; the admissibility of government 'interference' in fields unknown to earlier days—social, fiscal, administrative—is bitterly questioned; and, in brief, conceptions of the prerogative and obligations of the state and of its own optimum structure are, except in limited 'evolved' circles, very far from those generally accepted in the West. This wide difference is due, in general, to long ages of government based on unwestern, Islamic concepts, followed by centuries of arbitary maladministration or non-administration in substantial isolation from the main stream of world affairs. Our western axioms concerning popular representation, personal liberty, an independent judiciary, and human rights as applicable to political or governmental life, are not only not taken for granted as desiderata, they are commonly rejected, if not in words, then in action. Add to this that most of the nations of our region are essentially at quite different stages of their organic development from those of Europe or North America, differ widely in temperament, and are confronted with a dissimilar set of tasks and problems, and it will be apparent that hopes of merely transplanting to the Middle East western political or constitutional systems must be profoundly illusory—a fact too little realized in the last half century, both in the West and in our region itself.

The body politic in these territories is almost always plainly hetero-geneous. It consists of elements differing much more than superfici-ally in their strong, specific community loyalties, their economic interests and way of life, and—most important—their level of evolution and education. Society falls, if one may obviously over-simplify, into two parts: the smaller, that of educated men with more or less evolved ideas and desiderata in politics and society—that is, the intelligentsia and the literate bourgeoisie: and secondly, the numerically much greater part, that of the uneducated masses, rural and urban. The educated class itself contains a small minority of well-equipped potential statesmen, often of distinguished ability, and a large majority from the literate, politically conscious, almost entirely urban, middle and lower-middle class. The uneducated masses are commonly dismissed by western observers as of little political interest but as merely, at best, inarticulate folk misled by a 'handful of agitators'. This is an error. The peasant or tribesman has admittedly little information, backward (if any) conceptions in politics or government, and an absorbing interest, above all, in his own circle and in living: but politically he cannot be ignored. He is capable of accepting and following a leader, or at least of supporting his own local magnate or landowner; he can exhibit violent if uninstructed political emotion, can demonstrate and riot, can destroy governments or cause a reversal of their decisions; and many a political leader, disliked by authority in office, can find formidable support among the masses perfectly ill-equipped to judge the relevant issues.

This deep division in national society is doubtless diminishing, but will not soon disappear; meanwhile, added to local, sectional and community stresses and strains, it leads to that overall instability of political life, or indeed of government itself, which is the region's dominant and most disquieting feature. This instability is emphasized, or increased, by the clash of personalities (sometimes of clans or families) which is perhaps even more conspicuous in the Middle East than elsewhere: by the crudely divergent interests which different personalities or forces are publicly pursuing: by most political leaders', writers' and speakers' immaturity in statecraft, and their natural recourse to an extremism often competitive: by the constant elements of restless movement, splintering and regrouping: by, in fact, all the phenomena to which the excitable, intransigent, indivi-dualistic character of, at least, Arabs and Persians must inevitably lead in public life.

Political leadership belongs today in all these territories, except

Arabia and in some measure Persia, no longer to the old ruling class of rich landowners, merchants, urban magnates, wealthy ex-officials or blue-blooded aristocrats. These, their lives and property often in danger from vigorous reformists—as in Egypt since 1952, or 'Iraq since 1958—are not today, as they were for centuries, the repositories of power, even though in wide rural or tribal areas they may, through their influence over the tribesmen or peasantry, and in opposition to the government's policies, still constitute a formidable force of self-preserving conservatism. But overt political power belong nowadays neither to these nor to the mob (powerful role as this can sometimes play) but, except when temporarily suppressed by a dictatorship, to the urban (including the military) intelligentsia, from which spring practically all leaders, politicians, organizers, military and civil executives—and the dictators themselves.

It is often asked, is there or can there be any true Middle Eastern democracy? There is little guidance here, paradoxically, in the authentic Arab social tradition of equalitarianism, the accessibility of old-type rulers to the petitioner, desert freedom and the like; all this belongs to history, and often to legend. And such phenomena as a vigorous, often an ultra-violent, political Press, and mammoth street demonstrations, fail also to indicate the presence of true democratic instincts; most politicians and journalists exhibit these in no more than their speeches and leading articles, and demonstrators are available at little or no cost for any cause or occasion whatsoever, royalist, communist, hero-greeting, martyr-mourning, or any other. But if a true democratic régime demands a reasonably instructed, tolerably homogeneous electorate, this is absent. If it needs to express itself by political parties which stand for principles, or at least for coherent policies and programmes, these very rarely exist otherwise than in rootless and ephemeral forms, since few parties (except the communist) have a country-wide organization or continuity, or stand for much more than personal followings or tactical manoeuvres. Certain groups, it is true, in Lebanon, Syria, Egypt, Cyprus, Israel offer at least partial exceptions to this too-sweeping judgment; personal followings (as those of 'holy men' in the Sudan) can be permanent and fairly consistent: in Turkey the parties—or at least the Party, and the opposition to it—have both long continuity and a firm tradition, and in Persia both the (mainly Communist) Tudeh party and the conservative landlords' 'lobby' are seemingly permanent forces. But few profess a comprehensive, moderate programme to replace the current policies which they oppose, or can be conceived as an acceptable alternative government. If democracy, again, calls for a genuine system of popular representation, this is a most infrequent asset in the Middle East: if for a desire of political leaders to see power truly vested in the masses, this is rarer still, since nine-tenths of the statesmen who assert this as their ideal would reject with horror a veritable realization of it; indeed, the intelligentsia-politician has normally the lowest opinion of the brains or judgment of his illiterate fellow-countrymen. In spite of frequent advocacy by tyranny-hating orators of 'one man one vote', it cannot be pretended that democracy as a system (identified as it is, moreover, with the unpopular West) makes a seductive appeal to Middle Eastern ideologists; when not rejected as inefficient and sanctimonious, it appears with its debates, delays and squabbles as the enemy of national unity, and an impediment to dynamic progress. It will be long before Middle Eastern statesmen (unless, just possibly, in Turkey) can appreciate the value of a 'loyal opposition'; and even in Turkey the two-party system, installed in 1950, has had a tempestuous career.

We conclude at this point that, for the reasons given, the Middle Eastern political background is one widely dissimilar from that of most modern states in other regions: that the statal régimes, and their publics, are markedly heterogeneous, restless and unstable: that political power belongs today to the growing, literate middle class: and that the attainment of any democratic régime worth the name is far to seek. We pass next to deal with the question, what are the main political issues today disputed in these countries?

The first of these is evidently that of the struggle for immediate power in the state, for the individual, party or interest engaged. Such struggles take an infinity of forms and occasions, and, though always concealed under other names and pretexts, none are more bitter or recurrent. Their incidence occurs naturally in every sphere of government and public life—personal, procedural, financial and administrative, military and bureaucratic; and their frequency, normal in all politically-active societies, does not exhibit Middle Eastern politicians as lower or more self-seeking than others elsewhere, which they are not. On the constitutional side, habitual conflicts concern the general form of the government—monarchical or republican, 'popular' or oligarchic or dictatorial: the maintenance, or abolition, of a system of internal community balances as the basis of government (as in Lebanon): the limits or the achievement of popular representation: the wisdom, or alternatively the condemned weakness or folly, of allowing power or privilege to minority population-elements—Kurds, Druzes, Nusairis, or Sudani pagans—as against a policy of centralized uniformity. Behind this group of issues lie, more generally, the attitudes of those (found most commonly among semi-suppressed oppositions) who clamour for wide liberty of press and party action—in fact, for a free field for 'democratic rights'—and who resent all forms of authoritarian rule and all princely or shaikhly or ecclesiastical pretensions to extra-legal power. These or connected issues can take the form of autocracy versus so-called democracy, or of feudalism versus representative institutions; in extreme form they take shape as the forces of tradition or reaction against those of an extreme left-wing, or against Communism itself. The same issue merges, in the social-economic field, into the conflict between protagonists of a controlled or socialistic organization of society and economic life (such as the old étatists of Persia and Turkey or the new socialists of Egypt, Syria and 'Iraq) and those who prefer the freedom to run their enterprises under minimum control. In the agricultural sphere the same issue appears as between large-scale landlords and the advocates of state-imposed land redistribution.

A further type of divisive issue in Middle Eastern politics is that of foreign relations, embracing questions of antipathy to, or desire to amalgamate with, adjacent states: the tension of Persia's claim to Bahrain or between Sa'udi Arabia and its Gulf neighbours is one type, differing Lebanese, Syrian and Jordanian conceptions of a Greater Syria or every state's varying ideal conception of Arab unity itself, are others. Anyone of these or allied questions can be a frequent, hard-fought theme in local politics. Beyond them lies the whole field of foreign policy—western or eastern blocs, alliance or non-alignment, varying shades of neutralism: a field full of mutual recrimination but always united in wearisome denunciations of the sinister imperialism, colonialism, etc., attributed to whatever Great Power is for the moment most out of favour.

These, then, being the themes of political controversy, what are the methods characteristically in use? That of democratic elections must be placed first; yet, though popular elections are indeed frequently held and produce some sort of results, they are subject to various disabilities. Their processes can be blatantly falsified; they can be controlled under government orders by local officials; they can be limited to preselected candidates; they can be stultified by a boycott. Of all these phases of election-holding the Middle East can show abundant examples.

Of political parties, an indispensable element in any sound political system, we have spoken already. Apart from their habitual rootlessness and discontinuity they are readily suppressed by the dictator or dominant faction of the moment, or (as almost habitually with the Communist parties) are pronounced illegal and driven underground. But, inadequate as is the part they can play, they are prominent in the political field by their violence in speech and writing, their ready organization of mob and student demonstrations—the latter a constant and deplorable element—and often by their control of the (largely political) Trade Unions. The Communist parties are not unique in their possession of funds from abroad (to which their persistence is largely due), since subsidies to politicians or journalists, particularly in 'Iraq, Syria and Lebanon, are known to have accrued at times from staunchly anti-Communist (Sa'udi) sources.

Other political methods in use are those of inspired intervention from inside the country but outside the normal political world, such as can be organized from or by the forces of religion in their more militant forms—from Sufis in Turkey, Shi'i *mujtahids* in 'Iraq and Persia, revivalists in Egypt and Syria. The same applies to provoked tribal uprisings (as in 'Iraq and Turkey), a manoeuvre dear to town-bred politicians who, in the event, can rarely control the resulting violence, and often suffer by it. In international politics, and scarcely less in internal, the use of violent broadcasting campaigns has become usual in the hands of dominant parties or dictators; and in this field, after all allowance has been made for the tradition of eastern hyperbole in political exposition, and the immaturity of many political publicists, it is difficult at times not to be pained by their repetitive and often foolishly mendacious outpourings. The active support of fugitives from other countries is a common way of expressing one's own Arab patriotism and creating difficulties for one's opponents—as, for example, by a welcome and support, in Cairo, for the leaders of Omani insurgence. Another technique is the discovery, at home, of a conspiracy by political enemies 'against the State', followed by arrest of the alleged culprits (often described as 'imperialist stooges') and an upsurge of loyal devotion to the threatened hero. The latter attitude is produced also by organized 'personality cult' of the ruler in power, aided by all the means of publicity and persuasion at his disposal.

Of interventions by the Army modern Middle Eastern history contains a score of examples; indeed, no major country is without one, and in most of them military dictatorship, short- or long-lived, is, as the world has witnessed since 1946, a recurrent phase. Indeed, the establishment of these dictatorships seems to confirm, by its witness against the practicability of successful democracy, the lesson of the scarcely less authoritarian forms adopted in Persia and Jordan, and temporarily in Turkey—and, of course, the totally undemocratic patriarchies or theocracies of Arabia. One might add here, regretfully, the often-used weapon of simple assassination, of which, again, no single Middle Eastern country fails to offer recent examples.

With all this, let no reader forget that, within the heated, confused, too often unedifying scene of Middle Eastern politics, there are actors not only of high ability, but of genuine devotion and patriotism. It is the more tragic that these qualities, so obvious and so valued in the quieter interludes or in private discussion, have but a limited force amid the stresses of a political arena dominated by slogans, obsessive antipathies, and competitive promises or boasts.

### 4. *Going Communist?*

No question is more often asked by observers of the Middle Eastern political scene than one at which we have already hinted: what is the likelihood of one or more of these territories 'going Communist'? Why and how could it happen? This deserves some consideration, partly because it is revealing of the present political— and, to an extent, the social—scene, partly because a move to the Communist structure and way of life, if it occurred, would have important social effects.

It is certain that the whole region has long enjoyed a high priority as a Communist, and before that a czarist Russian, expansion area: that the efforts of the U.S.S.R. since 1945 to expand its influence and penetration by swollen diplomatic staffs, abundant propaganda, acquired Press and personal allegiances, visits and missions, have been conspicuous: and that Communist Parties, whether subsidized or not, and whatever their precise relationship to Moscow, exist on some scale in most Middle Eastern countries, some with official recognition but most illegally. Communist influence has seen a significant increase since June of 1967: Soviet willingness to re-create the Arab armies destroyed by Israel, and the Russian diplomatic championing of the Arab cause in world councils, have made it the 'most-favoured' power in the Arab Middle East, as well as giving it more specific, visible gains undreamt of a decade ago—such as military 'advisors' to the Arab armies whose powers doubtless exceed the purely advisory, or privileges of naval visit which amount to bases without being formally so called. Adding to this the small but important groups of intellectuals, journalists, students, trade unionists and army officers who think and speak in Marxist terms, one is forced to ask the question: will the Middle East, or one or more parts of it, 'go Communist'?

The Middle East, by virtue of the poverty and backwardness still prevailing among its masses, and the restless, unstable immaturity of its public in matters political, may seem a favourable area for Communist expansion. The political *dirigeants* proclaim neutralism and socialism, which means that they refuse Western allegiances and feel that the expansion of state power is the true way to modernization; and they desire maximum outside economic aid. The Soviets, because they have never invaded or controlled the Arab countries, are regarded by the public (with however naive an unreality) as nonimperialist. They have no past to live down in the region, as have the British, French, and Turks: no identification with the old, now dethroned, ruling class of landowners and the rich: no colour bar, no social taboos, no subjects, no local oil concessions or commercial interests. They refrain from singing the praises of that locally ill-regarded system, democracy: they are gratifyingly anti-Israeli as well as anti-Western. They are generous suppliers of arms (irrespective of how they may be used or misused), granters of low-interest, stringless loans, signers of favourable trade-agreements, buyers of otherwise unsaleable crops. Above all, they are a people whom their own adoption of Communism seems to have raised, in a generation, from poverty, oppression, and near-serfdom to their present power and status.

All this would suggest an easy triumph for the Communists—that is, for the U.S.S.R., since the Chinese are not yet seriously in the picture—in the Middle Eastern region. Nevertheless, this outcome remains unlikely. The nature of Communist rule, and of life under it, are inevitably better appreciated as time goes on and public information improves, and the Russians themselves are less popular as they become better known through their representatives—experts, planners, missions, workmen—in the host countries, as a number of episodes have already shown; and as loan repayments become due, and the fulfilment of accepted obligations is expected, and occasions of friction have multiplied, cordiality is likely further to decrease. Moreover, the neutralism of the Middle Eastern states is sincere; no status tying them to the East, any more than to the West, would be tolerated. The idea of agreeing to exclusive relations with a new, notoriously powerful, and active Big Brother, after successfully eliminating the powers previously dominant in their countries, is unacceptable on a permanent basis, even if temporarily necessary; there are signs that the Arab-Soviet relationship since 1967 is already being found galling to the Arabs. Finally, the powerful, emotional Nationalism of the states concerned, without exception, is bound ultimately to clash not only with the nationalism of Russia (which from some aspects has changed little since 1917) but also with the international element of Communism, a proclaimed world-creed; now that the 'struggles against imperialist powers' are safely over, in which the U.S.S.R. could support local aspiring nations, as such, against the West, it will be difficult to disguise the fundamental incompatibility between local nationalistic pride and entry into the Soviet system. For these and such-like reasons, here too briefly summarized, it is unlikely that any Middle Eastern state will allow itself to drift into permanent Communist-satellite status.

But a variant form of Communist influence in the Middle East has manifested itself with considerable success in the later 1960s. This is the emergence of political movements nationalist in their external orientation but Marxist in their economic and social predilections. Parties fitting such a description now exist in most of the countries of the region, and some, in the Arab states, are in power—with what degree of permanency one cannot say. Thus Egypt officially accepts much of the Marxist interpretation of history and progress, although it rejects the class struggle in favour of social solidarity; the Syrian Ba'th accepts more (and has acted on it), the 'Iraqi Ba'th less; and the new régimes in the Yemen and in Southern Arabia, countries where Marxist theory is fully as meaningful as it would be for Antarctica, proclaim themselves to be the builders of socialist societies. The growth and rise to power of movements such as these, however, can be considered a gain for Communism only in a very limited sense, in that such movements have borrowed ideas from historical Marxism and have used contemporary Communism primarily to aid them in achieving nationalist aims. Of the two great -isms of the modern world, Nationalism and Socialism, the former is undoubtedly far more important to the Arab revolutionaries of the 1960s: their primary allegiance lies to the national unit (however defined), with 'international Communism' (again, however defined) little more than a tool to be utilized in the realization of national goals.

CHAPTER NINE

# PRIVATE LIFE AND SOCIETY

## 1. *Why backwardness?*

THE world at large, in both hemispheres, finds the Middle East a
region of backwardness: picturesque perhaps but, as regards the
mass of the inhabitants, socially retarded as well as poverty-stricken.
The prevailing image (as the writer has found repeatedly in the
United States) is that of the Arab as a scraggy, night-gown wearing,
camel-riding nomad; that of the Turk as a truculent, water-pipe-
smoking, harem-dwelling murderer of Armenians: of the Persian as
a subtle, effeminate opium-taker. These pictures correspond very
little to the facts of Middle Eastern life; but that there has been a
lagging development in much of society as in public life, and widespread poverty, is all too true.

This backwardness, it is obvious, is not of uniform incidence
throughout the region. It is at its most apparent in peninsular
Arabia, in parts of the Sudan, in wide outlying areas elsewhere: and
is at its least in urban and suburban areas of the more developed
countries. Nevertheless, and although, thanks to the prevailingly
high level of intelligence among the populations and their age-long
contact with advanced civilizations, Middle Eastern backwardness is
never at the abysmal level prevalent in most of Africa and great
parts of South America, yet it is pronounced enough to justify the
enquiry as to why a high proportion of the people of territories of
such fame and outstanding cultural tradition should have allowed
themselves, or been allowed, to fall, in the material and many of the
cultural achievements of the modern world, so far behind those of
other peoples not more gifted, and illumined by far less ancient
glory.

The answer can be briefly summarized. The early and medieval
greatness of the Middle Eastern region was obliterated by the conquests and catastrophes which it underwent in the later Middle Ages.
The region, by nature poor and unfertile, and failing, after the
Mongol visitations, to recover and provide the means of wealth and
leisure, inevitably fell behind communities in the West, better
endowed and less afflicted; and when the centre of gravity of the

civilized world, notably after the discovery of America, moved west-ward to the Mediterranean and Atlantic, the Middle East became no longer central but peripheral to it. The discovery of a sea route to India had a similar effect. The region had not escaped in earlier days, though it had now long forgotten, the fertilizing influences of Greece; but it missed entirely those of the Renaissance, which coincided with its own darkest period, and it proceeded on its way as though this immense upsurge of the human spirit had never occurred. The reason for this apathy, or failure in communication, was the same as that which was responsible, more than any other, more indeed than all others together, for the present backwardness which we are dis-cussing: the dominance of, and age-long uncritical devotion to, the religion of Islam. Because of this faithfulness, a major part of the thought, speculation and scholarship of the Islamic peoples was canalized, after a period of unsuccessful attempts at freedom, into a narrow, often sterile religio-legal field. Their activity, whether in public or private life, was limited by a conservatism not far, at times, from stagnation; and the range of this was the greater by reason of the claim of Islam to cover, by prescribed rules which were invari-able, every department of human life. With this immobility—producing, as it did, a gracious but changeless manner of life—went the marked 'superiority complex' of the Muslim, to whom the cul-tures and societies of the West, teeming in fact with progressive dynamism, were unworthy, valueless aberrations and improprieties. The Islamic world clung for centuries to its slow tempo, its restricted horizons, its narrow education, its secluded women and lack of western-type home life: to its ignorance of, or aversion from, mech-anical and material progress: to its isolation from science, many of the arts, and modern economic, strategic and political forms. It was the victim of endemic, weakening diseases, among them malaria. It accepted with fatalism the callous mis-government of Sultan and Shah, and lived without security, justice or progress, until at last compelled, in self-defence, to call in too late the special skills and methods of Europe. These were accepted without discrimination or, often enough, without any comprehension extending beyond the most obvious and immediate. The process of catching-up, which has been the outstanding feature of Middle Eastern life for the last century and a half, is still far from complete; but it is well begun and will continue without, it is to be hoped, the loss of the spiritual values so abundantly represented in Islam.

## 2. Towns and town life

The traditional society of the Middle East was, as previous pages have suggested, conditioned by its peculiar and diverse geography, climate and resources, and notably by the great varieties in its land-surface. These created the environments in which life could be lived —by agriculture, gardening, nomadic or static pastoralism, fishing, and urban and village occupations—and determined the local density of population, from empty desert to packed city, from the menacing over-population of Egypt and Lebanon, to the man-power shortages of 'Iraq, Persia and Syria. The human history of the region bequeathed, with frequent changes of fortune and new ingredients, legacies of tradition and way of life; its religion imposed upon it a pattern only recently, but now progressively, in process of modification.

The factors by which this modification has proceeded have been suggested in an earlier chapter, where we mentioned the influences making for reform in nineteenth-century Turkey (p. 70 f.); they included all the channels and forces whereby western influences had by that time come to bear upon Middle Eastern society. Since then their action has been further intensified by other, and ever closer and more operative, links between the region and the western world, resulting in deeper penetration by the latter in almost every field of Middle Eastern society. This has occurred through the post-1919 Mandates, the constant flow of communication of every kind and level between east and west, the increase of international trade and industry, and widening education. Among such more recent factors one could emphasize the ubiquity of the motor-car, with its immense impulse to mobility and interchange: aviation, highly developed in the region, with its rapidity of travel and anni-hilation of frontiers and distance: the vast increase of newspapers, and of a literate public to read them: the never-ceasing broadcasts from western and eastern Europe: the cinema showing, in every city and town, scores of films of western society from which both the good and the bad—and too often the deplorable—features of Euro-pean society, morals and 'progress' are to be learned: and television, of which the same is true. These forces have operated unequally throughout society, which today in consequence presents the strange yet familiar spectacle of a region deeply divided in its manner of life, full of contradictions and anachronisms, and widely diverse as between its urban and its rural publics, between the old, traditional life and that of invading and prevailing modernity.

We pass, then, to review (with a degree of generalization too easily misleading, because allowing too little for great inter-regional varieties) the life of Middle Eastern towns, countryside and tribes, with the again-repeated proviso, however, that little of what follows is applicable to peninsular Arabia, where the ancient conditions, scenes and way of life are still (save in the small areas dominated by foreign industry) those of the Middle Ages: nor to Cyprus, culturally an outlying part of Greece and Europe: nor to Israel, a country totally remote (save in its Arab minority) from the region in which it has established itself. We speak here of the non-Arabian Arab countries, and of Turkey and Persia.

Middle Eastern towns of whatever magnitude owe their siting variously to the presence of an assured water-supply, to convenience as a caravan-staging-post in earlier days, to location at a point where some local resource could best be handled, to natural facilities for defence, or to some special sanctity (shrine or burial place) which attracted pilgrims and a resulting livelihood. To whichever of such origins, mostly now lost in remote antiquity, a given city was originally indebted, its present scale bears no visible relation to them, being due more probably to personal or administrative factors not always analysable. But in any event the region is one in which cities have played a dominant part in society, economics and government alike, and have maintained themselves as the providers of leadership, capital and social progress, if any, for thousands of years. And today, notably since 1945, the growth of urban populations, due to constant inward movement from the villages, is an outstanding feature of the times.

The urban life of the region is, evidently, the most changed, the least traditional, and furthest from the images of 'the East' dear to the uninstructed West. In its new setting, gone are the protective walls around the city, gone many (but not all) of the malodorous rubbish-heaps, the slums and the narrow alleys, the strings of load-carrying camels, the deep mud or swirling dust. Every Middle Eastern country today boasts its dozen or score of major and lesser cities in which can be studied, with many varieties, all that they have yet evolved in features of city life. Too often these cities are surrounded by an irregular ring of shabby, unfinished suburbs, by a mass or masses of shanty-towns where new arrivals from the countryside live in first hopeful, later despairing misery; but the inner areas of the city are very different. Apart from the still prominent monuments of the past—mosques, palaces, khans, barracks—there are everywhere signs of new town-planning, the pride of the local mayor and his council or of the central government itself. The new boulevards, parks, plantations, fountains are often of beauty and dignity, especially where helped by a favourable natural setting, and are the focus of a warm civic pride. Modern 'bus services run everywhere, taxis abound, private motor-cars and trucks throng the streets. Street lighting, upkeep and watering are a matter of course; so, though not everywhere, is a public sewage system. Well-planned, well-sited villas for the well-to-do, in whole streetfuls and quarters, replace their former town-houses, and modern-type housing estates have been developed in many cities to meet the needs of the public of the middle or lower-middle income ranges. Every government has provided itself and its cities with public buildings to its taste, which offer usually the greatest contrast to those even of half-a-century ago, and are the more diverse as state activities have increased. New mosques appear, though most of these conform to ancient pattern. New bank and office buildings, institutions, schools, clubs, hospitals, 'bus stations, garages, mark the contribution of private enterprise to the new scene, in which many cinemas and an occasional theatre or athletic stadium have their place. The hotels, mostly housed in new and grandiose buildings, give a high standard of modern service in the largest cities, and are nowadays usually reliable (not without occasional lapses) even in smaller provincial towns. Modern shops abound, with a range of European wares of every quality, as well as the familar merchandise of the bazaars. Restaurants admirably kept, and smart cafés, are among usual amenities attractive to 'the best people' and to foreigners. The latter, residents in or visitors to the city, and foreign diplomats if this is a capital, are a familiar element. Some state ceremonial may stir the citizen's pride, with a military band or a passing presidential cortège.

But this picture of the modern Middle Eastern city, varying in aspect with the scenes and taste of the country concerned, is part only of the truth; there remains always, on an important scale, remnants of the very different past. Such are the ancient, busy, noisy, arched or open bazaars, often miles in extent and scarcely changed in aspect for a millennium: old-type public baths and tea-shops, the craftsman in his workshop, the barber and the seller of cold drinks or vegetables: the archaic khan or caravanserai for the poorer wayfarer: the winding alleyways giving pedestrian access to windowless, airless dwellings: peddlars and street vendors, beggars, laden donkeys or mules, scores of ragged children and their black-clad mothers, and innumerable dignified, seemingly workless, sitters-in-the-sun. The easy co-existence in a single city of medieval and ultra-new, grandiose and sordid, eastern and western, progressive and static, with no boundary between them, and both wholly accepted, is to the new-comer a striking feature of life.

In the lesser towns, district or provincial capitals, the balance swings over to the ancient ways, as more of traditional building and planning—or no-planning—survive, threatened by less innovation. These centres are more compact because less magnetic to the drifting surplus rural population: more homogeneous, because unincreased by new-built quarters: more typical of the country in which they lie, because less cosmopolitan and more in unity with the surround-ing villages and tribes, for whom they form the natural centre and market-place. But all have, nonetheless, their share of new buildings, improved streets and gardens; the public services are well in evidence, with visible new-fashioned private ventures, and easy rapid com-munication to other centres. Thus, life is lived here half in the modern, half in the ancient fashion.

Within this general setting of part-modernized town-life, all the occupations normal in the modern world are practised. Religion keeps its own in mosque-staffs and seminaries, and in the officials charged with management of the extensive pious endowments. (Much the same is found, on smaller scales, within the Christian and Jewish communities.) Since every territory has its armed forces, these in all their ranks and branches occupy large numbers of the employable, as well as every type of supplier and camp-follower: and, with them, the gendarmerie, police and fire services. Reference was made elsewhere (p. 197 f.), to the importance of government service in all its departments and at every level, central, provincial or municipal; this, with the public services of every kind—teachers and medical staffs, engineers and transport workers—employs inevitably a large body of the citizenry who are, to their fellow-countrymen as to visiting foreigners, 'the Government'. Taking for granted the un-skilled or semi-skilled masses, pursuing their many livelihoods (but noting the recent appearance of an industrial proletariat created by new factory-type industry) and passing over equally the mere property-owner or 'idle rich', one may specify the diverse grades and varieties of skilled artisan in every industry, the technologists and managers who control them, and the capitalists who own and may direct such enterprises; and, with these, the executive as well as clerical grades in foreign-directed industry and commerce—banks, insurance agencies, travel-bureaux, and the oil industry itself. Add to these the practitioners of law or medicine, journalism or politics, and the executives and staffs of all the multifarious businesses normal in every city, from retail shops and humble *ateliers* to export houses, shipbuilding or transport enterprises, and wholesalers or middlemen in any and every commodity. The purpose of this list is not to be exhaustive but to suggest that urban life in Middle Eastern cities— conceived by some foreigners, it seems, as a simple affair of shaikhs or pashas and a mass of ragged underlings—is in fact, as elsewhere, a complicated and evolved microcosm. Closer examination of it would reveal new social features of some interest, among which three may be given as examples. One is the recent emergence of a new upper-class founded on industrial or commercial wealth, side by side with the old 'best families' who bear famous names. For some of the new-made fortunes the war and its opportunities were responsible, for others the immense influx of money through the operations of the oil companies. Another feature is the modified relationship between Muslim and minority-community society, a relationship now easier by reason of less fanaticism and more modern tolerance, but less easy through the upsurge of a Nationalism apt to reject the non-Muslim as not fully a patriot. And a third is the change of manners, among the younger middle-class, from their traditional forms of courtesy to consciously anti-traditional western fashions not always, one must admit, as pleasing: a change sometimes barely appreciable, sometimes striking, and in any case inevitable.

How do they all live? There is here the familiar dichotomy between old and new, running deeply through society. Among the proportion (highest, obviously, in the less advanced territories) who even in great cities keep the traditional ways of life, the clothes worn are the flowing, picturesque garments of the country, in varying pattern according to local usage, and in quality from rags to finery according to personal wealth and taste. The houses of this old-fashioned, and usually but not always poorer, city-element are of the ancient, en-closed pattern, with dark rooms, scanty furnishings, and few or no services of light, water or drainage. Their occupants eat but poorly, entertain at home rarely or not at all, isolate their women, observe the Islamic taboos against drinking and card-playing, travel by the crowded and noisy but not too inefficient public transport, conduct their social lives in coffee-shop and bazaar, and fail to share, for the most part, in such mixed blessings as modernity and the West have brought. Illiteracy still prevails (though less than ever before) among the lower orders, poverty is still oppressive, the death-rate among children needlessly high, malnutrition widespread, and disease commoner than it would be if the available medical services were fully used.

The line of demarcation between the exponents of the conservative way of life and those of the newer-fashioned, next to be described, is not merely one of wealth, since some rich families still prefer a little-modified version of the ancient way; it is one of education and calling. The followers of 'white collar' occupations are of the newer school, manual workers—but with many and increasing exceptions —are of the old, while in the middle, with a series of reasonable or awkward or sometimes half-comical compromises, comes the mass of the artisan and humbler clerical types. Ignoring these, one finds that the life of the modernizers—a substantial majority, in most cities, of those in easier circumstances or of modern upbringing—is characterized by the wearing by both sexes of dress of European type, often costly and well styled: the occupation of houses of western type equipped with all normal services, furnished à l'européenne, the scene of well-served meals (with local often preferred to European dishes) and pleasant social parties. These have, in fact, adopted living-styles either wholly European or of the agreeable Levantine pattern familiar among the socially élite (including Christian minority communities) in Turkey, the Lebanon and Egypt for centuries past. Their fashion of living is comfortable rather than luxurious, excess and ostentation are generally though not quite always avoided, the use of alcoholic drinks is far from universal, drunkenness rare though not unknown, gambling practised but by many disapproved. The two sexes, even in modernist circles, are still to some extent socially segregated by hard-dying custom. The more dashing members of such families meet in hôtels and cabarets, attend the cinema (as indeed does every class and age), frequent the racecourse if such exists, play cards (and play them extremely well), appear at athletic meetings, use freely their many and well-appointed clubs, delight in expensive motor-cars, and spend part of the hot weather abroad, or, where these exist, at the hill-stations of their own country. In their conversation, apart from gossip and personal matters, politics easily predominates; religion has little place, books and culture not much more. Literacy and a certain level of modern sophistication are assumed. The children, of both sexes, go as a matter of course to primary and probably to secondary schools, and often on to university or professional education, at home or abroad. The boys join the

Scouts and the local Youth Movement, play football and debate politics; the girls play tennis, follow the cinema, and accompany their mothers to their charitable societies and receptions or cocktail parties.

A recent feature of town life, which extends in large measure to the villages also, must be further specified; it is that of the changed position of women, so long a reproach, as many felt, to Islamic civilization. The movement towards emancipation, begun some decades ago, received great impetus from the legislation enforced by Kamal Atatürk in Turkey and Riza Shah in Persia, and from sympathetic but less conclusive movements in the same sense among the Arab countries. In the Middle East today the ancient restraints on veiled, uneducated, cloistered women, still prevail in the Arabian peninsula, in many country areas elsewhere, and, surprisingly, in some otherwise 'evolved' urban circles; and even in Persia and Turkey unveiling and emancipation, in spite of all laws and official sanctions, have far less than universal range, thanks mainly to the conservatism or shyness of the women themselves—the principal, if paradoxical, restraining factor in this field. Nevertheless, immense ground has been gained in the last forty years. The old polygamy of Islam is now relatively rare, and in 'evolved' circles is almost a curiosity. Full equality of opportunity for schooling or employment exists over a substantial, and increasing, area, and well-educated girls and women in open society, with thousands employed in clerical, technological and professional occupations, are now no longer an unfamiliar sight. (Significantly, the ancient theological university of al-Azhar, in Cairo, has now been opened to women students.) Less archaic conceptions of marriage, and a western type of home life, are fast extending. In her married state, in entering which she enjoys a freedom of choice unknown before, a woman benefits by much recently passed legislation which provides, in one country or another, for modification in her favour of the cruelly unequal rules for divorce, and those of polygamy itself. And the general, but still not universal, broadening of public opinion in favour of the new ways helps her, far more than laws—far more, even, than the vote which she can now, in most countries, cast in elections—towards a free place in society and the world.

## 3. Cultural Aspect

The Middle East has been, for centuries or millennia, a home of high culture and learning; but because much or most of its achievement belongs now solely to the historian (if not to the archaeologist), and because its immense and continuing contributions to Islamic law, religion and history stand clearly apart from the secular western world which here concerns us, the following pages will deal only with that part of Middle Eastern activity in the cultural field which links it to the present-day world: that, in effect, of the West.

The universities of the region which, mostly new but including some medieval foundations, exist in almost every country outside Arabia, are vigorous and thronged with students; and they contribute invaluably to enlarging the educated middle-class upon which these territories, administratively and economically, do and must depend. That they are making, also, valuable academic contributions to knowledge no one will wish to deny; but, not less undeniably, 90 per cent of students take a predominantly utilitarian view of their university work as the indispensable prelude to civil service or business appointments. Curricula are based upon European and American models. The language of instruction is that of the country, with English or French usually added—or, as in Lebanon, substituted. Premises and equipment vary from adequate to excellent. The status of the professorial staff is high. As in universities elsewhere, not all but most of the usual faculties and departments are represented, with less attention, obviously, to subjects little in demand, and less also to those requiring costly equipment or teachers of extraordinary qualification. Most universities, except the foreign, are state-financed and administered, though this does not prevent the seemingly endless addiction of the students to political demonstrations and strikes. The universities offer B.A., M.A., and Doctorate degrees. The standards of excellence for obtaining these can at some universities be respectably high, and a degree involves, generally, at least some study, some attendance at classes, and some intelligence. Nevertheless, the attainments of a high proportion of B.A. graduates are, it must be admitted, extremely moderate, and in at least some institutions the days when 'passing' was an unquestioned matter of course for every student are only now ending. There is, no doubt, as much variation between the merits and standards of Middle Eastern universities—Turkish, Persian, Arab, Israeli—as is familiar in North America. Among the best, by common consent, are such famous foreign foundations as the American University and the (French, Jesuit) University of St Joseph, both at Beirut; the (American) Robert College—not fully a university—at Istanbul: and the American University at Cairo. But these have no monopoly of excel-

lence. There were in 1969 forty-one institutions in the Middle East
using the designation of university: Cyprus and the oil shaikhdoms
had none, Jordan and Kuwait one each, Syria and the Sudan two,
Israel and Sa'udi Arabia three (and the Israeli Technion has the
standards of a university, even if not so called), Lebanon and 'Iraq
four, Egypt six, Turkey seven (including the Middle East Technical
University at Ankara, a centre for international development which
is full of promise), and Persia eight—some of which, however, are
new and small.

Sometimes affiliated to, sometimes separate from, the universities
are a wide range of colleges. These mostly offer, to approximately
university standard, a variety of 'arts', scientific, technological, professional and commercial subjects, which include, in one college or
another, law, fine arts, agriculture, economics, teacher-training
and pedagogy, music, engineering, medicine and dentistry,
veterinary science, oriental studies, and theology. The aggregate
contribution of these is very important. They help to produce the
membership of the numerous 'learned societies' and institutes to
be found flourishing in all the major capitals and provincial cities.
Some of these bodies are general in their cultural interest, some are
specialized to certain fields, such as local folk-lore and linguistics,
scientific (including medical) research, archaeology, education,
orientalism, sociology and philosophy. There are societies for the
practice and enjoyment of the fine arts and music, with exhibitions and teaching facilities. To these can be added the professional
associations and societies which embrace the graduate practitioners of
law, medicine, engineering, etc., and, finally, the official Academies
of the local languages, literature and history.

One or more museums, general or specialized, are to be found in
every major city. These are usually well maintained on modern lines.
Some are of strictly local interest, others, like the museums of Cairo
or Baghdad, have earned world fame. The more considerable are as
a rule state-owned, but the non-Muslim communities, or specialized
para-statal institutions, or private persons, are responsible for others.
There is an interesting observatory, of French (Jesuit) foundation,
in the Lebanon. The public or semi-public or collegiate libraries in
the territories have grown in recent years to importance; most can be
freely visited, some are of high value for serious students and contain
works nowhere else available.

A cultural activity highly characteristic of our region, and one
happily linking the interest of local and foreign scholars, is that of

field (as well as study and museum) archaeology. The immense wealth of the region in ancient and medieval sites and objects has led to many projects of excavation by European and American bodies. These have been conducted with great propriety and the highest skill, and rewarded by 'finds' of unique interest in fully two-thirds of the territories. In this work local scholars, now trained thereto, have in recent years taken a creditable part, as also in administering the connected museums and libraries. The general public, to whom a generation ago the whole activity was one of 'foreigners digging for gold'—and smuggling it away when found!—are beginning to see it in truer colours; to the educated it is a source of interested pride.

To describe, and even more to appraise, the current output in the Middle East of modern-type literary and artistic work seems not to belong to the scope of this book. It must suffice to remark that a considerable public interested in these things, as distinct from traditional arts and writings, had by the mid twentieth century come into existence even in those countries where it was, until recently, insignificant; both the producers of such work and its readers or critics are multiplying. Not only in those countries which have long possessed a strain of western art and writing as well as the traditional types (Egypt, Lebanon, Turkey), but in every territory outside Arabia, there are now a number of writers of political and economic essays, of archaeology and history, of philosophy, poetry and fiction, whose best output has sometimes fair, sometimes admirable, merit. This applies to women as well as men, and to all the main Middle Eastern languages, including Kurdish and Armenian. If much of this output is based on western models, this need not deprive it of all originality; it can nonetheless reflect the personal attitudes and gifts of the writer, which often include realism, humanity, and a reforming spirit. The most copious single element, that of political analysis or diatribe, is perhaps the most difficult for the non-nationalist outsider to read with enjoyment. The techniques of printing and book-production, though still indifferent or worse, have immensely improved during the last generation, especially in Egypt and the Lebanon; but book publishing and distribution as an efficient and service-rendering business are still strangely backward, and give authors little encouragement.

In the visual arts, there is already a body of interesting work, but, it would seem, few products yet of such merit as to call for international recognition. Nevertheless, the fine arts are now a subject of higher study which attracts pupils, patrons are found to assist young artists, and the latter study in Europe and can arrange exhibitions of their work. Both here and in modern architecture and, in a very limited circle, western-type music, our region, which was until lately one of near emptiness, is filling to a surprising and encouraging extent with interest and inspiration; outstanding performance, in the near future, would be no surprise. The ancient arts of the region, in miniature-painting, delicate metal work, ceramics, carpet-making and carving, keep their place in public esteem (and as tourist attractions), but seem to have generally declined from their highest level.

The Middle Eastern publics are served by an abundant periodical and daily press. The dailies are, in a few well-known cases, of high or reasonable standard as news-carriers and commentators, with a solid organization behind them and some years of continuity; but the great majority are, for financial reasons, without any serious pretence of a news-service, are without sufficient subscribers or advertising income to maintain publication, and are too often, it must be confessed, without reliability or serious content. The inferior sheets, which by their numbers far over-supply the public demand, almost all represent the politics of a faction or an individual by which or whom they are briefly subsidized, and are devoid of other interest; they are often pointedly or wittily written, commonly by under-employed lawyers or journalist politicians, but ill-produced and likely to enjoy lives of no more than a few weeks or months—or sometimes days. Government censorship is severe, 'freedom of the press' a rarity. The periodical press, consisting of monthlies, weeklies, and some appearing at irregular intervals, is of higher standard. It contains material—political, literary, professional, scientific, scholarly, commercial—of often considerable merit and interest. Such publications are extremely numerous, with a score of weeklies in Tel Aviv and Beirut, fifty per cent more in Teheran and Ankara-Istanbul, over two-score in Cairo, and dozens elsewhere. They cater, in appropriate languages, for all the main communities including the minorities, carry material from cartoons to scholarly articles, and in spite of limited readership can be a valuable educative force.

In broadcasting, no Middle Eastern state has failed to equip itself with one or more stations and transmitters of varying power. In this field, for once, the Arabian principalities are no exception. Programmes, among which the Egyptian lead easily both in abundance and (on the whole) in the standard maintained, consist of the usual ingredients, professionally edited and produced, but with music (oriental and western) as the principal time-filling stand-by, and with heavy doses of strongly, sometimes rabidly, nationalistic politics or propaganda; indeed this powerful instrument seems often to be regarded by its possessor, the government, as more a political than a social or educational weapon. It is probable that broadcasting in most of our territories fails generally, as does the daily press, to satisfy the more educated strata of the public; but this, it seems, is scarcely less true in most countries of the world. Television, highly popular wherever installed, is technically efficient but is forced for its programmes to rely largely on the use of films—and, again, on opportunites for propaganda.

Film-making has made great strides in the more advanced Middle Eastern countries since the Second War, and in particular has produced 'documentaries' of excellent style and content. The social effect of these can be very appreciable. In this field Egypt is unquestionably in the lead.

### 4. *Villages and Tribes*

Since, in spite of the striking growth of the cities and the increase of industry, agriculture in one or another of its forms remains by far the greatest of Middle Eastern sources of livelihood in terms of labour, capital and extent, the life of the villagers devoted thereto ought to be among the most significant objects of our study. In fact, the infinite variety of village settings, in farmland and steppe, mountain and sea shore, wetness and aridity, in all of our dozen countries, would render this the task of a lifetime; and the significant content which would emerge, in terms of Middle Eastern current changes and tendencies, would be relatively small.

The tone and pattern of the life of these many thousands of agricultural villages has in fact changed little in recorded history. Many stand upon relatively new sites, others on ground immemorially occupied. The type, shape and material of the houses, the single room shops, the mosques, coffee-shops and caravanserais have scarcely altered. The furnishings, poor and scanty, are little improved. The food of the peasantry is that, probably, of the last half-millennium—and not more plentiful. Social inter-relations are not less permanent, the position of women scarcely less depressed; in spite of all laws and urban innovations the village way of life is substantially that of past ages, with few gaieties, amusements, amenities or hopes of a wider horizon. The labours of the bread-winner are not less arduous, his methods largely unmodified, his rewards, too often, those of bare subsistence. Drought, locust visitations and other agricultural misfortunes can still intensify poverty and increase indebtedness. These matters are viewed by the peasantry with a resigned fatalism, and they oppose an extreme conservatism to all proposals for change not immediately attractive. The local government still demands its due of land-revenue, landlords (often absentee) have their claims for rent, crop-share and debt-recovery, and tribal authorities, where these persist, must be served or placated.

Such, at least, would be the impressions of a visitor, and they are largely true. Yet there are both hopes and some signs of changes for the better. Landlords, where these survive the break-up of large, multi-village estates now widely in progress, are becoming more amenable, more enlightened both as estate-owners and as citizens. Government officials are for the most part more modern-minded, humane, accessible; many are themselves reformist and public-spirited, security is better than of old, bandits and prowlers less to be feared. The terrors of rain-failure are mitigated, in favoured areas, by irrigation works; specialist work has been done on seed-types and anti-pest measures, demonstrators from the nearest Research Station may have paid the village a visit. There is easier transport of produce to the market-town, a better road, a truck instead of pack-animals. The country 'buses run daily, and fairly reliably. Some new and better-type houses may have appeared, a telegraph office or telephone-box where none existed, a postman, a repair-shop. In Turkey and in post-1952 Egypt Village Institutes, a valuable innovation, combine school and dispensary, library and recreation room; these are immense assets to the village. Far more rural schools exist, and with better teachers than ever before, though still far from sufficient; and this degree of education, now being extended, for the first time, to ever larger numbers of villagers by that revolutionary device, the inexpensive and easily obtainable transistor radio, and by relatively easy contact with the near-by town, is modifying village life at varying speeds wherever it penetrates, and stimulating the villagers to concepts of politics bound to threaten the restraining hold of the landlord or shaikh, agha or sardar.

These tribal authorities, just mentioned, lead us on to a consideration of tribalism. The tribe, as a simple, social group living and acting together under some form of patriarchy, is found in many parts of the world and many environments, but nowhere more characteristically, and with more instructive varieties, than in the

Middle East. Tribes exist on a major scale not only in all of the Arabian peninsula, but throughout the Fertile Crescent. In Egypt they are present, but in little force and on the outer fringes of the national life; in the Sudan, they are numerous, important and various. In Turkey there are today little more than fairly numerous traces; in Persia the tribes are never Persian, but the Lurish, Kurdish and Turkish tribes of the country bear famous names, and are too vital to be ignored.

The tribe is never nothing but a tribe; that is, the households which constitute it form at the same time an economically viable group by their own efforts (as graziers, farmers or otherwise), thanks to skilled use of their environment; they are also, administratively, subjects of their state and province, and, it may be, politically an element of some weight within it. The tribal loyalty which binds them together is habitually the closest and dearest tie of which they are conscious, far surpassing those of locality or nation; and both this and the tribe's special interest in uninhibited freedom, and aversion from 'government interference', result in that reluctant, imperfect integration of these communities with the rest of the public, of which governments and non-tribal publics commonly complain. Their introvert tribal loyalty is derived from their awareness of a common origin (whether true or mystical) and long inseparable common fortunes. Some tribes are, or claim to be, literally the blood-descendants of an eponymous eminent founder, with, obviously, miscellaneous accretions who quickly claim authentic membership. Others derive from a small original body, perhaps military or migrant from elsewhere or linked to a famous name, and have multiplied, and attracted incomers, until the tribal form with all its unifying myth is achieved. Some represent no more than the sedentary inhabitants of a valley or tract whom a leader, indigenous or immigrant, has come to dominate—or possibly has defended—so that a self-conscious 'tribe' results. Others are clearly traceable to the centripetal power of a holy man, or a shrine, around whom or which have clustered his relations, pilgrims and protection-seekers. Many groups, including the noblest in tribal estimation, are of great antiquity and tell ancestral tales of which history can make nothing; these go back to origins in primitive Arabia and, heedless of present poverty and fallen fortunes, claim high superiority in the tribal hierarchy, than which no more rigid yet accepted snobbery exists.

The tribe takes, oecologically, various forms: or rather, tribal nomenclature, and to an extent its organization, has spread in many areas from an environment where it was appropriate to one in which it could, to all appearance, be easily dispensed with; and indeed even city-dwellers to whom countryside, and even more mid-desert, life would be unthinkable not infrequently claim, as a social (occasionally a legal) asset, the name and prerogatives of tribesmen. Apart from these, the established classification of Middle Eastern tribes arranges them into four categories. The first is the long-range nomadic camel-owning tribe of Arabia; the second, the mainly migratory cattle-owning tribe, of Persia and Kurdistan and Turkey; thirdly, the largely-settled, agricultural but also, in some sections, sheep-grazing tribe on or near the fringes of the steppe: and fourthly, wholly agricultural village-dwelling communities which use a tribal name and hierarchy, and may be not less sincere in their long-established tribal loyalties.

The pure *badu*, found in true desert and the lightest steppe-country, migrate at all seasons to and between the grazing-grounds and water-holes which are theirs by right of unwritten desert convention. They have no fixed abiding-place, and no houses but their windy, insecure goats-hair tents. Their life is one of hunger, hardship and ignorance. Both food and clothing are simple and scanty, domestic equipment a traditional minimum, water rare and often foul. They live by selling the surplus of their camel-herds—no other animal could survive mid-desert conditions—and by buying grain and coffee and a minimum of cotton-cloth. The less 'noble' *badu* earn a pittance at times by services of carrying or escort. To four-fifths of these nomads contact with the world beyond the desert is not more than annual. Their own amusements are hawking and fireside talk, the pursuit of blood-feuds, and the traditional mutual raiding between hereditary foes. Their expert accomplishment is tracking, their pride is in their pedigree and tribal lore. Their lives are guided by the customs and rules of a millennary tradition, and to a slight degree by those of Islam—but never, if they can help it, those of the government! Their desiderata are the fullest freedom, a sufficiency of water and grass, the give and take of desert hospitality, success in raiding, deference to their status—and enough to eat. Their relations with government, conducted entirely by their shaikh, are as slight and infrequent as they can achieve; attempts by the state to penetrate their deserts and normalize their society are always resisted.

The cattle-migrants, or transhumants, of the hill-country share some features of the camel-nomads' life, but with wide differences. Their migration is six-monthly, to and from their higher mountain pastures and those of the low, warm country where they pass the winter. They move together for lesser distances, by prescribed routes and in formed parties, passing *en route* through settled agricultural country according to an established right which does not, however, exclude numerous quarrels with the crop-growing villagers. Inter-tribal fighting is less common, though hereditary enmities abound; living standards are less abject, tribal pride less immoderate. A part of the tribe-group, certainly including its ruling elements, may own houses and gardens, and often does not migrate; indeed, the proportion which moves annually is probably decreasing. These tribes, in Persia, have recovered much, but not all that they lost in lands, numbers and status during the period 1925–1940.

Of the category of sheep-owning but largely sedentary tribes, those on the Upper Euphrates in 'Iraq and Syria are typical. Most of the tribesmen, village-dwelling or housed in semi-permanent wood-built shelters, cultivate permanently on lands by the river-side while specialized sections (each also a sub-tribe within the tribe) graze the sheep of the community on the inlying desert pastures created by the rains, from mid-winter to late spring, or as long as the grazing and water lasts. These are inoffensive folk, ranked in the tribal hierarchy far below the authentic *badu*, exposed to ruin in case of drought, and more raided than raiding; but the tribal organ-ization and chain of command apply, and tribal pride and its mystique are not absent. This applies, with somewhat diminished force (by reason of dilution, and competition from other sources) but still essentially, to our fourth category, the wholly settled communities of villagers, whether in plain or foothill, farmland or mountain, where the structure and attachments of tribalism yet prevail. Here the sense of tribal solidarity can still be dominant, even when the shaikh or agha is also landlord and government agent, and the state has full powers of interference and coercion—and even though the tribal pretentions of the taxed, controlled, laborious villagers would be viewed with curiosity and scorn by 'Aniza or Shammar!

The minimum unit of tribalism is the single group obeying a single headman, who is chosen by majority opinion from the seniors of the community, in most cases from the sons or near relations of the former shaikh. This authority is normally, but without precise formulation, subject to known custom and to prevailing opinion within the tribe; unless of outstanding personality the shaikh can be no dictator, and in case of failure he can and will be replaced. His function is that of protector of all tribal rights and advantages, dispenser of hospitality for the tribe, occasional judge or arbitrator, leader in raids and in defence, policy maker and representative *vis-à-vis* the government, other tribes and the outside world. Upon him rests the cohesion of the tribe, a quality certain, in this region of intense individualism, to vary between the widest limits. Many shaikhs retain their authority for a lifetime, and bequeath it. The formation of groups and confederacies of tribes, with a common consciousness and group-name but composed of many constituent units, is very general; such often furnish, in all territories where tribes exist, the most famous of tribal names—Arab, Kurdish or Turcoman—and may keep their structure and allegiances for decades: indeed for far longer, when the prestige of the name and ruling family provide bonds strong enough to hold the group together in harmony and without (no uncommon event) secession. Every major tribe will prove, on examination, to contain within it, with an accepted order of precedence and distribution of authority, a variety of sub-tribes, themselves probably of differing scales and origins.

The policy of all modern Middle Eastern governments, except perhaps that of the Sa'udi rulers, to tribalism is instructively uniform: it is that of progressive tribe-breaking, with the aim of reducing all tribesmen to the status of normal citizenship. This policy, in force in 'Iraq since the mid-nineteenth century, and notably in Persia in the recent inter-war period, is undoubtedly shared by other concerned governments of today. It is justified by the consideration that tribalism, except in desertic regions scarcely susceptible of normal government, can have little or no future in modern states—as Scotland and other countries have found—because it necessarily, and indeed designedly, detracts from governmental authority; the tribe as such stands openly for conceptions of corporate life and administration inimical to what is nowadays accepted as civilized progress in equity, citizenship, law-enforcement, education and the public services. It is true that procedures of tribe-breaking and resettlement, if they are to be carried out with humanity, and above all to be succesful, call for more intelligent planning, more material aid and imaginative economic thought, more psychological appreciation, than have so far been forthcoming from impatient reformists; but, on a long view, there seems little alternative to such a policy. Its application will be aided by a number of factors affecting tribal life, such as are now visibly operating. These are the increasing sophistication and urbanization of many tribal leaders, with their motor-cars and town houses and amusements, whereby they lose true contact with their followers: the economically serious loss of demand for tribal products: the easier penetrability of desert areas to government transport, and therefore control: the spread of education, through broadcasts if not through schools, leading to a self-critical view of tribalism as archaic and unfashionable: and an increasing realization, by the rank and file of the tribes, that their life is one of hardship and misery from which softer surroundings may one day lure them. Meanwhile the tribes, of every type and scale, are very much alive, represent, at their best, a distinctive form of society, and pose no lack of problems.

# CHAPTER TEN

# LANDS AND FACTORIES

## 1. *Agriculture: a general view*

IN its devotion to agriculture, and dependence for livelihood upon it, the region which is our subject suffers—in contrast, it seems, to a general opinion—from serious drawbacks. These include not only its distance from the world's major markets for agricultural produce, but the very high proportion of its land-surface which is uncultivable desert, mountain or marsh; less than 15 per cent of the area is capable of bearing crops. The drawbacks include also the vagaries of a rainfall habitually insufficient for dry farming, and often practically non-existent. They include the prevalence of excessively light soils with inadequate organic content, and a tendency to salinate when habitually irrigated. With all these defects go the prevalence of pests and diseases, including those which afflict and debilitate the peasants: the rural conservatism which, linked to a crippling lack of capital, has perpetuated primitive methods and acquiesced in low productivity and inferior products: and finally, too often, land-tenure systems which deprive the worker of most of the fruits of his labour, and discourage effort and enterprise.

These factors do not, with all their force, prevent the agricultural life from being the favoured (because the only conceivable) livelihood of nearly all our territories. As a source of national income the agricultural industry is exceeded by others only in the oil-states of Arabia, in Israel, in Lebanon, and possibly now in Egypt; throughout the rest of the Fertile Crescent, and Cyprus, Persia, Turkey, Yemen and the Sudan, the largest share of wealth, and the livings of some 50 to 80 per cent of the inhabitants, derive directly from the land. And, with all their disadvantages, the farmers of many of our territories have cultures of interest, sometimes of merited fame, to show; such are, as all the world knows, the cotton of Egypt and the Sudan, the dates of 'Iraq, the citrous fruits of Israel, the coffee of the Yemen, the grapes and fruit of Turkey and the Levant.

Of the serious disadvantages mentioned above, some are manifestly intractable: that is, those deriving from the sheer facts of geography and climate—though, even here, the works of man can, and to some extent do, provide palliatives. Others of the current defects may with time, goodwill and money be partially curable. In any event, so close is the connection between agriculture, actual and potential, and social well-being in the Middle East that some pages must be devoted to these matters. First the basic troubles, almost region-wide, from which agriculture suffers will be more closely considered, together with possible lines of advance: then, a brief survey will be made of the agricultural performance of each territory as it now appears.

The provision of a greater acreage of cultivable land can, in evident cases, be effected by the terracing of mountain-slopes, already a characteristic feature, for long ages past, in the Lebanon, Turkey, the Yemen and Persia: by the costly and long-drawn draining of marshes in, for example, Syria, southern 'Iraq, ultimately the vast *sudd* of the Sudan, and well known localities in Egypt, Turkey and Persia: and, on a far greater scale than these, by the provision of irrigation for lands whose only fault is their aridity. This same method will often replace a precarious rain-cultivation with assured and possibly all-seasonal supply of water, with immediate doubling or trebling of productivity. Irrigation works on a very important scale have in fact been carried out over the last century, but more notably within the last generation, in 'Iraq, Egypt and the Sudan, and less projects have been completed in Turkey, Persia, Syria, Lebanon, Israel, and even the Southern Yemen. Moreover in all these, and in Cyprus, Sa'udi Arabia, Jordan, and Yemen also, more and more effort has gone into the increased provision of agricultural water by the time-honoured methods of tapped underground channels (the Persian *qanat*, Arab *kahriz*), of captured hill-streams, of wells and channelled springs, of animal and mechanical water-lift. Today major irrigation projects have been drawn up, and are actively in hand, in most of the major countries of our region—notably 'Iraq, Egypt, the Sudan, Turkey and Syria—while almost none of the territories is without one or a number of plans to increase, on an interesting scale, their acreage or its output. The familiar dangers of such projects, even when successfully completed, are those of salination of the soil, for which drainage, and avoidance of over-irrigation, are the cures: and (a more human aspect) failure to complete the unspectacular de-tailed canalization which secures maximum usefulness. And two other aspects of major irrigation-development are notable. One is, that it may lead to immediate social disturbance, by the shifting of popula-tion into the newly developed area and away from an inferior. Another is the economic aspect: that the crops to be grown must needs be such as to pay not only for the probably high cost of the work, but for its upkeep; and this, with only the traditional crops and methods, may be difficult.

For two other curses of Middle Eastern agriculture, inferior light soil with insufficient humus, and the prevalence of pests, one can but leave the solutions to the scientists. In this field, that of research (to be followed, one hopes, by the evolution of practicable techniques, and by popular instruction) the governments of our states are already active (p. 202) according to their lights. Few have failed to realize the present inadequacy of productivity and product-types (with, in consequence, restricted or low-priced demand) due to these causes, and to divert funds and energies to finding cures. Among these is, for example, the increasing number and efficiency of irrigation pumping-engines, the attempt by good landlords to introduce—and, much more difficult, to keep pure—new types of seed, and the now widely extended use of tractors in place of the ancient, infinitely slow, plough-animals. The government research-stations, experimental farms and field-schemes, wherever found, are full of interest and hope; but their entrenched opponents are not only the forces or shortcomings of nature, and the vagaries of plant-disease, blights and locusts, but also the deep conservatism of the peasantry, their ignorance, and their slow acceptance of superior methods which may call, perhaps, for greater effort or for dislocation of time-honoured routines. The inducement of the peasant intelligently to face new methods and conditions can be effected only, in general, as part of his own gradual evolution and education by school and college and all other instructional media; and, in particular, by practical proof, before his eyes, that the new ways demanded are to his own advantage. It is not to be forgotten that the low productivity of Middle Eastern agriculture, per head of workers, is at present a notable adverse factor; it is reckoned, indeed, as one-fourth, or less, of that of European or American workers. The cure for this seems to lie not only in improved methods, equipment and crop-types, but in a progressive improvement in human health and vigour, which better nutrition and living-standards alone could bring.

For the lack of capital which impedes, always and everywhere, the provision of better implements and facilities and the adoption of progressive plans, there appears no rapid cure, unless provided by an oil-enriched government ('Iraq or Persia) able itself to provide what is required, from major irrigation-schemes to tractor-main-tenance workshops. The diversion of more capital to agriculture depends in part upon willingness, by the rich, so to invest (and risk) their money: in part, on the slow increase of cultivators' own resources: in part, on direct governmental aid. In this field co-operative societies have, it seems, a leading part to play, once initial suspicions are overcome; and in fact this movement is now well established, and has achieved immediate results, not otherwise conceivable, in Turkey, Persia, Cyprus, the Levant States and the Nile Valley. It permits not only the communal acquisition and maintenance of tractors, harvesters and other costly implements not otherwise within reach, but also co-operative marketing and sometimes management, and even the acquisition of land-holdings by facilitated purchase. This is an important, and relatively new, factor of great value in Middle Eastern society. But, on a wide view, under-financing remains one of the major inhibitive factors in the region's agricultural progress.

Another, yet more serious and not less deeply rooted in the existing social régime, lies in the peculiarity—one might say, the evils—of the land-tenure systems. Not only have these an immediate effect on agricultural efficiency and productivity, but they deeply affect the whole life, morale and happiness of probably two-thirds of the peasantry of the region. In some territories there are areas of small holdings in which, apart from the abiding danger of excessive fragmentation due to inheritance, only minor problems arise; such are Cyprus, Jordan, much of Turkey, small parts of Persia and Syria, and the mountain areas of 'Iraq and Lebanon. There are, elsewhere, large estates, perhaps government-owned or corporation-owned, in which tenant farmers are reasonably well treated and content; and there are districts where peasant small-holding settlement has been, in recent years, carried out by government policy. In countries, or districts thereof, where estates have traditionally been extensive, and privately owned by landlords habitually absentee (as Egypt, Persia, 'Iraq), steps have been taken in late years by the governments to remedy by direct statal action the serious evils of this abused, anti-social and inefficient system: that is, by imposing by law a maximum holding of so-many acres (varying usually as between irrigated and non-irrigated land) per owner, and parcelling out the rest for sale, by instalments, to the ex-tenants. Such programmes of land reform have already been undertaken by four of the region's major states. Egypt was the first, imposing radical restrictions on private land-holding as early as 1952 and extending these in 1961 to a maximum allowable holding of approximately 100 acres per person. By 1966, a reported 765,000 acres of land had been redistributed to some

300,000 families under the Egyptian land reform. Land redistribution similar to the Egyptian programme (indeed, largely inspired by it) began in both Syria and 'Iraq in 1958. Of the two, Syria's has become the more stringent, limiting holdings to less than 200 acres; in 'Iraq the limits on individual estates can be as high as 1000 acres. In both of these Fertile Crescent states, however, the implementation of their decade-old land redistribution programmes has been hindered by political instability and the alternation of partially conservative with revolutionary régimes. The most recent large-scale effort in land reform is that of Persia; since 1963, the monarchy has been engaged in the heroic experiment of a 'White Revolution', in which the throne itself is attempting to break up the great, often multi-village, estates and to redistribute the land to the peasantry. With the increased powers of the modern state behind him, the Shah seems to be well on the way to success in his programme; in 1967 it was even claimed that four million families had received land. All of these reforms have shown a new willingness to deal with an ancient social evil, even though they have created also new problems for the cultivators in the fields of large-scale canal management and upkeep, and in the immediate finding of even minimum financing (for seed, animals, and interim existence) for the penniless and now landlordless new owner. But, morally and practically, the new position is, where it exists, undoubtedly more hopeful than the old.

Another undoubted need is that of a greater contribution by the State (since there is no other adequate authority) and, for some purposes, perhaps also by concerted inter-statal action, in the field of agricultural planning. This might cover, for example, the proportion of each main crop to be grown (as, for instance, between grain and cotton in Egypt), the prohibition of some profitless or damaging cultures, the encouragement of more 'mixed farming' integrated with stock-breeding and its products, the movement progressively from merely subsistence crops to cash-crops, the insistence on drainage, the organization of anti-pest efforts, the expansion of co-operatives, the observance of reputable standards in marketing and export: and many other matters. The part played by governments in this general field (p. 202) is already highly important; it will probably increase, as will their direct provision of more instructors and inspectors, more facilities for trial and experiment, more transport, storage and marketing organizations. Inter-government consultation could, as in a measure it already does, deal with the apportionment of river-waters (Euphrates, Nile, Jordan) between neighbouring states: with concerted anti-locust measures: perhaps with the expansion or limitation of acreage to be devoted to crops regionally in excess or in short supply. But the success of such consultation would evidently depend on factors far outside the agricultural sphere.

## 2. Agriculture: country by country

The crops, the methods and problems, the rural circumstances of our territories as they stand today, only half-way or less on their journey towards the greater development destined to be theirs, deserve a closer survey.

In TURKEY, some three-quarters of the population lives on and from the land, of which, in all, perhaps one-third (a high proportion for the Middle East) is said to be cultivable. With the exception of wheat, a recent rising demand for which has led to imports, the country is normally self-sufficient in cereals (barley, rye, maize, millet, oats) which are produced on a large scale. Rice is widely grown, but without exportable surplus. Excellent fruit, including citrous, is produced and sent abroad; Turkish raisins, sultanas and figs are famous, olives are ubiquitous, hazel-nuts a major crop. Part of the grape-harvest is made into excellent wine, welcomed in foreign countries. Tea, on the eastern Black Sea coast, is a useful innovation; experiments in coffee-growing are in progress. Opium poppies are grown, and, with due authority, their produce is marketed. Turkish tobacco, of high and characteristic quality, is a renowned product and in international demand; the main growing areas are those of Izmir and Samsun. But it is a relatively new crop, cotton, grown in the Izmir, Antalya, Aydin and Adana areas, which is now Turkey's leading export, averaging almost one-quarter of all exports in recent years. Land-tenure problems are less acute in Turkey than elsewhere; in spite, however, of an impressive increase of tractors and other mechanization in favourable areas, and development by irrigation in others, the general level of method and productivity is very low.

In PERSIA dependence on agriculture is equally general, the environments of its practice not less varied; but here not more than 10 to 15 per cent of the land-surface is cultivable, and a high proportion of this has been held (until the 'White Revolution') in large absentee-owned estates or crown-lands. Widely grown products are cereals of every type, sugar-beet, fruit and nuts, rice in the Caspian provinces, opium (prohibited but still profitably grown), tobacco, and oil-seeds. Limited quantities of good fruit are gathered, some cotton and a little tea. All the characteristics of Middle Eastern agriculture are exemplified in Persia, including particularly the long and difficult communications, persistently primitive (though in rare localities modernized) methods, and rural poverty at its grimmest. But study, capital and effort are now all being in some degree devoted to agriculture, with emphasis on rural credit (for which a Bank has been founded), on co-operative societies, and on discovering and conserving water-sources. The effects of the current attempt to break up the country's large estates should, if successful, vastly transform Persian agriculture, in ways not yet fully discernible.

In 'IRAQ, the date crop picked in the vast date-gardens of the centre and south is the most famous, rice perhaps the most prized by its growers, the winter grains (wheat and barley) the most widespread, of the country's products. A substantial export of dates (some ID 5,000,000-worth annually), cotton and barley is normal; of these, cotton is increasing the most rapidly. All the usual summer grains and vegetables are grown, with small quantities of fruit, and tobacco in Kurdistan. Cultivation is by rain in the north, by controlled canal or pump-irrigation in the centre and south, and by tidal irrigation in the Basra date-gardens. Whatever the contributions of oil-riches and of nascent industries, agriculture and horticulture remain the staple livelihood of the 'Iraqis who, in general terms, seem to possess the greatest agricultural potential of any Middle Eastern state, as well as the necessary capital from other sources (their oil) to help its development. A number of important irrigation and flood-protection projects have been already accomplished (the first in 1912) and others are planned, all on a scale truly impressive and indicative of the extent to which oil-derived Development funds have been so utilized. A multifold increase of cultivated acreage, through new canals and mechanical water-lift, throughout central 'Iraq has been brought about in the last generation, chiefly by private capital and enterprise. Much well-directed governmental effort has been spent in research and instruction, an Agricultural Bank exists, new cultures have been attempted, locust-destruction campaigns conducted, comprehensive anti-salination measures formulated, specialists invoked; nevertheless, the mass of 'Iraqi agriculture is still relatively primitive and wasteful. And the benefits of the redistribution of land, begun in 1930 and reactivated on revolutionary lines in 1958, are as yet but little apparent; some observers feel that it has created more problems than it has solved.

In SYRIA, endowed likewise with abundant cultivable acreage, with Euphrates and Orontes water, and with a normally sufficient rainfall for dry-farming in the north, cultivation has shown striking advances in area since the Second War. In the 1950s, agricultural effort concentrated on opening the steppe to cultivation, and re-markable strides were made in the raising of cotton, which indeed has been Syria's leading export for the past decade. The changes in land-holding begun in 1958 and extended thereafter were for long delayed in their carrying-out by political instability, doubtless to the detriment of both peasant and entrepreneur; only since 1963, under the régime of the Ba'th Party, has significant implementation been achieved. Agriculture in Syria, partially because of the open, level nature of the new lands in the steppe, is relatively highly modernized and mechanized. Irrigation works on a considerable scale have been carried out since 1945, more than doubling the area of irrigated land; the Euphrates Dam (p. 132) will, if finally built, open to intensive agricultural development a zone almost one-half as large as the current cultivated area. This same river already serves hundreds of water-lifting pumps. The main crops grown in Syria are wheat and barley—with usually, not always, an exportable surplus for needy neighbours—cotton, oil-seeds, sugarbeet (its production increased ten-fold in the last twenty years), grapes and other fruit (olives, figs, apricots, apples), summer grains and vegetables. The tobacco of Lataqiya is small in quantity, but world-famous.

In LEBANON, just over a quarter of the country is cultivated, a proportion reached only after much effort in drainage, reclamation and terracing; and in a small mountainous country no great further expansion can be possible. In the field of land-tenure, hundreds of holdings in the mountain districts are uneconomically small, those in the plains of the south and north are extensive and often absentee-owned; half the total cultivable land is said to belong to 200 owners. With exceptions, agricultural methods remain primitive. Cereal pro-duction is limited, and increasing but little; the population is dependent on imports. Some sugar-beet is grown, and most of the familiar vegetables; onions are a usual export. Lebanese fruit-growing is of more, and characteristic, interest; good apples are grown (though these are not easily marketable outside the country), and the citrous fruits, of excellent quality, furnish an export to Europe. The crop has increased strikingly in late years, and is now a third of that of Israel. Bananas manage to survive the winter, and

54. The harbour, Aden

55. The refinery, Little Aden

56. The Hadhramaut: the Sultan's palace at Sayun

57. (*Facing page*) Mecca: the Ka'ba

58. Abu I
Liwa sand
dunes

59. Trucial coast: Camel train, Abu Dhabi

indeed to increase in output; the grapes, also an increasing crop, produce a respectable wine. Figs and olives are locally consumed. A little cotton and tobacco are grown. With all this, Lebanon is an agricultural country to a less predominant extent than most in the region; about 40 per cent of its workers are cultivators, the rest being occupied in industry, commerce, and service activities. Trade, not agriculture, here provides most of the national income.

In CYPRUS, the case is similar; roughly the same proportion of the labour-force is in agriculture, which accounts for not more than one-quarter of national wealth. Small-holdings are the rule. The deficient rainfall makes irrigation desirable for most cultures, and this is achieved wherever possible by a numerous variety of small works—pumping, conservation of flood-water, and minor canalization. About one-sixth of existing cultivable land is or can be irrigated, the rest is exposed to the danger of drought and failure. No major expansion of cultivable area (now some 1,250,000 acres) can be hoped for. In the plain, mechanization by tractors and combine harvesters has made advances. Production costs are relatively high, the income of agricultural workers low, and a drift to urban employment results; agriculture, within Cypriot limits and problems, can barely, or cannot, support the population which successful measures of health-improvement have so greatly increased. The principal crops grown are cereals, grapes from which saleable wines and grape-alcohol are produced, citrus fruit—a considerable export—olives, carobs, potatoes, onions and other vegetables, and some tobacco.

The agricultural picture in JORDAN is, on the west side of the river, one of poor and largely eroded soil, well cultivated with terraces, trees and vineyards, while on the east lies less eroded and more extensive land still under a primitive and little productive régime of cultivation. Agricultural methods have seen considerable modernization in the 1960s: the number of tractors in use increased by five times from 1956 to 1967, and the use of chemical fertilizers grew almost as rapidly; but the prevalent agricultural régime is still that of tradition. Land-tenure problems, a field in which admirable work of settlement and stabilization was done under the Mandate (1920–1946), are limited to the too-exiguous acreage of many of the holdings. But Jordan's basic agricultural problem is that less than one-tenth of her cultivable land is irrigable, the rest being dependent on scanty and capricious rainfall. Some progress has been made in the 1960's in extending irrigation—the East Ghor scheme, a gravity-fed canal from the Yarmuk south, has added 30,000 acres, and the Mukhaiba Dam on the same river 18,000—and the state has plans for irrigating 200,000 acres more; but political questions of international water rights and the shortage of capital make any major extension in the forseeable future improbable. Only more laborious and more skilful farming, it seems, can increase production. The crops now principally grown are cereals, especially wheat—but in quantities necessitating the regular import of grain and flour to feed the population—on the East Bank, vegetables and fruit (especially olives, largely exported) on the West Bank.

Of the insistence on land-work in ISRAEL, for both ideological and economic reasons, we have spoken elsewhere (p. 190); and reference has been made also to the forms of agricultural settlement adopted, so different from those found elsewhere in our region. The Israeli community has tackled its agricultural problems with a wealth of energy and science, under the spur of necessity to feed its public and to save the cost of imports; it has enjoyed at the same time, to an extent wholly unknown to its neighbours or to the Palestine of earlier years, the advantage of massive financial help from outside. This has permitted expenditure on settlement-building, irrigation, mechaniza-tion, research, etc., on a scale to which the resources of the territory itself could never aspire. Much of the new state's energy has gone towards the extension of the cultivable area, a policy dictated by the rapid population increase. The draining of the Hula marshes in the far north in the 1950s resulted in the addition of some 15,000 acres, and persistent efforts have reclaimed desert, steppe and scrub forest wherever these touch the sown. The major hope for great agricultural growth, however, rests on the exploitation of the Negev, Israel's southern desert. The opening of this area to cultivation was one factor behind the construction of the National Water-Carrier, a massive conduit carrying the waters of the Jordan Valley east and south—and the source of constant political tension in the mid-1960s. It has indeed made possible the extension of agriculture into the northern fringe of the Negev, and may someday make it a veritable garden. In all, the state has almost tripled the cultivable land which it took over in 1948, as well as irrigating a proportion assessed at one-third.'

Israel, with a notably diversified and increased agricultural pro-duction, is now said to be self-sufficient in vegetables and dairy produce, though large imports of grain and meat are still necessary. Citrous fruit-growing (the famous Arab industry of such long stand-ing, based on the inimitable Jaffa orange) has been restored, after a

severe recession, to over its pre-1948 level; it provides Israel's most
valuable agricultural export. Other fruits grown and in part exported
are olives, grapes, apples and bananas. Crops grown on unirrigated
land are cereals, pulses, fodder-crops, oil-seeds; on irrigated, cotton,
sugar beet, ground nuts, tobacco. As much of all this as possible is
processed for export, by the industries established *ad hoc*: by the
manufacture, for instance, of wine, sugar, fruit juices and cotton
textiles.

The agriculture of EGYPT is of high importance not only for its
own sake as the sole support of about 60 per cent of Egyptian lives,
and the activity of some of the world's most skilled and industrious
cultivators, but as a field also of economic and political problems
whose range exceeds that of Egypt herself. The soil of the Nile
valley is of unusual fertility; but by reason of the sheer numbers of
the population, still growing at a minimum rate of 2 per cent a year,
intensive cultivation with two, three, or four crops a year is necessary
in the very limited irrigable areas. This has called, and calls, for an
agricultural régime radically different from that of any other Middle
Eastern country. The intensive use of fertilizers, which must be
imported and paid for, is widespread, costly and unavoidable; the
government's hopes for self-sufficiency in fertilizers by 1970 will
unfortunately not be realized. The conversion of earlier 'basin'
irrigation (by merely local and temporary capture of the annual
flood-water, in confined basins) into perennial irrigation (by vast-
scale imprisonment of high-season Nile supplies, by great river
barrages) has been proceeding for a century—the first Delta barrage
was built in 1843—and now covers almost all areas except those of
Upper Egypt; and it has called, and is still inevitably to call, for
enormous expense. At the same time the devotion of a high proportion of the restricted acreage to the most financially rewarding
crops, notably cotton, cannot but lead to diminished food-growing,
and therefore to greater dependence on imports.

In major irrigation works, to those existing at Aswan, Isna, Nag
Hamadi, Asyut and elsewhere has now been added the renowned
High Dam at Aswan, which was made possible by a 1959 Nile
Waters Agreement with the Sudan. The High Dam, the physical
construction of which was virtually completed by late 1968, must
rank among the greatest man-made phenomena in the world. Built at
a cost of nearly £400,000,000 (at least one-quarter supplied by aid
from the U.S.S.R.), it is a rockfill, sand and clay structure with an
impervious granite core, over two miles long, 120 yards high and

two-thirds of a mile thick at its base. It has created a reservoir, Lake Nasser, with a capacity of 130,000 million cubic yards of water. With its giant power installation of twelve Russian-built generators, it is expected to add over 1,200,000 acres to the cultivated area, transform another 750,000 from basin to perennial irrigation, eliminate the annual flood and replace it with a controlled flow, and more than double the country's hydro-electric capacity. Yet, when all this is achieved, the amount of agricultural land *per capita* will be less than that available in 1952—such being the dynamics of Egyptian population growth! A different type of project, but perhaps of equal long-range significance, is the New Valley, an attempt to develop, with the help of underground water, wide areas of desert land in the Western Desert parallel to the Nile.

The contribution of the Egyptian Government to its agriculture has not been limited to these works. It has embraced agricultural research, experiment, demonstration, control, and a policy, not always capable of implementation, of balancing internal needs against the advantage of added exports. It has embraced also, with social and political as much as agricultural exigencies in view, a radical redistribution of lands from the hands of the great landowners—sometimes admirable estate-managers, but not infrequently heartless exploiters of poor and indebted tenants—to those of the cultivators themselves. From 1952 to 1966, some 765,000 acres were so disposed of, with important psychological results and, as official figures suggest, appreciable gains to agricultural productivity. Dispossessed landlords, their estates cut down to a mere 100 acres, are compensated in treasury bonds. Some 4,000 landowners have been affected by the land reform programme, and one of the alleged major scandals of Egyptian society has thus been partly corrected. But the fragmentation of the smallest holdings, of which hundreds of thousands are less than a single acre, goes on, and many peasants are entirely landless. The minimum subsistence holding is two acres.

The crops grown in Egypt consist of both subsistence and cash crops. Among the former, wheat and maize are necessities for food, rice and onions are important both for local consumption and for export. *Barsim* (a clover fodder-crop), vegetables, pulses, dates, barley, millet and ground nuts are other products. Cash crops include grapes and citrus fruit of limited export value and, overshadowing all the rest, the famous Egyptian long-staple cotton. This crop, the object of intense care and great skill at every level, gives Egypt the rank of fifth among the world's cotton-producers, and an output of nearly half the world's long-staple cotton. The crop covers about one-fourth of the total cropped area and provides some 40 per cent of the national income from agriculture. The dangers of so great a dependence on outside demand and on uncontrollable, fluctuating prices are realized.

The SUDAN is strictly an agricultural country, where efforts are now being made to diversify produce and to lessen dependence on the cotton-crop, at present the country's most highly developed culture. In areas where rain-cultivation is possible, traditional methods still largely prevail, though mechanization has notably increased. The main crops grown on rain are maize and millet, sesame, ground nuts, and short-staple cotton. The characteristic, perhaps unique, method of grain cultivation in these districts is that of *hariq*—that is, by burning the grassy or weedy ground prior to planting. The problems of rainland farming are currently under close study and experiment. On lands irrigated by flood or by controlled gravity, or by human, animal or mechanical water-lift, the extent of which has grown greatly in recent years, most of the same crops are produced, with wheat, pulses and some barley, and dates; coffee, tea, tobacco, citrous and rice are all under major experiment. The outstanding success of irrigated agriculture, and of an imaginative venture in agricultural organization, has been the Gezira Scheme, a project involving the area in the triangle of the Blue and White Niles, irrigated since 1925 by the reservoir created by the Sennar Dam. This has been developed by an admirably managed threefold partnership of government, the Sudan Gezira Board (successor to the Sudan Plantations Syndicate), and the cultivators themselves, with careful regard to the rights and functions of each. A major extension of the Gezira estates southward into the Managil district, planned in 1957 and completed in 1961, has added some 750,000 acres. The area so far developed is some 1,850,000 acres, with hopes of reaching an eventual 5,000,000; the Roseires and Khashm al-Girba dams are part of this extension. Gezira cotton—though other crops than this are also grown—is the mainstay of Sudani exports and of the national agricultural income. Other governmentally organized projects are those at 'Abdul Majid, watered by a canal from the Gezira, another in the Gash Delta under a carefully regulated government-tenant partnership, another in the Tokar Delta similarly; others exist in the Nuba Mountains where rain-grown cotton is produced under constructive official control, and in the Rufa' district of the Blue Nile where pumped water irrigates cotton and food-crops. In no country, it would seem, is a visible agricultural effort being made with more determination or a more prudent adaptation to conditions.

In the ARABIAN PENINSULA, on the other hand, vast as it its area, agriculture plays, with interesting local exceptions, the minor part which alone Nature permits. In the SA'UDI ARABIAN kingdom there are fairly extensive date-gardens at the oases, with small yields of other fruits. A little wheat, maize, millet and lucerne can also be grown in these favoured but limited locations. There are current projects for small irrigation works at two or three places where sub-surface water is believed to exist. At the al-Kharj oasis south of Riyadh, American initiative has produced valuable fruit and vegetable cultures by well-irrigation. A major project, by Arabian standards, is that of an irrigation dam, at Wadi Jizan in the southwest, which will irrigate 20,000 acres when finished. The authorities are instituting research and instructional centres to foster whatever the best technical help can devise in agricultural enterprise; but this can, by the nature of things, be little. The YEMEN, as we have seen, is more favoured; if the lowlands are mostly uncultivable, except for dates, oats and most importantly cotton, highland districts are capable of growing admirably both irrigated and rain-fed crops, to which, and notably to the famous coffee, the moderate level of subsistence prosperity and (by Arabian standards) the dense population are due. Terracing is widespread, and small-scale irrigation works represent a long tradition of skilful husbandry. Among the hill-villages and around the chief towns, varieties of maize and millet are grown, with some barley, sesame and rice; the fruit are dates, grapes, apricots, almonds, citrous fruits, plums and apples. *Qatt* (p. 161) is widely grown. The country's immemorial dependence on coffee is gradually being reduced by the increasing value of cotton as an export crop.

The southern and south-eastern districts of Arabia contribute as little to the world's agriculture as almost any inhabited region on earth. The SOUTHERN YEMEN can show a little grain and vegetable cultivation, a very few fruit gardens, coffee of export value, and some not unpromising attempts at development in the Hadhramaut valley by pump-engine irrigation, the sinking of deep wells, and the culture, for the first time, of citrous and hard fruit. At 'Abyan to the east of Aden an important irrigation scheme was begun in the last decade of British rule, and 5,000 acres (out of a hoped-for 120,000) were opened to the cultivation of the long-staple cotton which has now passed coffee as the region's most valuable export. But further development projects, for which outside aid is imperative, are paralyzed by the country's uncertain political life.

The OMAN principality can boast its isolated but attractive seaside oasis of Dhufar, where wild vegetation is rich but agriculture (at least until recently) not encouraged. In the Jabal Akhdhar dates and fruits abound in the rare but long-established mountain settlements and the deep passes, where grain and fodder crops, rain-fed or irrigated from *qanats*, cater for man and beast. The same is true of the coastal strip of the Batina, from which date-export is, by Omani standards, considerable. Under the current development programme in the Sultanate, agricultural stations experimenting in the adaptation of a variety of crops (including cotton) to local conditions exist at Nizwa and Sohar, but wider development must depend on the exploitation of water-resources. In the Persian Gulf area, agriculture on the TRUCIAL COAST is limited to the few and small inland oases, and to an experimental station at Ras al-Khaima; BAHRAIN, as we have seen (p. 170), has its district of attractive and intensive cultivation, with dates and fruit, lucerne and vegetables; and QATAR and KUWAIT, with the wealth provided by oil, are prospecting now for water as well as oil—Kuwait is arranging to 'import' it from 'Iraq'—and building model, if expensive, farms where agriculture was unknown a decade ago.

## 3. *Industry*

Factors are not lacking which would seem to favour a major industrial development in the Middle East, even though density of population, a usual motive, is lacking except in Egypt, Israel and perhaps the Lebanon. The local governments favour such expansion for reasons of prestige, industrialization being reckoned progressive and anti-traditional; they hope also to lessen imports, increase exports, and give employment to the un- or underemployed rural and urban proletariat, as well as to the growing ranks of the *évolués* for whom politics or the overcrowded professions seem to be otherwise the only outlet. Governmental encouragement to such enterprise has therefore been freely given, in most of our territories, by fiscal privileges, by government participation, by an *étatiste* policy (as in Turkey, Persia, Israel and Egypt), and by customs-tariffs calculated to exclude competition. At the same time, the public are equally well disposed to the same development, and can point to considerable private initiative, a modicum of industrial skills, and a local purchasing power increased, in some territories, by the recent and continuing boom in oil prosperity.

Why, then, is it more prudent to treat industry with caution when offered as the panacea of Middle Eastern economic, and perhaps social, troubles?

The reasons, some foreseeable *a priori*, others already demonstrated in practice, are clear enough. Local purchasing power, if higher than of old, is still wretchedly small. Local manufactured products, with very few and special exceptions, can scarcely hope to reach, for some time, competitive international standards; and if forced upon foreign markets (itself no easy task) by sheer lowness of price, they would show little profit. Raw materials exist only in a narrow range, and are of indifferent quality—for example, wool and (save in Egypt) cotton; and they include few ores. Technology is generally backward, individual skills of high quality exist only in rare categories. Capital is notably scarce, the moneyed public is little accustomed to the risks of industrial investment: they prefer to hoard, or to buy real-estate; and foreign capital, a clear necessity for any major development, is more often scared by insecurity and political threats than it is attracted by governmental or promoters' blandishments. Finally, the planning of industrial enterprises, when undertaken on any major scale, as in Turkey, Egypt or Persia, has shown endemic defects of over-optimism, insufficient study, defective financing, uncalculated markets; and even when quick profits have been realized they are all too likely to prove short-lived.

The factors thus enumerated, which are unlikely soon to disappear, make it improbable, or inconceivable, that factory-industry will, for many years, have a dominant part to play in the Middle East. Such it may have in small, highly differentiated communities such as Israel and possibly the Lebanon; it may play an important though always a subsidiary role in Egypt, on a scale almost certainly less than confident Egyptian ministers hope today. It can make a contribution, and valuably diversify national life, in Turkey, Persia, 'Iraq, Syria, Cyprus. It is unlikely to lead more than a marginal existence, which need not, however, exclude all such enterprise, in Jordan, the Sudan, or Arabia.

Of countries today pressing forward in industrialization, only Israel, the Lebanon, and perhaps Egypt derive more of their national incomes from that source than from agriculture; next in order would come Syria and Turkey, followed by Persia and 'Iraq. In all, both public (governmental) and private funds have been employed; in all, the state has shown keen interest and helpfulness, most notably in Egypt, Turkey, Persia and 'Iraq. In Israel both statal and para-statal funds as well as copious investment by non-resident supporters have been available. In the Lebanon, and until recently Syria, private enterprise has borne the main burdens. (The governmental background organization of financial support, in the form of Industrial Banks, Development Boards, Economic Development organizations, Seven Year Plan organizations, and so on, does not here concern us.) The scale of factory construction and organization has varied widely; most plants are small, the great majority employing less than fifty, and few more than five hundred workers. But it should be emphasized that the unfamiliarity of industrial installations in these territories and of the industrial way of life itself, and the interest and hopes (perhaps illusions) excited by their appearance, are far greater than in developed countries, and they therefore represent a more striking social contribution than their scale or economic value would suggest. For better or worse, they proclaim change and progress, and seem to offer an alternative to the age-long, almost static, agricultural life hitherto without rival. The numbers of workers employed in industry may vary from not far less than a million in Turkey, and a not much inferior figure in Egypt, to a very few thousand in Cyprus, still fewer in Jordan or the Sudan, and mere hundreds in the Arabian states.

By reason of lack of metallic ores, and shortage (in most countries) of fuel, and perhaps undemanding domestic markets, heavy industry at present is limited to Turkey, with her iron and steel works at Karabuk and Eregli, to be followed by another at Edremit; to Egypt, with similar facilities at Halwan; and to Israel, with a steel rolling-mill at Acre. But others are now entering this field; Persia with an iron and steel mill at Isfahan, 'Iraq with one at Baghdad, and even Sa'udi Arabia with a rolling-mill at Jidda. The manufacture of arms and ammunition and the construction of lorries and cars (or their assembly from imported parts) is in progress in Turkey, Persia, Egypt and Israel. And the semi-heavy industries of brick- and tile-making, stone and marble quarrying, and (most widespread of them all) cement-making, are found in almost every territory. That all have their thermal, or rarely hydro-electric, power-stations, constantly growing in scale and numbers according to increasing demand for electricity, needs no insistence.

The wide range of light industries favoured by many or most of our territories can be no more than briefly listed. They include notably textiles—that is, the spinning, weaving, dyeing, etc., of cotton-cloth, usually from local cotton and intended predominantly for the local market. This is on an important scale, and with very few territories excepted; in some the textile industry is the most developed branch of their industrial life, as in Persia, Egypt and Syria. Woollen cloth is produced in Egypt, 'Iraq, Israel, Persia, Syria and Turkey; jute in Persia; silk in Turkey, Persia, Syria and the Lebanon; and rayon in Israel, Egypt, Syria and the Lebanon.

The food-processing industries, using raw materials of the country and varying in their product with the local produce available, have established a useful, perhaps a growing, place. Wines, beer and spirits are all produced in diverse grades of excellence and quantity. Tea comes from Turkey and Persia. Vegetable oils are prepared for the market from sesame, cotton seeds, the olive, sunflowers and ground nuts; cattle-cake is a by-product of some of these. Sugar-refining is widespread, and renders much of the region self-sufficient in sugar. Date syrup is exported from south 'Iraq. Fruit- and vegetable-canning occupies dozens of small plants in many countries, with the confection of sweets, jams and cakes. Flour mills, bakeries and biscuit-factories are numerous. Soft drinks and mineral waters cater for the Muslim abstainer from alcohol. With these food-industries may be grouped those (if indeed worthy of a place in the industrial picture) devoted to preparing natural products for export: these are, for example, hides, skins, wool, mohair, incense, gums, oyster shells, liquorice, intestines and dried fish.

Industries connected with building, additional to brick-making, etc., already mentioned, are those of bitumen-preparation, joinery, sheet-metal production, the making of glazed tiles and plate-glass, electrical equipment and refrigerators, woodwork and furniture, ply-wood and plasterboard. These are all widely represented. Less so is the manufacture of explosives, fertilizers and insecticides, refined sulphur, industrial alcohol, and petrochemical products including plastics. These, or some of them, are found in Israel, Egypt, Turkey, Persia, 'Iraq, and being initiated in Sa'udi Arabia and Kuwait.

A complete census of factories and plants throughout the region would probably reveal that an actual majority of workers and resources was being devoted, if not to the food-processing industries, then to those providing consumer goods, almost wholly from local materials, to the limited local public able to afford them. These include cigarettes and tobacco: footwear, hosiery and clothing: glass ware and ceramics: soap: pots and pans of aluminium and tin: leather goods, paper and matches: buttons and artificial teeth. The last-named, from Israel and Cyprus, is an item designed principally, one may assume, for export: and in this it resembles the diamond-cutting and polishing industry established in Israel, the drugs and toilet preparations in the same country, and, most famous perhaps of all Middle Eastern manufactured articles, the carpets of Persia, prized throughout the world for their design, colour and craftsman-ship.

Some of the same factors which operate to limit the export of Middle Eastern products—that is, foreign competition, and changing tastes—have served also to diminish the importance of the home or cottage industries of the region. Many of these, as other pages of this book have mentioned, were for centuries highly prized in the form of local textiles and brocades, carpets, needlework, carved or worked metal, jewellery and painted panels. These, mainly luxury products, and the humbler industries of tribal rug-making, pottery, reed mats and blankets, still survive; but both their output and, one cannot but observe, their quality also have been for some time in decline.

To sum up, the Middle East industrial picture (from which we have reserved the vastly important petroleum industry for separate treatment) is full of interest, of variety, of laudable initiative and confidence. It has a part to play in the development and uplifting of these territories; it can do something to increase national wealth, afford employment, satisfy needs, save foreign exchange, and act in some measure as an educative and modernizing agency. But it would, for reasons already indicated, be an illusion to suppose that the factors are widely present in the Middle East which could enable it to achieve more than a moderate potency in solving economic or social problems in the foreseeable future.

# CHAPTER ELEVEN

# OIL

## 1. *Facts and Comparisons*

THE vast Middle Eastern oil production, and its even more impressive available reserves, affording as they do the region's outstanding source of wealth, suggest various comments. Such could be the extreme remoteness of these supplies from the world's major markets: their occurrence in a region previously innocent of all modern industry: their creation of sudden affluence for communities hitherto deep in age-long poverty: and their capricious distribution as between these territories, with Nature's bland and total disregard of human populations, needs, or development. One may admire also the industrial achievement, carried out with highest technological and organizational prowess—and to high standards of commercial and personal conduct—by the great international companies responsible for it.

The region's oil-contribution to the world is certain to be prolonged as well as massive, unless adverse conditions, regional or world-wide, should supervene to prevent this. If the world in 1968 used approximately 2000 million tons of petroleum and its products, it will probably use 3000 million in 1975; if the Middle East supplied in 1968 570 million tons of crude—or 28·5 per cent of the world's output—it is likely to supply 1100 million in 1975 and perhaps 1500 million in 1980. In response to the civilized world's insistent demand, which other regions, on all present indications, will be unable to meet because fully occupied with their own and each other's requirements, but which must be met, the Middle East's contribution is bound to grow in volume, absolutely and proportionately, and with all the force of sheer indispensability. It has grown already from nothing in 1910 to 7 million tons in 1932, 15 in 1942, 104 in 1952, 305 in 1962 and 570 million in 1968. These figures, as representing a rate of increasing output of a major product in a single region, are without parallel. Moreover, the area's own needs in oil consumption being still relatively humble though steadily growing, some 90 per cent of crude output is available for export and thus for the winning of abundant foreign exchange.

Earlier pages of this book have referred in passing to some effects of the region's new-found wealth; we pass now to consider these more fully, beginning with some of the present facts and figures of the industry.

Not by coincidence but in obedience to the basic geological conditions necessary for major oil-accumulation, which are found in unique perfection in the Persian Gulf geosyncline, the principal area of Middle Eastern production is situated in the territories in, and bordering on, that outstanding geological feature. It follows that a number of Middle Eastern countries other than these—at least as far as yet revealed, and to their own puzzled chagrin—are oil-less. These are CYPRUS, the LEBANON, JORDAN, the SUDAN, the YEMEN, and the territories of southern and part of south-eastern ARABIA. In these, all the processes of exploration and testing have been active for some decades, in vain. The Lebanon, traversed by trunk pipelines (p. 129) which bring her a comfortable revenue, possesses also important loading terminals (Tripoli and Sidon) and two refineries. The city of Aden has likewise a refinery of much importance. Jordan is crossed by 'Tapline' (p. 137) and by now derelict pipelines from 'Iraq, but has no terminal and only one small refinery. The Sudan has, and Cyprus will soon have, each a single refinery; the Yemen has nothing.

In a second group of territories oil has indeed been discovered but in quantities of only minor or very moderate significance. The first of these is SYRIA whose two small oil-fields, producing one million tons in 1968, are far inland and call for a long pipeline. A small Czech-built refinery is at Homs. The pipelines from 'Iraq (p. 132) cross the territory, heavy transit-fees being payable by 'Iraq Petroleum. The latter's loading-point is at Banyas, the Syrians' own at Tartus. ISRAELI production amounted to a mere 100,000 tons in 1968; the country has, by inheritance, a major refinery at Haifa, now under enlargement, while a smaller unit is being built at Ashdod; crude supplies arrive by pipeline from Eilat. Long and intensive search has revealed no considerable indigenous crude to add to that of a small field, Heletz, discovered by the 'Iraq Petroleum Company in 1948. EGYPT which since 1967 has deprived itself and the world of the valuable oil-traffic of the Suez Canal, and lost to occupying Israel half of its small but useful Gulf of Suez coastal oilfields, has lately welcomed interesting discoveries by its American and Italian partners in the Western Desert; these will render the country more than self-sufficient in crude, as it already is in refining capacity. All oil operations are administered by a government corporation, which has enjoyed much Russian help. TURKEY, where Turkish and foreign seekers have for years spent much effort and treasure in prospecting, has still sadly little to show; some 3 million tons of crude production was obtained in 1968 from a number of small, inferior, ill-situated fields. Its refining capacity however has been greatly increased by a number of foreign-owned, as well as Turkish, plants at Mersin, Izmir and elsewhere, while the search for crude sources, if slackening, is by no means at an end. BAHRAIN Island, another small producer since 1934 from a single field, with a current output around 3·5 million tons a year, is also an important refining centre for its own and Sa'udi crude, and benefits greatly thereby.

None of the ten territories so far named, or all of them together, could give the Middle East its leading importance in the oil world. That falls instead to three major countries of the Persian Gulf region—'Iraq, Persia and Sa'udi Arabia—and four lesser states, Kuwait, Qatar, Abu Dhabi, Oman. These will be considered in turn in slightly greater detail.

The industry in 'IRAQ is conducted, under three regional concessions from government, by an international British-American-French-British/Dutch Company, the 'Iraq Petroleum Company and its two identical sisters. These operate highly important fields in northern 'Iraq (Kirkuk) and in southern (Zubair and Rumaila), exporting from the latter by tanker and from the former by trans-desert pipelines across Syria/Lebanon to the Mediterranean. Lesser fields in both main areas are also in production and linked by pipeline. Total production in 1968 was 74 million tons. The 'Iraq government, which itself undertakes refining and distribution in the territory, and moreover exploits a small field of its own (formerly British-operated) on the Persian frontier, receives at present upwards of £185 million or $450 million from the I.P.C. group in royalties and taxes. The National 'Iraqi Oil Co., founded in 1962, intends to undertake operations of exploration and exploitation (in territory abruptly confiscated from the I.P.C., being 99·5 per cent of its concession-granted acreage) and will doubtless co-opt foreign partners and operators for such work.

In PERSIA, operations are divided between, first, the National Iranian Oil Co. which represents the government and intends to produce and sell oil on its own, when it can, from fields which it has discovered and proved in central Persia (Qum area): second, eight companies formed in 1962–1966 by N.I.O.C. jointly with American,

Italian, British, French or German partners for oil production in Persian Gulf off-shore licensed areas—in two of which successful production and export, on small or medium scale, had been achieved by 1968: and thirdly, and by far the most important, an international consortium of eminent British, American, British/Dutch and French concerns as successor, since 1954, to the Anglo-Iranian Oil Co, which was, from 1901 onwards, the true pioneer of the whole Middle Eastern oil industry. The Consortium's production from its great range of fields in the Khuzistan province in the southern Zagros was in 1968 some 135 million tons, bringing some £325 million to the Persian treasury. Recent discovery and development has added to the already vast resources of this area and enterprise. The Consortium operates also the giant Abadan refinery, but takes no part in distribution or marketing in Persia, which are the concern of N.I.O.C., itself now a medium-scale refiner, notably at Teheran. Nor does the Consortium as such export or market oil abroad, these being the functions of its constituent companies.

In KUWAIT, the enterprise on land is that of a single joint Anglo-American company which, after a career of phenomenally rapid growth, produced and exported 120 million tons of oil in 1968 and operates also a refinery of some ten million tons annual capacity, largely for bunkering requirements. Conditions for production in the Amirate (other than climatic or scenic!) approach perfection, and every advantage has been taken of these. There is one outstandingly rich and extensive field (Burgan), with others of considerable scale. The industry and its resulting flood of wealth for the Amir and his people cannot but completely dominate the Kuwaiti scene and outlook (p. 171). The ruler's direct revenue from the K.O.C. is of the order of £310 million a year. An off-shore concession in Kuwaiti waters was allotted in 1960 to the Shell group who, after prospecting and drilling, failed to find oil. The mainland of the Kuwait-Sa'udi NEUTRAL ZONE has, since 1948, been the scene of operations by two American companies, under separate concessions; in 1968 some 6·5 million tons of crude was exported, its royalties (£15 million) being divided between the grantors. Two small refineries handle a proportion of this oil. Off-shore, a Japanese consortium obtained rights in 1957, discovered an important field and began export immediately, all to Japan. This amounted in 1967 to 17 million tons. A second field has recently been located.

The oilfields in the al-Hasa province of SA'UDI ARABIA, located over a wide area in a variety of desert settings and also off-shore

under the shallow waters of the Persian Gulf, are on a scale of the
greatest magnitude and productivity. The Arabian-American
('Aramco') enterprise, born in 1934 and constituted of four of the
great internationally operating companies, is all-American. Major
fields, with others in reserve likely to rival them in scale, are under
exploitation to the limit of market demand. Production of crude in
1968 amounted to 140 million tons. Export is by tanker from the
Sa'udi coast, by submarine pipeline to Bahrain for refining, or by
trans-desert pipeline—the famous Tapline, 1,070 miles in length—to
the Lebanon for shipment. A large refinery is also operated in Sa'udi
Arabia, and a second, smaller, is under construction. Efforts are made
to develop Sa'udi industries ancillary to Aramco's own enterprise
which itself produces hitherto unimaginable revenues, currently some
£350 million (or $840 million) per annum paid to the Sa'udi treasury.
Areas relinquished are now being granted to other foreign concerns.

In the QATAR peninsula a mainland field (that of Dukhan) has
been in production since 1960, in the hands of a company identical
in all but name with 'Iraq Petroleum. Export is by tanker from Umm
Sa'id terminal, constructed *ad hoc*. Production in 1968 was of
8·5 million tons, producing a revenue for the Shaikh of some £20
million. An off-shore concession over waters east of the peninsula,
allotted in 1952 to the Shell group, has also been successful, two
mid-sea medium-scale oilfields being placed in production. From
these an output of 8 million tons of crude, and an income of £18
million for the ruler, is realized.

In the extensive, sparsely inhabited shaikhdom of ABU DHABI
(p. 167) an off-shore field was discovered in 1959 by its Anglo-French
concessionaires, and export of oil began in 1962; meanwhile, two
more mid-sea fields had been located. The marine operations
produced nearly 9 million of crude in 1968. On land, a company of
the 'Iraq Petroleum group, after years of search, found a major
oilfield at Murban in 1960, and within three years established it in
important production; indeed by 1968 Abu Dhabi had become the
Middle East's fifth-greatest exporter, with fantastic wealth—and all
its problems!—accruing to the ruler of a few thousand half-starving
tribesmen. In 1968 some 15·5 million tons was exported from the
mainland and around £42 million gathered by the Shaikh. In the
neighbouring, but tiny, shaikhdom of Dubai, under rights granted by
its ruler to a multi-national consortium, oil at an off-shore location
was discovered in 1966, and steps were taken which would lead to
production in 1969.

60–63. Four types in the Hadhramaut: village woman, basket-maker, retired seafarer, mercenary soldier, Shibam

64. Trucial coast: a guide

65. Abu Dhabi policeman

66. School children: Abu Dhabi

67. Abu Dhabi: one
of Sheikh Zaid's
retainers with falcon

68. Trucial coast:
Dibai creek

69. The new
Kuwait

In the backward isolated Sultanate of OMAN, three medium-scale oil-deposits were found in 1963–1964 by a Shell company, after years of frustrated search. Immediate measures were taken towards development, including a 150-mile pipeline to the sea, and the Sultan's principality joined the ranks of major oil-producers in 1967. Eleven million tons were exported in 1968, worth perhaps £25 million to the Sultan. The effects of this on the society of the territory cannot but be profound—and dangerous.

Most of the territories, venturing nowadays more deeply into industrial activities and western domestic standards of living, are consuming increasing quantities of their own or their neighbours' oil, to a present extent of some 50 million tons a year. Most states are now undertaking refinery operations through official corporations, to a throughput of some 100 million tons p.a.; the largest-scale plants, as those in Persia, Kuwait, Sa'udi Arabia, Bahrain and Aden, are company-owned or -operated, others in these countries or elsewhere are state-owned, as in Egypt (partly), 'Iraq, Syria and Israel (partly), or are enterprises of the local public. In the backward territories all refining-plants are those of foreign companies. The discovery of new oilfields continues year by year; the region has perhaps not yet revealed the half of its secrets. Its oil-reserves, even as already located and physically and economically available, far exceed those of any other region—upwards of 33 billion tons out of a world total of some 57 billion; that is, 60 per cent of the whole world.

Output of Middle Eastern oil was in 1968 570 million tons in the year, or 11·5 million barrels a day: detail by countries is given in Appendix B. Far greater output than this, however, will be available when demanded by the world's markets; and this condition will undoubtedly continue for many years, as long as not unduly compromised by the policies or exigencies of the host governments. Meanwhile, a total of some £1350 million a year, or $3750 million, is being paid to the local Treasuries by the operating oil-companies; details of this are given in Appendix B. To these payments to state treasuries must be added, of course, the very large disbursements to labour, staff, local suppliers and contractors. A fuller picture of the industry as visible locally, however, must include, in a wide variety of physical surroundings, a fragmented yet interconnected mass of wells and pipelines, storage tanks and multifarious industrial buildings, plants and installations, ports and jetties, stores and offices and laboratories, domestic quarters and clubs, hospitals and schools and training-centres, streets and gardens and sports-grounds. These things, and the presence of hundreds of foreign—mainly American and British sometimes Dutch or French, more rarely Italian or Japanese—experts, managers and technicians, as fellow-workers in the industry at all levels with its local labour-force and executives, must inevitably be a leading social influence in the areas of their operation, and far beyond them.

## 2. *The Nouveaux Riches*

It is clear that if the oil industry is merely one among many others in Egypt, Turkey and Israel, and if it makes in Syria, Lebanon and Jordan not more than a fairly substantial contribution, by way of small-scale production, of ton-mile transit-dues and terminal loading-fees and payments for services of all kinds, it is on the contrary a vastly important factor in the economies of 'Iraq and Persia and Bahrain, and a completely dominant element in those of Sa'udi Arabia, Kuwait, Qatar, Abu Dhabi and Oman—doubtless soon to be followed by Dubai. Since it is in these latter nine territories that Middle Eastern oil in its most massive volume is produced, and since in these too the local characteristics of the industry—the services it tenders and the attitudes towards it—are most fully developed, we pass next to comment on these aspects.

The attitude of the Companies' many thousands of workers to their industry is generally loyal and satisfactory; long and exemplary service is common; the Companies' efforts to be just, generous, considerate employers are not unappreciated; and in fact the oil companies, thanks to their pay-rates, terms of service, offer of hopeful careers, training and miscellaneous benefits, are, without known exception, by far the best employers of labour in all these territories. The general public also is, in normal times, complacent or well-disposed, except in so far as inflamed at times by xenophobic voices among the politicians; and this attitude would seem a natural consequence of the very substantial benefits derived by the local public in any area of oil industry activity, in the diffusion of employees' wages and salaries, the profitable contracts given locally for works and supplies, the extensive purchases from wholesale and retail suppliers, the industrial training freely given, and often the substantial aid offered in many forms to local institutions and amenities. The central governments of the enriched states might be expected, for much the same reasons, to take a similar view, especially since the whole of the new wealth, which has transformed their governments and countries, has been discovered, financed, produced and developed without risk or trouble to them at any level; and further because, beyond all question, the immensely costly tasks of exploration, development, transport, marketing, etc., must at all times have been, and admittedly still are, a whole world beyond the financial, technical, organizational or commercial powers of any local or national body or authority whatsoever. If not for this reason alone, then, a favourable governmental attitude to these enterprises might have been expected because of the rapid, fantastic enrichment itself; because the unbroken continuance of the complex of operations to perpetuate the profits now enjoyed by all parties is a clearly shared, indivisible interest of company, public and government: and because this heaven-sent wealth permits the fortunate states not only to achieve an outwardly superior status (in their diplomatic and military establishments, for instance, and in all the 'things that show') but also, and far more important, to develop their countries on lines of benefit to all their inhabitants, whether near or far from the oil-fields—in improving agriculture and extending irrigation, in fostering industry, in perfecting communications, in providing superior public services (schools, hospitals, town-improvement), in achieving a more honest and reliable civil service and judiciary. Every project, every major enterprise and improvement without exception in these nine countries depends on the continuance of their income from this single source. Especially since sheer poverty has been the age-long curse of these territories, it is not easy to exaggerate the social and economic benefits, direct and indirect, which this oil-wealth, wisely used, is capable of conferring on them in almost every material—and also, if less directly, cultural—sphere of their lives. The services rendered to these countries by 'the Companies' have, indeed, been of extraordinary value, and could in practice have been afforded by no other means; and they have been accompanied by the genuine goodwill of the companies' managements and staffs. Nevertheless, the attitude of governments and many politicians and writers, and much of the articulate part of the public, is too often suspicious or hostile to these benefactors. Why should this be?

This attitude, which is clearly predominant though neither continuous nor universal, has importance because it creates a sense, or fact, of insecurity directly inimical to further investment and development, and because it can, in some of its phases, physically impede the field-work and export upon which all benefits depend. The attitude, amounting at times and places to a specifically anti-Company policy (as in the 'Iraq of 1961–1962, or the Persia of 1951–1954), is chiefly due not to coolly reasoned considerations but to a complex of emotions. They are those of antipathy to a looming, *foreign* industrial giant in their midst, and to envy and dislike of its so evident success: to distrust of the attraction felt by many company's employees and well-wishers towards a non-governmental, foreign, focus of loyalty: to hints or rumours that the Company is 'interfering in politics' (a wildly improbable event); to feelings that 'the Company' enjoys too favourable a concession, which ought therefore, in the eyes of all good patriots, to be annulled. Such feelings are exacerbated by a widespread inferiority complex *vis-à-vis* prosperous, complacent foreigners (always suspected of 'colonialist' policies), by minor frictions in the daily running of the industry, by government's endless demands for more money and participation, and its scant regard for signed and sealed agreements. In the aggregate such feelings create, too often, an unquiet atmosphere in government-company relations, damaging to confidence and continuity. Meanwhile, the Organization of Petroleum Exporting Countries (O.P.E.C.), which dates from 1961 and includes all the concerned states except Oman—with Libya, Venezuela and Indonesia—is vigorous in pressing claims for vaster revenues, less company privilege and acreage, more statal control or share; and shows scorn rather than respect for old-fashioned notions of legality or commercial ethics. The would-be united governments follow suit.

The industry is, if ever one existed, a goose laying golden eggs; and there is proverbial advice as to how not to treat that rare and sensitive bird, which hot-head xenophobic nationalists in the countries concerned would be wise to heed. Present, admittedly foreign, concessionaires and their merits or demerits apart, there seems no alternative currently in sight to the operation by them of the oil industry in these Middle Eastern territories, least of all at a time of global over-supply of petroleum. These far-flung, integrated companies alone possess the capital, the technological and organizational command, and above all the worldwide markets, which are indispensable; and they have been and are, as it happens, conducted on reasonable, sympathetic and humane (as well as highly efficient) lines by men of probity and goodwill. The interested observer can but hope that, by the efforts of both sides, present imperfections in the atmosphere as between 'the authorities' and the operating companies can and will be removed, and their immensely important, inter-dependent enterprises will enjoy a favourable environment and cordial inter-relations.

The imperfect government-company relations so far considered arise chiefly when, as in all the earlier and greater concessions given by Middle Eastern governments, the 'blanket concession' method was *faute de mieux* adopted: that is, the grant of oil-rights over very wide areas of territory to a single company for a long term, as was done in Persia, 'Iraq, Sa'udi Arabia, and the Gulf States. Such concessions have, of course, been repeatedly reconsidered, renegotiated and modified (always in the states' favour) since their original grant; and in some cases later-coming outside concessionaires, to cover unallotted or abandoned territory, have additionally been introduced, as in Persia, the Neutral Zone (off-shore), Qatar (marine areas), Kuwait, nearly all the Gulf states, and Oman. The same process is now under way in Sa'udi Arabia and 'Iraq. In Turkey, Israel and Egypt some of the odium of foreign near-monopoly has been avoided by an equal-for-all-comers system of exploration (followed by exploitation) licences, covering lesser areas and shorter periods than the old 'blankets'. In all these countries, whatever the form or detailed provisions of the government-company agreements, acceptance of the principle of effective statal participation in a joint enterprise is now a government demand; indeed, the position may one day prevail in which the company acts as a mere contractor for government, on terms securing for the former a bare minimum profit. Meanwhile, some of the joint ventures, notably in Egypt and Persia, have already achieved production. It is notable that many of the recently incoming entrepreneurs represent not only companies new to Middle Eastern industry (for instance, American non-majors) but also countries hitherto strange to the oil-fields of the region—German, Spanish, Indian, Italian, Japanese. The U.S.S.R. has been active in offering technical aid and equipment to the National Companies.

Resentment at the great foreign companies' success and, in some territories, their exclusivity of oil-operation would be substantially diminished by the undertaking on the part of government itself of an increasing range of activities in this field. Already in most of the Gulf territories, including 'Iraq and Persia, a National Oil Company deals with refining with local distributing and marketing functions, and, in Persia (which other countries are following) those also of prospecting and production. Most of the governments take a proportion of their agreed royalty in the form of crude oil, which they are free to market or to sell back to the company. It is foreseeable that such active participation in the industry by local governmental or, if possible, private enterprise will increase; it is educative, it affords outlets for the employment (in addition to that offered by the companies) of local technicians, engineers and executives; it helps to destroy the galling picture of 'foreign monopoly', and to substitute a local interest and achievement. The example of the N.I.O.C. might well be widely followed, though the countries' lack of a position in foreign markets, and of available capital on an adequate scale, must prevent them for some years to come from enterprise of the largest magnitude. Nevertheless, the possibility or dream of a great, integrated, foreign-operating, inter-statal, all-Arab operating company has been suggested by imaginative Arab oil-experts.

We have referred above to some of the social benefits obtainable by the diffusion of the industry's local expenditure, and by country-wide governmental measures thus financed; is, or will be, the local political world—so closely bound to the social—equally a beneficiary? This is more doubtful. Greater wealth, while not conferring greater wisdom or more statesmanlike qualities, must complicate public life and administration, widen the fields of controversy, and make more attractive than ever the rewards of personal success in terms of power and glory. In few of the enriched territories does it appear that their new material circumstances have tended to stabilize or strengthen the constitution, or the body politic, or its leadership; indeed, the lessons of 'Iraq and Persia tell a sadly different story, and the precipitate emergence of Sa'udi Arabia, Kuwait, Qatar, Abu Dhabi and Oman—and soon Dubai—into the stresses of the modern world, due solely to their respective prolific, golden-egg-laying geese, will probably tend to threaten rather than to consolidate their patriarchal régimes of government. This need be no subject of present despair; weaknesses apparent today may prove to be but passing phases, and should be as nothing compared with the undoubted blessings to which oil-derived wealth, *wisely used*, can and should lead in other and broader fields of living.

Internationally, the effects of an oil-wealth which some states possess while others totally lack, are much as would be expected. There has been imaginative generosity by some to the needy or hard-pressed: there have been safety-seeking presents from rich but weak states to poorer but more powerful, perhaps menacing, neighbours: there have been large sums made available, especially by Kuwait, for 'development' in sister territories. The gratitude thus earned is probably no more than moderate, and short-lived; not improbably the too-human instincts of greed, jealousy, egoism and abuse of power, will continue to haunt international Middle Eastern scenes (as they do the wide world over), and to enjoy many occasions to manifest themselves.

# CHAPTER TWELVE

# CONCLUSION AND PROSPECT

IT will not be easy for the writer, after fifty years of close connection with the countries of the Middle East, to select, and to compress into a few paragraphs, what seems to be most worth saying, most likely to be valid for some period at least, of the situation, prospects and hopes of these territories.

The region's geographic situation is, in human terms, unchangeable; its land-surface can be modified only in local detail, by routes, bridges, dams, afforestation or reclamation; its climate, unless by humanly unforeseeable, uncontrollable changes, must remain what it is, even though science, by prophylactic medicine, air-conditioning and other means, can mitigate its severity.

Even with such differences as may be effected by rapid ubiquitous air-travel, closer and instant telecommunication, nuclear weapons and other not-yet-evolved factors, the region cannot but retain more than a little of its central, tri-continental importance, political and strategic. It must continue to command east–west global routes by sea and land; it will remain close to the centres of eastern-hemisphere power and wealth on the one side, and the dozens of weak but aspiring new states of Asia and Africa on the other; its possession of unique reserves of petroleum will give it more, not less, importance with passing decades. The fortunes of its populations will continue to be watched with exceptional keenness by co-religionists and sympathizers throughout the world, and it will continue, no doubt, to be an object of concern, possibly of ambition or cupidity, to stronger powers or blocs. These facts, and the local unease and stresses to which they may conduce, cannot be without consequences in the social and political life of the area. This will never be among the happy regions which have no history.

In spite of factors which might seem to make for closer inter-country relations, perhaps ending with political unity—the sense of Arab brotherhood and (non-political) homogeneity, the common front against 'imperialism' and against Israel—the not less real, and seemingly even more effective, disparities between the Middle Eastern states in their geographic and economic circumstances,

stages of evolution, vested interests and foreign contacts, combine
still to keep them apart and disunited; nor is it possible, at the time
of writing, to see cause to expect any major change in this regard.
All, or almost all, of the states of the region are still far from having
reached a stage of national development in which they would be
willing, unless temporarily and exceptionally, to accept any diminution of their national sovereignty. Pacts and alliances will doubtless
be made from time to time between two or more governments, but
these may well prove as short-lived as in the recent past. Artificial,
or even imposed, 'unions' or confederations of small units, such as
those of the Trucial Coast, may be proclaimed and brought into
existence, but can contribute little to the area as a whole unless in
diminishing the vulnerability of a single sensitive area. A weak state
with a precarious ill-based régime, such as Hashimite Jordan, may
imaginably be annexed by a stronger neighbour—Egypt or (improbably) Syria, and the world is aware of the proclaimed ambitions of
Persia to annex Bahrain, of 'Iraq for Kuwait, and of Sa'udi Arabia
for at least parts of Oman. But these are not signs of movement towards, or toleration of, greater regional unity. Possibly the present
Egyptian conception of some form of bloc of 'democratic' socialist
Arab states, feasible only if and when they adopt an equivalent of
current Nasirite policies, may prove to be a more centripetal force.
In the case of Syria, the attempt failed; in that of Jordan, it may
some day be made; in the Yemen it was tried, but its success or
failure is still uncertain; and the history of 'Iraq since July 1958
indicates that anti-monarchical revolution need not be synonymous
with a move into the Egyptian orbit.

Current world opinion, and the global organization of United
Nations, have decreed that these states should face, each by and for
itself, the stresses and problems of the most difficult and dangerous
of periods through which human society is now passing. Their
administrations, central and local, give today, as earlier pages have
suggested, some grounds for satisfaction and hope; the governments,
here in accord with articulate public opinion, are aiming in every
field at higher standards than of old, are using to advantage the
improved class of better-educated and more public-spirited officialdom, are providing law and order and social and technical services
to the best of their often considerable ability. That in all these fields
there will be steady—certainly not rapid or sensational—improvement and expansion can be a confident hope. The less attractive

picture is that of the constitution of the states themselves, and the world of politics; here, optimism is not easy to achieve.

Most of these countries have still only a limited élite class of educated, modern-minded citizens with some real acquaintance with the present-day world, its facts and standards; the masses are still largely illiterate, leading lives scarcely different from those of past centuries and, over wide areas, far from habituated to the processes and standards of law and civil discipline. There are in fact, politically and socially, the two co-existent worlds, medieval and modern, western and eastern, progressive and conservative. Temperamentally, a large majority are highly individualistic—an outstanding feature of the Arab character—emotional, and peculiarly averse from self-submission in any form; and they are fed by their politician-leaders on a diet of phrases and catchwords—independence, imperialism, colonialism, etc.—of, too often, little real content or present relevance: or on self-glorifying myths and promises. At the same time, it is taken for granted, even in the least advanced and least opulent state, that a fully-developed, western, modern-type administration and range of public services is their right, and must be their ambition. The exigencies of a vigorous and competitive political life, where this is permitted, lead to much public denigration of the western foreigner as the traditional oppressor, and thus unnecessarily alienate foreign sympathy.

The rival claims of discipline and liberty, which in all governing régimes are notoriously difficult to satisfy simultaneously, are at their most antagonistic in Middle Eastern administrations; 'discipline' easily takes the form of oppressive dictatorship denying all popular rights, 'liberty' becomes lawless licence. In all the circumstances of the modern Middle East, internal, regional and global, the conduct of a reasonably liberal and secure administration, in any one of the territories, cannot but be a task of quite exceptional difficulty, and one which demands from the outside observer more informed sympathy than scornful criticism. It may be many years—and here perhaps Latin America offers a precedent—before an acceptable stability is achieved; for the present weaknesses of Middle Eastern political and social structure—deplored, needless to say, by their own most enlightened citizens—there is no simple or single cure. They are likely to last for many decades to come, until gradually corrected by the spread of education, enlightenment, experience, and a widely improved standard of living.

Meanwhile, and additionally to the general, region-wide shortcomings in stability and in orderly political-constitutional life, each separate territory, as previous pages of this book have sufficiently suggested, has its particular problems, to few of which an easy solution appears. In Persia, some power still resides in the rich landowning class who distrust 'progress', much corruption flourishes in the public service, the army is or may become doubtfully loyal, the monarchy has many discontented critics. In Turkey, the economy has for years been overstrained, and indeed sacrificed for party-political ends; a stable form of government and administration, acceptable to a solid majority of Turks, still awaits realization. In Cyprus there is a continuance of inter-community rancour, even if at times concealed or dormant. In 'Iraq a dictatorship combining an unintelligent rigour with inefficiency deprived the country of all political and much personal liberty (1958–1963), and sadly lowered the good name of the country abroad; today the restoration of confidence, sound administration and a tolerable pattern of public life appear less improbable, although most basic factors are unchanged. In Syria, where much ability and goodwill are devoted to public affairs, there is, with a marked regionalism, a singularly restless and divided public life with sharply differing objectives; it remains to be seen whether a form of representative government worthy of the name can be established and maintained. Lebanon, of the Arab states the least devoted to international Arabism, has found no shared basis on which to achieve a true national unity, and remains an unstable congeries of its Christian and Muslim communities. Jordan is a weak and indigent state, united only within its monarchi-cally-minded minority, and dependent for its livelihood and its sur-vival on foreign friends. Israel, feared and detested by all its neighbours, will survive as long as the remittances from abroad to pay its bills and finance its development continue to arrive in their present abundance—and/or as long as the Jewish pressure-groups of North America and Europe possess their present formidable power. Egypt is facing its gravely difficult economic and demographic situ-ation with vigour and, with however inadequate an administrative machine and with whatever deficiencies of justice and prudence, is seriously attempting to improve its people's standard of life. In the Sudan, after a period of comparatively mild but politically repressive dictatorship, the years 1964–1969 saw a revival of political life—although the *coup* of May 1969 has thrown all into question once again; there is here a tradition of, and a general preference for, good administration: but the absorption of the non-Muslim south in a Sudani nation poses a task demanding much patience and high-mindedness. The Sa'udi Arabian theocratic monarchy will probably be able to maintain itself for a further period, thanks to its prestige and its monopoly of the only wealth in the territory; but, as long as it does so, any general enlightenment or improvement in the conditions of the Sa'udi population can scarcely be looked for; the régime's most dangerous enemy will possibly prove to be not popular discontent, but dissidence, with foreign support, in the royal family itself, or in the army. The future of the Yemen is, at the time of writing, quite uncertain: even if a modern-type (which may here mean a Nasir-type) government establishes itself in replacement of the Imamate, it must be many years before the country can play any significant part even in Arabian affairs. On the People's Republic of Southern Yemen it is too soon to comment, though since it lacks every qualification and resource essential for a modern state, its survival seems doubtful. The petty states of south-eastern Arabia, continue to present the seemingly insoluble problem of— what to do with them! Only in the cases of Kuwait, Qatar, Bahrain and Abu Dhabi is the problem, on the contrary, that of—what to do with the money? Means must be found, it seems, to distribute a proportion of the available wealth (that is, the oil-revenues) of the region so as to benefit the poor and deprived, and to move towards freely accepted closer association between the tiny, traditional units now so embarrassingly anachronistic. Such steps can scarcely be made conditional on the consent of the present rulers of the 'have' statelets; they could properly be a task for the Arab League, if only this were a wise and effective body.

The social as well as the political development of the Middle East must depend in considerable measure on its economics: which means on the actual wealth which the countries are able to produce and to devote to intelligent development and beneficent services. After centuries of grim poverty, the need for rapid economic uplift is paramount: not only are there pressing needs of every kind in each country's affairs and services, but the mere equipment of the territories with adequate works and buildings, housing and institutions, routes and facilities—the whole complex of national fixed assets upon which developed nations have been spending their money for centuries past—must call for expenditure of a magnitude at present far out of reach. Ignoring for this purpose such lesser sources as the tourist traffic, entrepôt and commercial services, and remittances from abroad, the possible production of greatly increased national wealth can, within the domestic purview, be envisaged only as coming from agriculture, from natural (mineral or other) resources, or from industry. Of these, agriculture will certainly remain the greatest subsistence-occupation of the region; but, as we have shown, it seems unlikely, in any one of the states, even after much greater development and specialization than at present, to do more than contribute moderately to the Treasury or to private wealth. Industry has and will have, it is believed (pp. 247–51), a helpful and useful but never a dominant place in the future of the region. Of natural resources, only petroleum is of really major importance, and the substantial wealth from this source, already in process of full realization, provides (except in the Gulf statelets) no superabundance even for the happy possessors. The essential seems here to be, firstly, that there should be no interruption of the working of the oil industry such as to jeopardize its output of wealth; secondly, that some machinery should be devised whereby the 'haves' should, willingly, aid the development of the 'have nots'. This is no new idea, and it is realizable on commercial lines, given reasonable inter-country amity and confidence. Of one other possible fertilizing source of wealth for the region, material aid to be offered by other countries or by world organizations, it must be realized that, important as such aid can be locally and temporarily, and considerable as may be the part it plays —and, on every ground of humanitarianism and policy, ought to play—it cannot take the place of (nor could it ever be relied upon with as much confidence as) wealth produced and developed by the recipient country itself. Nor, it must be confessed, have ways yet been devised whereby both giver and receiver of such 'aid' can be counted upon to emerge cordial and satisfied from the deal; experience, hitherto, has been sadly otherwise.

The economic resurgence of the Middle East is, it seems, likely to be slow rather than rapid, and lack of wealth will long remain a chief and resented factor restrictive of progress.

Enough has been said elsewhere (pp. 201, 216 ff.) of the considerable changes in the urban—and, not negligibly, in the rural—social life of these countries. These developments will certainly continue until they spread to remoter parts and to all strata, and progressively modify the dominant, traditional ways of life everywhere: in literacy, in housing and clothing, in private and public amenities, in social habit and intercourse. Much that is, to foreign eyes, pleasant and gracious may be lost in the process; an old-time way of life will disappear from the world: much in the new, westernized scene may seem characterless or merely imitative. But such changes will, on the whole, benefit those who form, under the ancient social régime, the most depressed classes of the populations, and will be part of the modern tendencies and forces capable of offering them a less depressed, narrow, insecure existence.

What the region may prove able to bring to the world in the form of cultural output, in its narrower sense, cannot be foreseen. The likelihood of a more valuable contribution will increase with the wider spread of education, power of expression, broader appreciation of the world and humanity at large. The Middle Eastern populations are gifted with an exceptional degree of natural intelligence and sensitivity, and they contain—indeed, have never not contained—an élite fully capable, as their past and present output has shown, of artistic and literary achievement. This, it is certain, will increase; and it will form another link, of which there are now too few, between these confident, aspiring—if also puzzled and unstable—national societies in the Middle East, and their many friends and well-wishers elsewhere in the world.

## MINOR POLITICAL UNITS IN THE
## PERSIAN GULF (SOUTHERN SHORE)
## AND SOUTHERN YEMEN

(a) *Persian Gulf Coast* (other than Kuwait, the Neutral Zone, Sa'udi Arabia, and Oman):

The Bahrain Islands; the shaikhdom of Qatar; the Trucial shaikhdoms of Abu Dhabi, Dubai, Sharja (with Kalba, formerly independent), 'Ajman, Umm al Qaiwain, Ras al-Khaima and Fujaira (independent since 1952).

(b) *Southern Yemen* (until 1967, the Aden Protectorate).

  (i) *Western* ex-Protectorate.

   The sultanates, amirates and shaikhdoms of the 'Abdali (with Lahaj), Amiri (with Dhala), Audhali, Fadhili, Upper Yafa'i, Lower Yafa'i, Haushabi, Mausatta, Dhubi, Maflahi, Hadhrami, Shaib, Qutaibi, 'Alawi, 'Aqrabi, Upper Aulaqi (sultanate) (with Nisab), Upper Aulaqi (shaikhdom), Lower Aulaqi (with Ahwar), Baihan, and Dathina.

  (ii) *Eastern* ex-Protectorate

   State of Shihr and Makalla (Qu'aiti), with H.Q. at Makalla. State of Sayyun (Kathiri), H.Q. Sayyun. State of Qishin and Socotra (Mahri), H.Q. Socotra and Saihut. State of Balhaf and Bir'Ali (Wahidi), H.Q. Maif'a.

  (iii) *City* and immediate suburbs of Aden.

(i) *Successive periods in Middle East Oil Production* (*in million-tons per year*)

| Country | 1911 | 1920 | 1930 | 1940 | 1950 | 1960 | 1968 |
|---|---|---|---|---|---|---|---|
| Egypt . . . | 0·003 | 0·16 | 0·28 | 0·91 | 2·31 | 3·23 | 11·0 |
| Persia . . . | — | 1·38 | 5·94 | 8·62 | 31·75 | 51·8 | 141·0 |
| 'Iraq . . . | — | — | 0·12 | 2·65 | 6·50 | 46·7 | 74·0 |
| Bahrain . . | — | — | — | 0·94 | 1·51 | 2·76 | '3·7 |
| Sa'udi Arabia . | — | — | — | 0·68 | 25·9 | 61·10 | 140·0 |
| Turkey . . | — | — | — | — | 0·01 | 0·35 | 3·0 |
| Qatar . . | — | — | — | — | 1·62 | 8·20 | 16·5 |
| Kuwait . . | — | — | — | — | 17·0 | 80·60 | 120·0 |
| Neutral Zone . | — | — | — | — | — | 7·2 | 23·0 |
| Israel . . | — | — | — | — | — | ·13 | ·1 |
| Abu Dhabi . | — | — | — | — | — | — | 24·0 |
| Oman . . | — | — | — | — | — | — | 11·7 |
| Syria . . | — | — | — | — | — | — | 1·0 |
| TOTAL MIDDLE EAST | 0·003 | 1·54 | 6·34 | 13·80 | 86·60 | 261·0 | 569·0 |
| WORLD . . | 44 | 94·5 | 194 | 289 | 518 | 1,079 | 2,000·0 |

(ii) *'Proved Reserves' of oil in M.E. countries* (*January 1968*)
(in *billion*—i.e. thousand-million—*tons*)
    Sa'udi Arabia, 10·5: Kuwait, 9·5: Persia, 6·5: 'Iraq, 4·9: Neutral Zone, 1·6: Abu Dhabi, 1·1: Qatar 0·5: Egypt, 0·27: Oman, 0·27: All others, each less than 250 million. Total Middle East, 34 billion tons. *Other areas for comparison:*—U.S.A. with Canada 6·5: Latin America, 3·9: Western Europe, 0·45: U.S.S.R. and friends, 5·0: Africa, 5·6: Far East etc., 1·5. World, 57 billion tons. Middle East, with 34 billion, has thus almost 60 per cent of the world.

(iii) *Refinery Capacity per M.E. country, in late 1967*
(in barrels per stream-day)
    Persia, 554,000: Kuwait, 360,000: Sa'udi Arabia, 285,000: Bahrain, 205,000: Aden, 175,000: Egypt, 169,000: Turkey, 134,000: Israel, 115,000: Neutral Zone, 80,000: 'Iraq, 77,900: Lebanon, 36,500: Syria, 22,000: Qatar, 600.
    Total, 2,221,700 bbl, or nearly 300,000 tons

(iv) *Approximate annual payments by* (*foreign*) *companies to local host governments, as in 1968* (irrespective of non-recurrent lump sums).
    In Iran, £365M., Sa'udi Arabia, £350M., Kuwait, £335M., 'Iraq, £200M., Abu Dhabi, £62M., Neutral Zone, £55M., Qatar, £50M., Oman, £35M., Egypt, not ascertainable, Bahrain, £11M., Turkey, £6M., Syria and Israel, not ascertainable.

# SOME BOOKS FOR FURTHER READING

With no attempt at even a partial bibliography of the Middle East, which would necessarily fill volumes, a few suggestions are here offered as to recent, accessible books in English, with which some reader may care to extend his knowledge. With some exceptions, historical and political works are omitted; the same is true of official handbooks, statistics, etc.

### GENERAL FOR THE MIDDLE EAST

(a) *Books of reference*

Bullard, R. W. (ed.), *The Middle East*, 3rd ed., London, 1958.

Fisher, W. B., *The Middle East: a physical, social, and regional geography*, 5th ed., London, 1966.

Hogarth, D. G., *The Nearer East*, London, 1905.

*Statesman's Year Book*, 105th ed., London, 1968.

*The Middle East and North Africa*, Europa Publications, 15th ed., London, 1968

*Oxford Regional Economic Atlas: The Middle East and North Africa*, 2nd ed., London, 1960.

(b) *Other general works*

Antonius, G., *The Arab Awakening*, London, 1938.

Atiyah, E., *The Arabs*, London, 1955.

Baer, G., *Population and Society in the Arab East*, N.Y., 1964.

Berger, M., *The Arab World Today*, N.Y., 1962.

Berque, J., *The Arabs: their history and future*, N.Y., 1964.

Bullard, R. W., *Britain and the Middle East*, London, 1950; *The camels must go*, London, 1961.

Fisher, S. N., *The Middle East: a history*, 2nd ed., N.Y., 1968; (ed.), *Social Forces in the Middle East*, Ithaca, N.Y., 1955

Gibb, H. A. R., *Mohammedanism*, 2nd ed., London, 1953.

Halpern, M., *The Politics of Social Change in the Middle East and North Africa*, Princeton, N.J., 1963.

Hershlag, Z. Y., *Introduction to the Modern Economic History of the Middle East*, Leiden, 1964.

Hitti, P., *History of the Arabs*, 8th ed., N.Y., 1964.

Hourani, A., *Arabic Thought in the Liberal Age*, London, 1962; *Minorities in the Arab World*, London, 1947.

Issawi, C., with Yeganeh, M., *Economics of Middle Eastern Oil*, London, 1962.

Karpat, K., *Political and Social Thought in the Contemporary Middle East*, N.Y., 1968.

Khadduri, M., with Liebesny, H. J., *Law in the Middle East*, Washington, 1955.

Kirk, G., *Short History of the Middle East*, 7th ed., N.Y., 1964.

Laqueur, W. Z., *Communism and Nationalism in the Middle East*, London, 1956; *The Soviet Union and the Middle East*, London, 1959.

Lewis, B., *The Arabs in History*, London, 1954; *The Middle East and the West*, N.Y., 1966.

Longrigg, S. H., *Oil in the Middle East*, 3rd ed., London, 1968.

Nuseibeh, H. Z., *The Ideas of Arab Nationalism*, Ithaca, N.Y., 1956.

Qubain, F. I., *Education and Science in the Arab World*, Baltimore, 1966.

Smith, W. Cantwell, *Islam in Modern History*, N.Y., 1957.

Warriner, D., *Land reform and development in the Middle East*, 2nd ed., London, 1962.

CYPRUS

Balfour, P. (Lord Kinross), *The Orphaned Realm*, London, 1951.

Barclay's Bank D. C. O., *Cyprus, an economic survey*, London, 1960.

Durrell, L., *Bitter Lemons*, London, 1957.

Foley, C., *Legacy of Strife*, London, 1964.

Grivas, G., *Memoirs of General Grivas*, London, 1964.

Kyriakides, S., *Cyprus: constitutionalism and crisis government*, Philadelphia, 1968.

Xydis, S. G., *Cyprus: conflict and conciliation*, Columbus, Ohio, 1967.

EGYPT

Abdel-Malek, A., *Egypt: military society*, N.Y., 1968.

Ayrout, H. H., *The Egyptian peasant*, Boston, 1963.

Hansen, B., with Marzouk, G. A., *Development and economic policy in the UAR (Egypt)*, Amsterdam, 1965.

Holt, P. M. (ed.), *Political and social change in Modern Egypt*, London, 1968.

Hussein, T., *The Stream of Days* (tr.), London, 1948.

Issawi, C., *Egypt in Revolution*, London, 1963.

Lacouture, J. and S., *Egypt in Transition*, London, 1958.

Little, T., *Modern Egypt*, 2nd ed., London, 1967.

Mansfield, P., *Nasser's Egypt*, London, 1965.

Marlowe, J., *Anglo-Egyptian Relations*, London, 1954.

O'Brien, P., *The Revolution in Egypt's Economic System*, London, 1966.

Saab, G., *The Egyptian Agrarian Reform*, London, 1967.

Thomas, H., *Suez*, London, 1966.

Wynn, W., *Nasser of Egypt*, London, 1960.

IRAN: *see* PERSIA

'IRAQ

Ainsrawy, A., *Finance and Economic Development in Iraq*, N.Y., 1966.

Arfa, H., *The Kurds*, London, 1966.

Edmonds, C. J., *Kurds, Turks and Arabs*, London, 1957.

Fulanain, *Haji Rikkan*, London, 1927.

Harris, G. L. (ed.), *Iraq, its People, etc.*, New Haven, 1958.

Khadduri, M., *Independent Iraq, 1932–58*, 2nd ed., London, 1960.

Langley, K. M., *The Industrialization of Iraq*, Cambridge, Mass., 1961.

Longrigg, S. H., *'Iraq 1900 to 1950*, London, 1953; (with Stoakes, F.), *'Iraq*, London, 1958.

Qubain, F. I., *The Reconstruction of Iraq*, London, 1959.

Salter, Lord, *The Development of Iraq*, London, 1955.

Stark, F., *Baghdad Sketches*, London, 1939; *Beyond Euphrates*, London, 1951.

Stevens, E. S., *Folk Tales of Iraq*, Oxford, 1931; *The Mandaeans*, Oxford, 1937.

Thesiger, W., *The Marsh Arabs*, London, 1964.


ISRAEL

Barbour, N., *Nisi Dominus*, London, 1946.

Bar-Zohar, M., *Ben-Gurion: the armed prophet*, Englewood Cliffs, N.J., 1968.

Ben-Gurion, D., *Rebirth and Destiny of Israel* (tr.), N.Y., 1954.

Bentwich, N., *Israel Resurgent*, London, 1960.

Eisenstadt, S. N., *Israeli Society*, N.Y., 1967.

Fein, L. J., *Israel: politics and people*, 2nd ed., Boston, 1968.

Friedmann, Georges, *The End of the Jewish People?* N.Y., 1967.

Horowitz, D., *The Economics of Israel*, N.Y., 1967.

Laqueur, W. Z., *The Road to Jerusalem*, London, 1968.

Orni, E., and Efrat, E., *The Geography of Israel*, N.Y., 1965.

Peretz, D., *Israel and the Palestine Arabs*, Washington, 1959.

Prittie, T., *Israel: miracle in the desert*, London, 1967.

*Stastical abstract of Israel*, Jerusalem, annually.

Sykes, C., *Cross Roads to Israel*, London, 1965.

Weingrod, A., *Reluctant Pioneers: village development in Israel*, N.Y., 1966.

Weizmann, C., *Trial and Error*, London, 1949.


JORDAN

Abdullah, H. M. King, *Memoirs* (tr.), London, 1950.

Deardon, A., *Jordan*, London, 1958.

Glubb, J. B., *A Soldier with the Arabs*, London, 1957; *The Story of the Arab Legion*, London, 1948; *Syria Lebanon Jordan*, London, 1967.

Harris, G. L. (ed.), *Jordan, its people . . . etc.*, New Haven, 1958.

Hussein, H. M. King, *Uneasy lies the Head*, London, 1962.

Philby, H. St. J. B., *A Pilgrim in Arabia*, London, 1946; *Arabian Jubilee*, London, 1952; *Sa'udi Arabia*, London, 1955.
Sanger, R., *The Arabian Peninsula*, Ithaca, N.Y., 1954.
Winder, R. B., *Saudi Arabia in the Nineteenth Century*, N.Y., 1965.

### SUDAN

'Abbas, M., *The Sudan Question*, London, 1952.
Barbour, K. Q., *The Republic of the Sudan*, London, 1961.
Bashir, M. D., *The Southern Sudan: background to conflict*, London, 1968.
Cunnison, I., *Baggara Arabs*, N.Y., 1966.
Duncan, J. S. R., *The Sudan*, Edinburgh, 1952; *The Sudan's Path to Independence*, London, 1957.
Gaitskell, A., *Gezira*, London, 1959.
Hasan, Y. F., *The Arabs and the Sudan*, Edinburgh, 1967.
Henderson, K. D. D., *The Sudan Republic*, London, 1965.
Holt, P. M., *A modern history of the Sudan*, London, 1962.
Langley, M., *No woman's country*, N.Y., 1951.
Macmichael, H. A., *The Sudan*, London, 1954.
Said, B. M., *The Sudan: cross-roads of Africa*, London, 1966.
Shibeika, M., *The independent Sudan*, N.Y., 1960.
Trimingham, J. S., *Islam in the Sudan*, London, 1949.

### SYRIA and LEBANON

Atiyah, E., *An Arab tells his story*, London, 1946.
Fedden, R., *Syria and Lebanon*, London, 1966.
Glubb, J. B., *Syria Lebanon Jordan*, London, 1967.
Gulick, J., *Social structure and culture change in a Lebanese village*, N.Y., 1955; *Tripoli: a modern Arab city*, Cambridge, Mass., 1967.
Hitti, P. K., *History of Syria*, London, 1951; *The Lebanon in History*, London, 1957.
Hourani, A., *Syria and Lebanon*, 2nd ed., London, 1954.
Longrigg, S. H., *Syria and Lebanon under French mandate*, London, 1958.
Salibi, K. S., *The Modern History of Lebanon*, London, 1964.
Sayigh, Y. A., *Entrepreneurs of Lebanon*, Cambridge, Mass., 1962.
Seale, P., *The Struggle for Syria*, London, 1965.
World Bank (IBRD), *The Economic Development of Syria*, Baltimore, 1955.
Ziadeh, N., *Syria and Lebanon*, London, 1957.
    [*N.B. The great bulk of the (European) literature on these two countries is, of course, in French.*]

### TURKEY

Berkes, N., *The Development of Secularism in Turkey*, Montreal, 1964.
Frey, F. W., *The Turkish Political Elite*, Cambridge, Mass., 1965.
Heyd, U., *Foundations of Turkish Nationalism*, London, 1950.
Karpat, K., *Turkey's Politics*, Princeton, N.J., 1959.

Kirkbride, A. S., *A crackle of thorns*, London, 1956.
Patai, R. (ed.), *The Kingdom of Jordan*, Princeton, N.J., 1958.
Vatikiotis, P. J., *Politics and the Military in Jordan*, London, 1967.

### LEBANON, *see* SYRIA and LEBANON

### PERSIA
Arberry, A. J., *Classical Persian Literature*, London, 1958; (ed.), *The Legacy of Persia*, London, 1953.
Avery, P., *Modern Iran*, London, 1965.
Baldwin, G. B., *Planning and Development in Iran*, Baltimore, 1967.
Binder, L., *Iran*, Berkeley Calif., 1962.
Cottam, R. W., *Nationalism in Iran*, Pittsburgh, 1964.
Frye, R. N., *Iran*, London, 1954.
Lambton, A. K. S., *Landlord and Peasant in Persia*, London, 1956.
Lockhart, L., *Famous Cities of Iran*, London, 1939.
Mohammed Riza Shah, *Mission for My Country*, London, 1961.
Sykes, P. M., *History of Persia*, 3rd ed., two vols., London, 1930.
Vreeland, H. H. (ed.), *Iran*, New Haven, 1957.
Wilber, D., *Iran: past and present*, 6th ed., Princeton, N.J., 1963.

### ARAB STATES of the PERSIAN GULF
Albaharna, H., *The Legal Status of the Arabian Gulf States*, Manchester, 1968.
Belgrave, C. D. *Personal Column*, London, 1960.
Dickson, H. R. P., *Kuwait and Her Neighbours*, London, 1956.
El Mallakh, R., *Economic Development and Regional Cooperation: Kuwait*, Chicago, 1968.
Hakima, A. A., *Rise and Development of Bahrain and Kuwait*, Beirut, 1964.
Hay, R., *The Persian Gulf States*, Washington, 1959.
Holden, D., *Farewell to Arabia*, London, 1966.
Kelly, J. B., *Eastern Arabian Frontiers*, London, 1964.
Mann, C., *Abu Dhabi: birth of an oil sheikhdom*, Beirut, 1964.
Marlowe, J., *The Persian Gulf in the Twentieth Century*, London, 1962.
Wilson, A. T., *The Persian Gulf*, London, 1928.

### SA'UDI ARABIA
Armstrong, H. C., *Lord of Arabia*, Beirut, 1962.
Butler, G., *Kings and camels*, N.Y., 1960.
De Gaury, G., *Faisal*, London, 1966.
Dickson, H. R. P., *The Arab of the Desert*, London, 1949.
Hogarth, D. G., *History of Arabia*, London, 1922.
Lipsky, G. A. (and others), *Sa'udi Arabia*, New Haven, 1959.

Kazamias, A. M., *Education and the Quest for Modernity in Turkey*, London, 1967.

Kinross, Lord, *Ataturk*, London, 1964; *Turkey*, London, 1959; *Within the Taurus*, London, 1954.

Lewis, B., *The Emergence of Modern Turkey*, 2nd ed., London, 1968.

Lewis, G. L., *Turkey*, London, 1955.

Luke, H., *The old Turkey and the new*, London, 1955.

Makal, M., *A Village in Anatolia*, London, 1953.

Mango, A., *Turkey*, London, 1968.

Orga, I., *Portrait of a Turkish family*, London, 1950.

Robinson, R. D., *The First Turkish Republic*, Cambridge, Mass., 1963.

Sterling, P., *Turkish Village*, London, 1965.

Stark, F., *Ionia*, London, 1954; *Lycian shore*, London, 1956; *Riding to the Tigris*, London, 1959.

Szyliowicz, J., *Political Change in Rural Turkey*, The Hague, 1966.

World Bank (IBRD), *The economy of Turkey*, Baltimore, 1951.

Yalman, A. E., *Turkey in my time*, Norman, Oklahoma, 1956.

## YEMEN, SOUTHERN YEMEN, OMAN

Bethmann, E. W., *Yemen on the threshold*, Washington, 1960.

Hamilton, R. A. B., *The Kingdom of Melchior*, London, 1949; (as Lord Belhaven), *The Uneven Road*, London, 1955.

Hickinbotham, Sir T., *Aden*, London, 1955.

Holden, D., *Farewell to Arabia*, London, 1966.

Jngrams, D., *Survey of the social and economic condition of the Aden Protectorate*, Asmara, 1949.

Ingrams, W. H., *Arabia and the Isles*, 2nd ed., London, 1952; *The Yemen: Imams, rulers and revolutions*, N.Y., 1964.

Johnson, C., *The View from Steamer Point*, London, 1964.

King, G., *Imperial Outpost—Aden*, London, 1964.

Landen, R. G., *Oman since 1856: disruptive modernization in a traditional Arab society*, Princeton, N.J., 1967.

Little, T., *South Arabia: arena of conflict*, London, 1968.

Macro, E., *Yemen and the Western World since 1571*, London, 1967.

Paget, Julian, *Last Post: Aden 1964-7*. London, 1969.

Scott, H., *In the High Yemen*, London, 1942.

Stark, F., *Seen in the Hadhramaut*, London, 1940; *The Southern Gates of Arabia*, London, 1936; *A Winter in Arabia*, London, 1940.

Thesiger, W., *Arabian sands*, London, 1959.

Trevaskis, Sir K., *Shades of Amber: a South Arabian episode*, London, 1967.

Wenner, M. W., *Modern Yemen, 1918-1966*, Baltimore, 1967.

| | Agronomy | Area: Population | Climate: Topography | Communications | History | Industry |
|---|---|---|---|---|---|---|
| ADEN (S. YEMEN) | 162 f., 234, 246 | 162 ff. | 19 f., 162 ff. | 163 | 74 ff., 86 | 163 f. |
| CYPRUS | 18, 233 ff., 241 | 185 f. | 185 f. | 187 | 29, 40, 60, 66, 70, 76 ff. | 248 ff. |
| EGYPT (U.A.R.) | 18, 144, 233 ff., 243 ff. | 139 f. | 20, 142 | 146 | 29–68, 72 f., 76, 83 f. | 144, 247 ff. |
| 'IRAQ | 18, 234 ff., 239 | 123 f. | 15, 17 f., 19 f., 123 ff. | 126 f. | 28–69, 72, 76, 79 f. | 125 f., 248 ff. |
| ISRAEL | 233, 242 f. | 188 | 15, 188 f. | 192 | 35 ff., 40 ff., 72, 76, 82 ff., 137 | 247 ff. |
| JORDAN | 135 f., 234, 236 | 134 ff. | 15, 17 f., 134 f. | 136 f. | 35, 40, 76, 81 f., 137 ff. | 136, 249 ff. |
| LEBANON | 233 f., 236, 240 f. | 127 ff. | 15, 17, 127 | 129 | 13, 69, 72, 76, 80 f. | 247 ff. |
| MUSKAT AND OMAN | 165, 247 | | 16, 162 ff. | | 55, 69, 74 f., 86 | |
| PERSIA (IRAN) | 18, 175 ff., 233 ff., 238 f. | 172 f. | 15, 17, 19 f., 172 f. | 178 f. | 27–70, 75, 78 f. | 247 ff. |
| PERSIAN GULF STATES | 166, 247 | 166 ff. | 15, 20, 166 | 167 ff. | 69, 87 | |
| SA'UDI ARABIA | 18, 157, 234, 245 | 154, 156 | 15 ff., 19 f., 154 ff., 162 | 158 | 47–64, 66, 68 f., 73 f., 76, 85 f. | |
| SUDAN | 149, 234, 245 | 148, 150 f. | 148 ff. | 152 f. | 44, 73, 83 f., 85, 147 | 248 f. |
| SYRIA | 18, 132, 234 ff., 240 | 130 f. | 15, 17, 19, 130 f. | 133 | 29–69, 72, 76, 80 f. | 248 f. |
| TURKEY | 18, 179 ff., 233 ff., 238 | 179 f. | 15, 17, 19 f., 179 f. | 184 f. | 29–60, 66–77, 104, 106 | 247 ff. |
| YEMEN | 18, 233 ff. | 159 f. | 16 f., 20, 159 f. | 161 f. | 46, 53, 55, 66, 68 f., 73 f., 85 f. | |

# INDEX